Dependence and Transformation

Dependence and Transformation

The Economics of the Transition to Socialism

by Clive Y. Thomas

Monthly Review Press
New York and London

Library of Congress Cataloging in Publication Data
Thomas, Clive Yolande.
Dependence and transformation.
Bibliography: p.
1. Economic Development. 2. Marxian economics. 3. Underdeveloped areas—Economic policy. I. Title.
HD82.T493 338'.09172'4 73-90081
ISBN 0-85345-317-9

First Printing

Monthly Review Press
62 West 14th Street, New York, N.Y. 10011
21 Theobalds Road, London WC1X 8SL

Manufactured in the United States of America

This book is dedicated to:

The workers, peasants, and
revolutionary intelligentsia
of Tanzania where I lived during
its preparation and writing;

Josh Ramsammy, who survived the
assassin's bullets;

other socialists everywhere who
because of their commitment
are being killed, maimed, and
hounded into all manner and
types of coves and warrens,

and

the future—Raúl's world

Acknowledgments

This book was written, apart from these prefatory statements, entirely in Tanzania during my first visit to my original homeland, Africa. Although it is difficult to trace the origins of such a work, I believe that this single circumstance, more than any other, has been responsible for the unique form and conception it has taken.

While in Tanzania, I not only managed to live for the first time in a society where the urgency of the issues raised in this book seemed real, but in addition I was fortunate in receiving considerable support from my comrades and colleagues there. Walter Rodney has been, at all times, a major source of guidance. Indeed, he was responsible for introducing me early during my stay to the Sunday ideological classes held by the TANU Youth League at the campus of the University of Dar-es-Salaam. This book began with a lecture I was invited to give to one of these classes. It was subsequently expanded into a paper presented to a staff seminar at the University of Dar-es-Salaam during November 1972. Called "The Transition to Socialism: Issues of Economic Strategy in a Tanzanian-Type of Economy," it received a large number of comments and criticisms which in one way or another proved invaluable in helping me complete the work.

Among those whose comments I especially valued were Mark Segal, Bill Luttrell, Jay Mandle, Andrew Coulson, and

Manuel Gottleib, all of whom provided detailed written comments. Paul Sweezy also provided extremely valuable comments and encouragement in our exchange of correspondence. Justinian Rweyemamu, Phillip Raikes, John Loxley, and Aidan Foster-Carter helped me clarify some points in numerous verbal exchanges. Marc Wuyts's help was particularly valuable, since at all stages of the work he seemed amazingly able to grasp what I was striving for, even when this was not much more than a tentative and poorly articulated exploration. Specifically, he was of great help in making concrete some aspects of Chapter 4.

My indebtedness to those in Tanzania would not be complete if I did not further acknowledge the help Justinian Rweyemamu provided in securing me financing from the university to have the manuscript typed. I am also very grateful for the great patience and skill Linda Nunes exhibited in the preparation of the manuscript under great pressure of time.

Although this study was written entirely in Tanzania, and indeed was not discussed with any of my colleagues in the Caribbean until after I returned in the summer of 1973, the contributions I derived from our long association are considerable. In particular I feel that wherever the work might be original, it comes from an extension of ideas on development, dependence, transformation, and socialism which we have collectively helped to formulate in the region. Whether it will mark a discontinuity in Caribbean scholarship (as some who are acquainted with it feel it may), or a further development, is left for the readers to judge. However, it seems to me that whatever differences exist, these must be a product of the change in the objective conditions facing the intelligentsia almost everywhere in the so-called Third World.

For creating the opportunity for me to discuss this work with my colleagues in the Caribbean, I am very grateful to George Beckford, Marshall Hall, and Alister McIntyre, who arranged a short visiting professorship to the University of the West Indies at Mona, Jamaica.

Despite this long list of people to whom I feel indebted, readers should not assume that the list is either complete, or that the people and institutions mentioned necessarily endorse the ideas or the manner in which they are presented.

C. Y. Thomas

Georgetown, Guyana
1974

Contents

Introduction

If we were to consider seriously the present state of economic science, we would find, despite a voluminous outpouring of literature over the last two decades and more, that there has been little of worth contributed to the concrete tasks of working out a rational strategy for coping with those problems which center on raising the levels of development of the productive forces of the small dependent underdeveloped economies. Apart from the popular, and essentially trivialized, distinction between "growth" and "development" —to which a long literature has been directed—it is surprising how little attention both neoclassical and socialist analyses have paid to developing a consistent strategy aimed at providing a planning frame to deal with the multidimensional problems of underdevelopment and material exploitation in the *specific context* of the small dependent economies, which have been surviving so far mainly as appendages, on the periphery of international capitalism.[1]

The poverty of neoclassical economic theory in this area is understandable, and indeed one might even argue it is to be expected. Given its ahistoricism and its preoccupation with the technics of keeping capitalism prosperous and crisis-free, little in the direction of the interests expressed here could really have been achieved. However, the failure of socialist economic theory to grapple with these problems, even if this is understandable in the historical circumstances, is certainly not forgivable. As a science which deals with the laws of development, socialist economic theory has always stood for a methodologically integrated treatment of philosophy, political economy, and the methods of socialist construction. One would therefore hope that such an approach would constitute the most powerful scientific basis for dealing with the phenomena of dependence and transformation.

We are forced to admit, however, that in the field of economic strategy, planning, and policy in these economies, neither socialist nor neoclassical economic theories have risen above attempts to apply the successes of the "typical" capitalist or the "typical" socialist economy. Inevitably, where specific and vital socioeconomic formations—such as national size—exist they do not permit the direct transfer of these models. The result is that these two approaches are left hanging in the air. In some cases—such as Brazil and India—the direct application of these models is not impossibly strained or excessively unreal and an approach along the lines of the "typical" capitalist or "typical" socialist path of development may yield useful insights. But in the small dependent underdeveloped economy seeking to transform its material structure of production, exchange, distribution, and consumption during the present era, dominated as it is by neocolonial economic relations, it is not much use to aim at the simple replication of other successes.

The profound implications of this limitation of existing theory for the further development of theory and practice manifest themselves in a number of ways, often surprising. Consider the following quotation from a recent review of the problems of socialist transformation in Cuba by Diáz-Alejandro:

> Suppose a being from Jupiter was faced with the following description of an economy: an export to GNP ratio of about one-fourth with an even higher import to GNP ratio; an export list dominated by one primary product, accounting for roughly 80 percent of all receipts, so that staple also accounts for a high GNP share, with other primary products responsible for the rest of

> exports; two or three closely allied major (and powerful) customers purchasing about two-thirds of all exports and supplying an even higher share of imports; imports providing very high proportions of the absorption of fuel, machines, weapons, and new technology, and significant shares of consumption for some foodstuffs; an agricultural growth rate having trouble keeping up with that of population; an expansion of exports seriously lagging behind that of the national foreign debt; heavy reliance on foreign resources for capital formation; and finally, less than full and efficient use of available labor, land, machinery, and raw materials. Our alien creature, especially if it had kept up with the literature on neocolonialism and dependency, could diagnose the situation as typical of deformed underdeveloped capitalism, and might suggest immediate revolution, with bold land and other structural reforms. The consensus view on the whole agrees with this evaluation of 1958 Cuba. But, add Mesa-Lago and others, the parameters listed still describe the Cuba of 1972. The size of the economy, rather than social systems, may explain their stubborn persistence.[2]

This paragraph not only betrays the general confusion in neoclassical literature about a number of important theoretical issues, but its very manner of expression also highlights certain universally held, and, as we shall see, unsubstantiated preconceptions about the nature of the small dependent underdeveloped neocolonial economy and its capacity to be materially transformed. While analyses of these and other relevant matters form the main substance of this book, a few introductory observations at this point may be helpful in alerting readers to some of these confusions and prejudices.

To begin with, let us look at the nature and significance of size in these economies, a point which Diáz-Alejandro dramatizes in the last sentence of the quotation. The concept of size has not been subject to much systematic study in the literature. Indeed, in much neoclassical and socialist economic analysis size appears, as it does in the quotation, to be capable of operating as a force of nature, alone and independent of the social system—readers may be surprised at the number of examples presented later in the text that support this point of view, and at how broad is the spectrum of approaches to the study of social phenomena they represent.

They all lead, at least by inference, to the following proposition: *that it is impossible for the small dependent underdeveloped economy to achieve a basic transformation of its structure of production, exchange, distribution, and consumption.*

As we shall ourselves argue, smallness is a factor of crucial *social* importance, but it is not the force of nature alone. We shall seek to demonstrate that it can and will operate as an insuperable social barrier to the development of the productive forces only when the framework of production relations that governs these efforts seeks to develop some form or other of indigenous capitalism. Such factors as market constraints, the social costs of development accompanied by private appropriation of material output, allocation based on the criteria of private profit, etc., rule out the possibility of raising the level of production forces from those which presently characterize these social systems to a reasonably developed level of industrial capitalism.

Apart from these somewhat negative conclusions, one of the positive tasks of this book is to demonstrate how, despite the size constraint, a transformation from dependence to socialism (with all this implies about the *degree* and the *correspondence* of development of productive forces, the quality of the instruments of production in use, etc.) is possible. Indeed, our task is the major one of demonstrating that it is only on the basis of a planned socialist transformation that underdevelopment and poverty on a world scale can be overcome—always bearing in mind that the small dependent underdeveloped economies account for the vast majority of states in the present world order.

Pursuing these objectives necessarily requires that we add what we believe to be a very important dimension to the existing approaches to the study of underdevelopment and poverty in these societies. To readily comprehend this point, let us first of all recall that even the strictest capitalist "free" enterprise and neoclassical analyses of these countries would concede the fundamental significance of the distinction between "growth" and "development." What this of course means is that increases in per capita material product may not mean improvements in the quality and standard of living of the broad mass of the population, or equity in the distribution of income and wealth, or a sufficient degree of differentiation in the structure of output so as to favor self-sustained increases in material production.[3] A number of so-called prosperous petroleum, tourist, and mineral-exporting economies, enjoying "boom" conditions in capitalist markets, attest to the significance of this distinction.

The substitution of "development" for "growth" is therefore the universal approach to the study of these economies. It is this substitution which permits the explicit incorporation of social and political issues into neoclassical economic analysis, but even here social issues are added as an *adjunct*. Thus, not surprisingly, they end up simply being indicators of the need for a bit of social engineering, here and there, in order to iron out the distinction between private and social costs.

A little reflection on the implications of the views advanced so far allows us to perceive that if material transformation is only possible in the context of a struggle to establish socialism (i.e., to seek to develop productive forces and the relations which govern production simultaneously), then our methodology cannot rest on a trivialized distinction between "development" and "growth" and the "gap" between private and social costs. Instead, our methodological approach must incorporate the theoretical and practical issues posed by attempts to support *the transition from one social system to another*. In other words, the theoretical base for considering the elimination of poverty and underdevelopment for this large a number of states is the study of the transition between social systems.

There is at least one very important result of identifying the issues in the way outlined here, which is that we are also able to establish, for the purposes of this study, the dependent and peripheral countries of international capitalism as the focus of our approach to the economic issues of worldwide socialist construction. In other words, we are in a better position to grapple with the problems of socialism in the periphery, without ourselves falling prey to the frequent transgression of treating these issues as peripheral to some other major thesis.

Reverting to our earlier argument that in both socialist and neoclassical economic theory smallness makes the development of the small dependent underdeveloped economy impossible, evidence of the prejudices supporting this view are readily observed in the very different ways in which the issue of size is dealt with in the literature of the small European socialist societies. Consider as an example the contrasting ways in which size impinges on the analysis of two small economies seeking to establish socialist societies: Cuba and Rumania. In his study of Rumania, Montias observes that during the 1951-1955 plan this largely rural economy had directed 57.5 percent of state investment into industry. State investment in transport and communications averaged 11.1 percent and in agriculture only 10.4 percent.[4] At the same time, in every year during the 1961-1965 period Cuba invested less in industry than in agriculture; yet the 1961-1963 period has been described as the adventurous years of "instant industrialization."[5] While there were no doubt ill-conceived projects in Cuba and a number of post-revolutionary euphoric excesses, much of the objection in the literature, as indicated in the phrasing of comments, seems to be directed to the idea that Cuba could seek to industrialize at all! The concern about Rumania is, however, different: there the drive for industrialization is taken for granted, and the analysis focuses, quite properly, on the problems of method, institutional organization, etc.

There is little doubt, at least in this author's mind, that one of the major factors affecting our consciousness about the possibilities of industrializing in an economy such as Cuba's is the absence of any theoretical and analytical framework within which this has been demonstrated, and from which we might concede such a practice possible. It is therefore one of the major aims of the theoretical and analytical work in this book to provide just such a cognitive framework.

If the analysis of economic theory and the development of

an economic strategy are to be concerned with the problems posed by the transition from one social system to another, it is to be expected that these considerations will dominate the various criteria and the method of calculus as they affect such important matters as resource allocation and use, consumption and accumulation, income distribution, etc. But what has been the actual practice? We find it alleged that in Cuba

> the essential error in the industrialization program drawn up under Minister of Industries Guevara was that the wrong criteria were used for the selection of industrial investment projects. The criterion employed was the peso value ranking of the commodity concerned in Cuban imports.[6]

When this growth strategy ran into inevitable difficulties, we find the following developments:

> It was recognized that this second growth strategy was a departure from the traditional Soviet growth model. Autarkic development was now seen to be appropriate for a large nation such as Russia undergoing a highly effective economic blockade. But the objective of industrial self-sufficiency was inappropriate for a small country which had the opportunity to trade with a group of fellow socialist countries. Similarly, the "proportional" growth of different industrial sectors in the Soviet schema, that is (i) the primordial emphasis upon heavy industry—iron and steel and heavy engineering—as the fount of real economic growth and (ii) the de-emphasis on consumer and light industries, was perhaps opportune for a country as large as Russia and with as broad a resource base. "Proportional" development, however, had proven to be unsuitable for Cuba, which had neither a sufficient resource base (it lacked the basic industrial resources such as iron ore, coal, a cheap source of power) nor a sufficient accumulation of technical and managerial expertise to install a broad range of heavy industries quickly. *On the other hand, Cuba did have long experience with sugar production and her resource endowment was admirably suited to sugar production. Thus sugar production was to perform for Cuba the same function as heavy industry had in Russia—to comprise the dynamic leading growth sector.*[7]

The above quotations highlight with remarkable clarity

some of the issues we have introduced. First, we can observe the lack of a theoretical framework consistent with the task of transformation in the unscientific (unhistorical) gropings for a developmental strategy. Second, in the absence of the appropriate framework, the developmental strategy adopted was very much derivative of either (1) crude adaptations of the ECLA import-substituting industrialization strategy,[8] (2) the Soviet model of "heavy" industry and "proportional" development, or (3) in recent years, neoclassical notions of comparative advantage and the nature of the factor endowments which are the bases from which this advantage is established.

Third, the above points also indicate, as we shall develop at some length further in the text, the fundamental importance of industry and its role in the development of the productive forces under socialism. Finally, we can observe in these quotations the trap involved in planning on the basis of *current* requirements, i.e., projecting the existing market for goods and services into the near future or the immediate planning horizon. Such a method must reproduce criteria of resource allocation, accumulation, etc., which are strongly derived from the status quo. This means that at best it can do little more than reproduce the existing patterns of production, *even if the forms of exchange and consumption change.* Yet it is clear that one cannot establish socialist relations to govern exchange and consumption if the productive structure remains basically neocolonial. Obvious as this view may seem, it nevertheless constitutes the main prevailing Utopian dream in almost all the so-called Third World countries.

Identifying issues such as these, and developing a strategy to cope with the problems they represent, are not only important to the development of socialist consciousness, but are also of vital importance to the theoretical advancement of the social sciences, and in particular economic science. The distance, if any, which we have been able to cover here, we leave for the reader to judge as he proceeds.

Notes

1. For some views on this, see William Demas, *The Economics of Development in Small Countries.*
2. The review by Carlos F. Diáz-Alejandro appears in the *Journal of Economic Literature.* The books reviewed are: *The Theory of Moral Incentives in Cuba*, edited by R. M. Bernardo; *Revolutionary Change in Cuba*, edited by Carmelo Mesa-Lago; *Man and Socialism in Cuba: The Great Debate*, edited by Bertram Silverman.
3. Although not emphasized, the notion of self-sustained development in the neoclassical literature implies that development is sustained on the basis of production for profit.
4. See J. M. Montias, *Economic Development in Communist Rumania.* The data are taken from Table 1.7, p. 25.
5. See A. R. M. Ritter, "Growth Strategy and Economic Performance in Revolutionary Cuba: Past, Present and Prospective." The second section of this paper is headed: "The First Strategy, 1961-63: Instant Industrialization." In Table 3 (p. 320), it is interesting to see that by 1963 actual investment in agriculture was 24.3 percent and industry 25.6 percent of total investment, but that by 1965 the figures were 40.4 percent for agriculture and 18.1 percent for industry.
6. Ibid., p. 319.
7. Ibid., p. 324.
8. One might say, given the criterion in use, that this was import substitution with a vengeance.

Part 1

General Analysis

1

Dependence and the Transition to Socialism

Colonialism, poverty, war, hunger, racism and genocide—all these and more have been both cause and effect of the worldwide spread of the capitalist mode of production. The progressive socialization of global production which this has *objectively* entailed, together with its form of private appropriation of both the means and objects of production, at first seemed capable of sustaining an unlimited expansion of the world's productive forces. Despite its early period of tremendous vigor, however, capitalism contained within itself an unanticipated dynamic of underdevelopment. By underdevelopment we refer to the present peculiar conjunction of productive forces and production relations among the "poor" countries, which at the prevailing levels of human technological development constitutes the *objective* basis of their poverty and of the growing inequalities of income and wealth which the world system of production and exchange naturally reproduces.

This study is primarily devoted to an examination of two basic issues which derive from these historical experiences—or, perhaps more accurately, two fundamental aspects of the same set of social phenomena. On the one hand, it is concerned with providing a broad analysis of certain economic aspects of dependence and underdevelopment in order to indicate the ways in which these factors interact on societies struggling to develop their productive forces during the "transition to socialism." On the other hand, it attempts to design an economic strategy to cope with the enormous problems of developing indigenous productive forces in the process of transforming the mode of production from one of dependence and underdevelopment to socialism. These two issues are examined in Parts 1 and 2 respectively. Since economic issues cannot be scientifically considered in isolation, certainly not outside of the context of such political and social issues as class and organization, which lie at the heart of production relations and are particularly crucial during periods of fundamental change, references to the wider context of social and political relationships appear throughout the book. However, in Part 3 we isolate a few of these issues for further treatment.

It will be evident to readers as they proceed that while these separations have been devised for analytical convenience, our intention has been to integrate both analysis and prescription at all stages of the main argument. In view of this overall approach, it would seem logical to begin by delineating quite clearly the sort of societies to which our analyses and prescriptions are directed, and the specific range of historical experiences with which we are concerned. In this way we may be able to avoid some of the unfortunate terminological confusion which has too often characterized such endeavors.

At the outset it should be firmly established that we shall be dealing exclusively with the problems of developing the productive forces that would confront what would contemporaneously be described as an underdeveloped economy during the "transition to socialism." It is recognized that in actual practice the notion of the "transition to socialism" has been applied to a much broader range of circumstances and a wider variety of present-day societies than are dealt with here. It has been employed in the study of the industrialized socialist states of Eastern Europe at all stages of their development since the October Revolution and has been used in reference to China, Cuba, Mongolia, North Korea, Chile, and

Tanzania, as well as to a wide gamut of Third World economies, such as Egypt (at one time), Algeria, Zambia, etc. Indeed, it has been used wherever it has been believed that progressive policies were being actively implemented.

For our own part, we are definitely not interpreting the notion of the "transition to socialism" in the sense of the now famous Sweezy/Bettelheim debate.[1] In those exchanges the analyses made were largely confined to the industrialized East European societies (and to a lesser extent China), where forms of socialist government practicing variants of scientific socialism have already been well established and where the problems of the development of productive forces are presently of an entirely different order. Our deliberate avoidance of concern over these problems of the industrialized socialist states should not be construed as a flat denial of the possibility that some readers might find what is written here relevant to the study of these societies. It is simply that we are purposefully avoiding focusing on these societies because it is our conviction, as will be indicated later, that the political, social, and economic processes that have characterized the recent history of these societies are qualitatively different from those of underdevelopment, which presently characterizes the societies we are seeking to encompass in this study. It follows that many of the problems which we shall identify here are not likely to be strictly comparable.[2]

There is indeed no real difficulty posed by this decision to exclude this class of societies from the study. Where a genuine difficulty seems to lie is in the categorization of the other societies—the Third World countries—since the practice has been to apply this phrase very loosely. To our mind this situation has developed because often it seems as if the major criterion used is simply whether the political leader (or leadership) describes himself, or his country, as being socialist or aspiring thereto. It does not require much reflection to realize that such a criterion is clearly of limited analytical value although it has been ingeniously suggested that the popularity of this form of self-description among Third World states is of significance to socialism. Thus the Hungarian economist

Szentes takes the view that this usage represents an explicit nationalist position, and an implicit recognition by the leadership of these countries not only of the universal imperatives of poverty, exploitation, and liberation, but also of the incapacity of the international capitalist system, given the way their societies are integrated into it, to eliminate underdevelopment and initiate autonomous and self-reliant development of the broad mass of their peoples. In other words, it constitutes another demonstration of the power of experience to teach:

> It is needless to emphasize again that without fighting for economic independence and the cutting down of the income drain as well as for the transformation of the economic and social structure, there is no chance at all for overcoming "underdevelopment," this peculiar and complex socioeconomic product of a lopsided development. The recognition of this truth does not require *a priori* socialist consciousness, not even a democratic, anti-imperialist approach from the outset. As it follows from the objective logic of development, *life and practice* may teach all those who are keeping in view, the *national interests* of their own country.[3]

While there is no doubt some truth to this view, it can easily be, and perhaps has been, overstated. It would appear more accurate to interpret the practice of such regimes to represent themselves as socialist as indicating not much more than a stratagem designed to mask the actual neocolonial character of these societies by suggesting that the present leadership is, or can be, representative of liberationist social and political forces at home. On this basis we can see that it has been employed mainly to serve the propagandist aim of creating a political platform for establishing the internal and external legitimacy of these regimes. That this tactic has met with not inconsiderable success, there can be little doubt. Much "radical" opinion (not to mention bourgeois opinion) has been swayed by pronouncements of this sort, whose fraudulent character has only later been exposed by historical experience. Thus we find the labels proliferating: Arab Socialism, African Socialism, Cooperative Socialism, and so on.

Again it is important that we do not detain ourselves on this score and allow the issues to degenerate into a purely terminological debate. Surely this phenomenon can only be confusing at the most naive level of social analysis. Accordingly, in view of these vague and unsatisfactory usages, the second dimension by which we shall delineate our area of study is by confining our attention not just to underdeveloped economies but to those in which a *political revolution has been initiated and has succeeded in transferring state power to a worker/peasant alliance, thereby fundamentally altering production relations so that the struggle to bring the productive forces under their control and direction, to disengage from international capitalism, and to raise the material levels of welfare of the population are the central economic issues at that stage in constructing socialism.* It follows from this delineation of our area of analysis that even though immense political and social problems still remain—such as defining the working relationship between the two classes, containing the local petty bourgeoisie and the bureaucracy, etc.—these problems, even where they may be important, are subsidiary to the major political issue of state power, which we shall take as being solved at the outset. It is only by making such an assumption that we can genuinely isolate for consideration the period of the transitional development of productive forces.

In addition to the specifications that the dominance of a worker/peasant alliance has been established and that the society we are dealing with is in the category of underdeveloped countries, two further characteristics are used to specify our area of concern. These are: that the societies we shall be considering are assumed in general to be small, and that the struggle to establish socialism is expected to take place during the present historical phase where their international relationships are of a neocolonial form. While, as we shall argue and demonstrate, smallness affects many of the manifestations of underdevelopment and the policies called for, the neocolonial situation is also of crucial importance since it constrains the real possibilities confronting these states within the international economy.

Smallness is not interpreted here as an attribute of material reality capable by itself of creating social forms. On the contrary, it is interpreted simply as constituting, in a certain sense, an additional dimension to underdevelopment, while underdevelopment itself can in turn only be explained in terms of historical dialectics. Thus size is not simply and crudely a constraint imposed by nature on social development. Smallness essentially manifests itself as one aspect of the context of relations between classes and groups in a society, and their own relationships to the material environment of their political unit. Smallness is therefore not the cause, but the spatial, demographic, and resource context in which social relations are formed and developed and the mode of production is organized. For our own purposes we suggest that smallness as an additional feature gives a qualitatively different character to two major manifestations of underdevelopment. One is the present nature of the structural dependence of the small underdeveloped economies on international capitalism. The other is the constraints which size and structural dependence together place on the material base of these societies, and hence on their material capacity to be transformed. By structural dependence we mean the extent to which the economic structure of these economies depends on foreign trade, payments, capital, technology, and decision-making to generate domestic economic processes.[4]

Smallness can be roughly measured as a composite and appropriately weighted index of population, national output—including its distribution between persons and its spatial concentration (dispersion)—and geographical area. The underdeveloped economy is then small when national expenditure on an important range of producer goods (and some consumer goods) imposes a serious constraint on the national capacity to establish certain plants which have been instrumental in the transformation of such socialist economies as the USSR. Deliberately, a great deal of precision is not being attached here to the measure of smallness. The use of such concepts as "constraints," "certain plants," etc., is deliberate, since in theory it cannot be denied that any plant can be established virtually anywhere and that how the social costs incurred would be measured—interpreted—would differ in different societies. Therefore, pursuing the measurement of smallness with any theoretical precision could also easily lead to endless terminological debate and perhaps sidetrack us from the real issue this study hopes to take up. It would also be unscientific to seek to give an absolute valuation to what is essentially a relative concept. The notion of smallness has to be given a historical perspective which allows for dynamic changes in population, resources, output, technology, and even geographical area (either through conquest or the merging of nation states). Given this, what is seen as small now may not be small in the future. Past history abounds with examples which show that size is not a constant factor.

For our purposes it is sufficient for readers to recognize that the size factor varies in such a way that it is generally—and, as we shall indicate, uncritically—accepted that the material prospects for, say, a China-type underdeveloped economy to transform itself in the present historical epoch are very different from those of, say, Cuba or Tanzania, as indeed their recent historical experiences readily show. In support of this view one has only to note the emphasis put by China on heavy industry in its economic program—an emphasis that has been taken to be natural and acceptable, in contrast with the way Cuba is taken to have "mishandled" its economic planning by abandoning its comparative advantage in sugar, or at best agriculture, and by pursuing "adventurist" industrialization policies. The partial reversal of the Cuban economic strategy would seem to support the argument advanced here. If this were not enough evidence, one can also examine "socialist" economic policy in Tanzania and study the various reasons advanced concerning the inability and irrationality of pursuing an economic program which places heavy industry first.[5] Thus, in an almost gratuitously scathing reference to the Cuban leadership, Karol points out:

> And so they persuaded themselves that quick industrialization was the cornerstone of Cuban socialism, and that everything else would follow in due course. There were many voices to warn them against the social upheavals their four-year plan was bound to create, but they refused to listen.[6]

Meanwhile, K. N. Raj reports approvingly of the greater emphasis immediately put by China, as compared with India, on its "machine-tool sector" (defined as the sector which manufactures capital goods for producing other capital goods) during the First Five-Year Plan. Thus he remarks: "China has attached very high priority to machine-building, and to the 'machine tool sector' within it, from the very beginning of its development program." He goes on to note that the First Five-Year Plan specified that "the machine-building industry is the key to the technological transformation of our national economy," and to comment on the Second Plan as follows:

> The emphasis on machine-building was continued in the Second Plan. Though information on the progress made during the period 1958-62 is much more scanty than for the preceding few years, there is general agreement that there was spectacular growth of industrial production in the first three years of this period.[7]

Further evidence of this policy of rapid industrialization in China is also provided by Wheelwright and McFarlane:

> The aims of the First Five-Year Plan were to lay the foundations of a comprehensive industrial structure as rapidly as possible. Priority of investment funds (over 50 percent) was given to the capital goods industries, which were planned to grow faster than the consumer goods industries although output of the latter was also to be increased. The proportion of the state budget devoted to agriculture was relatively low (6.2 percent), but investment in agriculture by the peasants themselves was not included in the state budget. *The economic strategy followed was that pioneered by the Soviet Union.*[8]

Contrary to popular impressions even during the Great Leap Forward, the policy of "walking on two legs" was not based on "the sacrifice of the development of big industries and the large plant sector in the interests of rural industrialization." In fact, "large industry continued to make the decisive contributions in iron, steel, heavy machinery, machine tools, and power."[9]

While these approving descriptions are being made, Huberman and Sweezy comment on Cuba as follows: "*By committing herself to a program of industrial diversification, Cuba would in effect be condemning herself to industrial backwardness.*"[10]

We shall be taking up the discussion of these points in greater detail later on and also will provide further examples of the widespread view to be found in both neoclassical and socialist economic theory that the small underdeveloped economy is virtually incapable of industrial transformation. Such a view would seem to leave virtually no scope for these economies—as compared with the larger underdeveloped economies—to develop their productive forces under socialism. We shall of course be concerned with pointing out the incorrectness of these views and offering a strategy which explicitly incorporates the constraining factor of size.

Another example of the importance the literature attaches to the size context in which social relations develop is the tendency for economists to concede (or at least to be more flexible in their approach) that an indigenous capitalism *might* develop in one or another of the larger underdeveloped areas (e.g., Mexico, Brazil) which, as in the case of Japan, would have a capacity to raise substantially the level of material output and establish in the process a modern industrial structure. Although the greater likelihood of a bourgeois revolution in such countries is of course not a function of size, if a bourgeois revolution does occur in states with a sufficiently propulsive industrial base for the capitalists to capitalize on, then the development of an industrial capitalism in these states cannot in principle be ruled out. However, if such a development does occur, it *can only be an exception* so long as the overriding balance of capitalist relations on a world scale is not drastically altered beyond its present form.

A final observation which we would like to make at this

stage on the question of size is that an examination of the world map would reveal that potentially the societies we propose to deal with in this study represent the vast majority of states in the present world order. They could possibly include all the underdeveloped societies (allowing for borderline cases) except China, India, Indonesia, Mexico, Brazil, Pakistan, and Bangladesh.

Given the potential number and range of such societies it is necessary for us to acknowledge that some very major difficulties exist. One of these is that these societies would be confronted during the "transition to socialism" with the fact that Marxist economic theory, as it has developed so far, does not deal satisfactorily, or indeed specifically, with the problems of developing the productive forces of such economies during the transition period. More specifically, we may say that socialist economic theory does not deal adequately with the problems of designing an economic strategy for transforming underdeveloped economies which, in addition to all that this implies, are also small and must undergo this transformation during the present neocolonial phase. Furthermore, since the experiences in this field are also fairly recent and largely confined to the economies of North Korea, Cuba, North Vietnam, and to a lesser extent Tanzania, there have been only limited opportunities for forging the required theoretical apparatus through practice.

Although this study and the responses to which it may give rise would represent efforts to fill part of this void, it is worthwhile for us to note some of the general factors which have been responsible for the present lack of theoretical development in this area. First, socialist economic theory has for much of its history tended to be preoccupied with the growth of industrial capitalism within the "center" countries, and only comparatively recently has there been evidence of an increasing amount of research and study directed toward the economic problems of the "periphery." Now, as we shall indicate in the course of this study, some of the central mechanisms which Marx has identified in regard to classical industrial capitalism, and which he has analyzed so effectively in that context, do not operate in the same form, if they operate at all, in the economies under consideration. This ought not to be surprising, as these societies do in fact clearly represent different socioeconomic systems from that of industrial capitalism. So, although the Marxian *method* of scientific analysis would hold, the results obtained from a study of industrial capitalism cannot, without serious qualification, be directly applied. One important consequence of this is that it clearly determines the limits to the prescriptive usefulness of existing socialist theory.

Such a recognition on our part does not imply that Marxian economic theory, and the subsequent elaboration and development which followed from the continuing analysis of capitalism, particularly monopoly capitalism and imperialism, has not been invaluable in aiding our understanding of the historical development of dependency, underdevelopment, and neocolonialism. On the contrary, it has been, and during the course of this study we shall be relying extensively on socialist theory and research in this area.

It is to be noted that, despite its general preoccupation with capitalism—and by extension with imperialism, neocolonialism, and so on—when socialist economic theory has turned its attention to the study of the economics of the transition period, the focus has been the Soviet Union and Eastern Europe. None of these countries were underdeveloped in the sense in which we speak of underdevelopment today, and their transition did not occur during the neocolonial phase, in the more-or-less total absence of an indigenous industrial and technological capacity. Indeed, even in terms of overall participation in international trade, the European socialist countries in 1938 contributed only about 6 percent of world trade, while having 20 percent of the world area and at least 20 percent of its total output at that time. These qualitatively different features of the economy have to be taken into account when drawing upon their experiences.

The second reason for the difficulties we have noted is that there has been a correct tendency, stemming from the historicological bases of Marxian theory, to avoid "writing recipes" for the future, particularly when the future is very distant. To have considered theorizing on the prescriptions for transforming a typically small underdeveloped economy, even thirty years ago when neocolonialism was only establishing its roots, would certainly have constituted "recipe-writing" for the future. Now, however, the historical future of the societies with which we are presently concerned has effectively caught up with the need for recipes. Already some of them (e.g., Cuba, North Vietnam, and to a much lesser extent Tanzania) seem to represent fairly closely the type of societies we are seeking to analyze in this study.

A third reason for the present underdevelopment of socialist theory has been the virtual freeze on creative writing in the field of economics for relatively long periods in the history of socialism in Eastern Europe, chiefly up to the late 1950s. Caught in the vortex of a dogmatic presentation of Marxist theory, a situation actually developed in which, although Marxian theory gave the only scientific explanation of past international economic history, Western neoclassical economic theorizing nevertheless seemed to be offering more practical tools for economic transformation. It was even the case that some of these tools and techniques offered by neoclassical theory (e.g., programming and activity analysis) were actually first developed in the socialist countries and, although clearly more useful and effective in the context of the kind of comprehensive planning possible only in these societies, they nevertheless lay dormant until they were finally brought into active use by Western scholars and subsequently adapted and applied to underdeveloped economies. The tragic irony of this development is that it was Lenin who, in his development of Marx's work, gave the first systematically scientific analysis of imperialism and the role of the colonial and semi-colonial territories in the process of the global expansion of capitalism. Thus these developments meant that a great deal of theoretical headway was lost during the great freeze.

This point of view has been supported by Mandel:

The most fertile period of Marxist economic theory was that between 1894 and 1914. After the publication by Friedrich Engels of Volumes 2 and 3 of Marx's *Capital*, and the assimilation of these volumes, after the publication by Kautsky of Marx's *History of Economic Doctrines* . . . in an atmosphere of rapid advance of the labour movement and of intense ideological struggle between "Marxists" and "revisionists," there came out, one after another, Lenin's work on the development of capitalism in Russia, Kautsky's on capitalism in agriculture, Parvus's first studies of imperialism, the debates among the Russian "legal Marxists" on the theory of crises, and then, the culmination of this entire epoch, Rudolph Hilferding's *Finance Capital* and Rosa Luxemburg's *Accumulation of Capital* . . . The bulk of these studies constituted a "bringing up to date" of Marxism in face of the structural transformation which had taken place in the world market as well as in the imperialist countries themselves in the epoch of monopolies . . . A second phase of development of Marxist economic theory, less fertile than the first, extended from the end of the First World War to the beginning of the great economic crisis of 1929-33. Two categories of problems held the center of attention: those of a society in transition between capitalism and socialism (that is, of Soviet economy), and those of imperialism . . . But at the very moment when the bankruptcy of traditional bourgeois political economy became plain, and when bourgeois economic thought made its pragmatic turn, Marxist thought, far from taking a fresh leap forward, itself experienced a pragmatic transformation, at least in the Soviet Union and in every milieu dominated by the Soviet Union. From being an instrument of research into objective truth it was degraded to the role of justifying *a posteriori* the political or economic decisions taken by the government of the USSR.[11]

Dobb, commenting on the same period, is equally frank:

One thing, at least, seems quite certain: after a fairly long period of dormancy, there has been in the last few years quite a remarkable revival (one is tempted to use the word renaissance) of economic discussion and theoretical activity in the Soviet Union, as well as in other socialist countries, and signs of a new and more

> creative approach to the problems of a socialist economy . . . After the animated debates of the 1920's, it seemed as though a pall had descended over economic discussion during the next two decades. At first one was inclined to consider this to be not unnatural in view of intense preoccupation with practice in the "heroic" pre-war decade and the decade of the war and its aftermath . . . There were some straws in the wind, however, that caused one to think there might be more to explain than this. On the one hand, there were recurrent complaints about the low level of economic theory, the prevalence of "narrow practicalism" and purely descriptive writing, and the failure to generalize the experience of a socialist economy . . . On the other hand, when occasional *ex cathedra* pronouncements on matters of economic theory were made, the subsequent commentaries on them, alike in the USSR and other socialist countries, were surprisingly empty of content.[12]

Both these long quotations from two economists who, starting from different theoretical perspectives, have made intensive studies of the Soviet Union since the October Revolution, note the decline of theory and the absence of significant theoretical and research work relevant to our chosen field of inquiry within the industrialized socialist states of Eastern Europe.

Despite the importance of all three of the reasons advanced so far, it is the fourth and final one which we believe is ultimately the most significant for explaining the existence of the theoretical and analytical void we are attempting to rectify in some small way in this study. Stated simply, it is that in many of these societies under consideration it is only now that a first generation of modern indigenous scholarship has begun to take root. This has been the product of a variety of circumstances, all basically bound up with their (until very recently) colonial status. Indeed, the absurd situation exists that most of these countries have only had their own universities during the last thirty years or so. As one would expect, when a large proportion of mankind is cut off from the opportunity to acquire skills with which to examine their own societies, the result has been a severe restriction of the growth of an indigenous scientific tradition. But society always pays a price for such deliberate stultification of its own growth. In this instance it has resulted in a wide gap between social reality and the development of the theoretical apparatus to understand it. Despite the belated proliferation of recent studies in this field, enormous lacunae remain to be filled.

One important by-product of these analytical omissions of socialist economic theory is that in many of the underdeveloped societies—even in those where at times the balance of social forces has been in favor of progressive "socialist"-type policies (e.g., Ghana, Egypt, Somalia, Guyana, Sri Lanka)—both economic planning and policy have been strongly derived from bourgeois theories of underdevelopment. Although this situation cannot be attributed simply to the absence of adequate socialist theory, this absence has not helped the struggle for socialism within these countries. Indeed, from the point of view of practical politics, neoclassical economic theories and policies have managed to maintain a nearly impregnable predominance in these countries.

The extent of this hold is even today not always fully recognized, and so it is important for us to be clear about the full implications of this position. It is doubtless true, as some would argue, that the limitations of economic planning, policy, and changes in these societies have been, and are being, strongly and effectively exposed by socialist, and other, theorists. Indeed, despite the only very belated attention focused on this area, socialist theorists have been particularly devastating in their analysis of the inability of present policies to cope with underdevelopment in the Third World. Yet the problem remains that, while social and political theories are well developed and hence are in this sense truly radical *both* in terms of analyzing the present weaknesses of the political and social systems of these societies and of identifying and elaborating clear alternatives, these radical political and social theories have yet to be combined and integrated with an equally radical economic theory which encompasses both the negative aspects (exposure of limitations) and positive aspects (constructing a strategy of transformation) of social reality. This has left socialist economic theorizing largely on the defensive, and it is with the problems to be faced in remedying this that this book concerns itself.

Notes

1. See C. Bettelheim and P. M. Sweezy, *The Transition to Socialism*, passim.
2. In an exchange of correspondence on an earlier draft of this study, Paul Sweezy pointed out that the study was really opening up the broad field of transition economics and was therefore of a wider compass. While it is true that I am directing my attention to the broad class of transition economics, it nevertheless remains that it is my present intention not to interpret and prescribe outside of the experiences indicated in this chapter. Inevitably, however, my theoretical argumentation has benefited from the transition experiences of these other societies.
3. T. Szentes, "Status Quo and Socialism" (emphasis in original); see also by the same author, *The Political Economy of Underdevelopment.*
4. For a useful discussion of size and development see A. McIntyre, "Some Issues in Trade Policy in the West Indies." McIntyre defines structural dependence as "the dependence that arises because of the size and structure of the economy" in contrast to "functional dependence," which "arises as a result of particular policies chosen." For further discussion of this approach see L. Best, "Size and Survival," and W. Demas, *The Economics of Development in Small Countries.*
5. See Cho-min Li, "China's Industrial Development"; E. Preobrazhensky, *The New Economics;* E. Boorstein, *The Economic Transformation of Cuba;* K. S. Karol, *Guerrillas in Power;* and H. Helleiner, "Socialism and Economic Development in Tanzania."
6. Karol, *Guerrillas in Power*, p. 539.
7. K. N. Raj, "Role of the Machine Tools Sector in Economic Growth," pp. 219-20.

8. E. L. Wheelwright and B. McFarlane, *The Chinese Road to Socialism*, p. 235 (our emphasis).
9. Ibid., p. 47.
10. L. Huberman and P. M. Sweezy, *Socialism in Cuba*, p. 74 (our emphasis). We shall be taking up this analysis more fully in Chapter 6.
11. E. Mandel, *Marxist Economic Theory*, pp. 722-23.
12. M. Dobb, *Capitalism, Development and Planning*, pp. 140-41.

2

Underdevelopment, Size, and the Neocolonial Mode of Production

National Independence, National Size, and Socialism

Despite its anarchic, erratic, chaotic, and immensely costly growth, the level of technological attainment of capitalism (together with the more recent and more systematically planned contributions of the socialist countries) places within the compass of human achievement enough knowledge of technical, biological, chemical, and other processes for man to be capable of a planned elimination of worldwide hunger, disease, and poverty—or certainly capable of drastically reducing their prevalence. The continuing existence of poverty, underdevelopment, and the systematic reproduction of inequalities is neither the result of nature nor a divine condition, as some would have us believe, but is instead the specific result of the conjuncture of production relations and productive forces on a world scale. It is this conjuncture which makes manifest and supports the gap between the prevailing level of material output and that level available with the full use of the productive forces at the present level of technological attainment.

Historically, this conjuncture has its origins in the political and social processes that have accompanied the worldwide spread of capitalism. It is supported in the underdeveloped countries by the national alignments of social classes and productive forces that have evolved through colonial and imperial domination. As we shall see, these social classes are incapable of generating a transformation, partly because of their origins, partly because of the absence of an indigenous material base for their existence, and partly because the internal dynamic of world capitalism is against them.

The present era of underdevelopment has also been, by and large, the era of self-determination and of the drive to create and consolidate *national* states out of what were formerly colonial or semi-colonial possessions. But once the historical process gathered social momentum in favor of national states, it inevitably had to follow that the national market, national size, and national resources all became important elements in the ability of capitalism to *generate* increases in the level of material production.

In the light of these historical realities, support for national self-determination has always been an important feature of socialist thought. This was unarguably the case after the appearance of Lenin's vigorous article, "The Right of Nations to Self-Determination." There, in refutation of Semkovsky, Liebman, and others who relied on Rosa Luxemburg's theses, Lenin argued:

> For the complete victory of commodity production, the bourgeoisie must capture the home market and there must be politically united territories whose population speak a single language . . . Unity and unimpeded development of language are the most important conditions for genuinely free and extensive commerce on a scale commensurate with modern capitalism . . . for the establishment of a close connection between the market and each and every proprietor, big or little, and between seller and buyer. Therefore the tendency of every national movement is toward the formation of *national states*, under which these requirements of modern capitalism are best satisfied . . . for the entire civilized world, the national state is *typical* . . . consequently if we want to grasp the meaning of self-determination of nations . . . we must inevitably reach the conclusion that the self-determination of nations means the political separation of these nations from alien bodies, and the formation of an independent national state.[1]

As soon as nationalism and self-determination constituted major historical forces, and as soon as socialist thought recognized the progressive character of this development, the national market and national size had to be incorporated into the contextual relations of the analyses of both capitalism and socialism. This follows from the self-evident fact that the nation, as a political unit, *is defined within a geographical framework, and production relations and productive forces are reproduced within this context. This is the case even though the conjuncture of productive forces and production relations may, in contradiction, generate transcending forces above and beyond the nation state.* The justification for our explicit incorporation of the notion of size is therefore supportive of well-known historical forces, and is indeed incontestable.

In the previous chapter we saw from the comments of Sweezy, Huberman, Karol, et al., quoted in the text, the way in which the issue of size (i.e., the national market) has implications for the analysis of socialist countries, in spite of the variety of theoretical perspectives behind these studies. The general impact of national size has been seen by these authors in terms of a strongly prejudicial assessment of the material capabilities of small countries.

Although all of the quoted works have arrived at their positions by focusing on individual countries, the impact of size also emerges, implicitly if not explicitly, from studies which focus on capitalism on a world scale. A recent and excellent study that provides a good example of this is Arghiri Emmanuel's *Unequal Exchange.* Assuming a tendency toward the equalization of profits on a world scale, Emmanuel locates the basis of inequality and nonequivalence in wages. Indeed, he argues that the level of wages is the crucial factor in economic development. Moreover, the determination of the wage rate is *independent* of the price of the output of labor, the level of technological development, and the degree of industrialization. One does not have to accept the strong consumptionist implications of his theoretical propositions to see that this is another powerful assertion of the impact of market size and national expenditure on the process of the development of capitalism in the underdeveloped countries:

> There are many examples where technological progress and industrialization *do not precede* the increase in wages, but follow it. This was the case in the United States in the eighteenth century . . . Development then appears not as the cause but as the effect of high wages . . . The capitalist world cannot show a single instance of a high-wage country that has had to reduce wages owing to failure to develop, or a single instance of a country that has been able to develop while keeping wages low . . . that famous "blocking" of development that is characteristic of capitalism in the peripheral countries. Why has this blocking happened? . . . Quite simply, because the wages and so the standard of living of the population of those countries being low, these consumer-goods industries have not developed extensively enough to provide adequate outlets for a local heavy industry, and also because this heavy industry would entail such high organic compositions both of capital and of labor that the low wages of the local laborers would not compensate.[2]

Emmanuel is very careful to point out that this analysis does not hold true for socialist planning since, as history shows, socialist states have "achieved exceptional growth rates while keeping wages down to a low level for a long period." However, he continues: "This does not reveal a contradiction in the conclusion of my analysis, but rather the objective contradiction between a competitive economy and a planned one."[3] The argument to be stated here is, therefore, the other side of the coin, since it relates market size via wage expenditure to the capacity of capitalism to transform the underdeveloped economy, whereas the earlier works were directed toward an evaluation of the capacity of socialism to transform the material base of the small underdeveloped economy. The question we may rightly ask is, where does this leave the vast majority of states in the present world order? Are they condemned to the perpetual limbo of dependence and neocolonialism?

Underdevelopment: Neoclassical General Theories

This conjuncture of production relations and productive forces generated by the rise and spread of capitalism, which is at the base of our theoretical understanding of the development of underdevelopment, is not acceptable to bourgeois analysis. Certainly its offshoot, neoclassical economic theory, does not see the economic process in these terms. Instead, and on the face of it, there appear to be a wide variety and multiplicity of theories which purport to explain the phenomena of underdevelopment.

First we have the "overpopulation" theorists, who seek to explain underdevelopment in terms of high population-to-land ratios in the underdeveloped economies. These high ratios, combined with rapid demographic growth (i.e., a high birth rate and a rapidly declining death rate) and a highly dependent population structure, are supposed to account for the failure of incomes to grow, poverty to be alleviated, the pressure on resources to be eased, and employment opportunities to be created in sufficient quantities. The basic policy prescriptions derived from these theories are obviously those aimed at containing this so-called demographic "explosion" through appropriate family planning procedures. When applied to small underdeveloped economies, these arguments and policy prescriptions are expected to hold *a fortiori.*

Theories of geographical determinism seek to explain underdevelopment as a product of the limitations of the physical environment (i.e., in terms of soil, climate, and natural resources). Thus the tropical countries are poor because they are tropical and have debilitating climates, poor soil, and unknown resource endowments. One is then encouraged to take a philosophical view of the natural and enduring nature of poverty in these societies. Again, when applied to the small countries, these arguments apply *a fortiori* since, given a random distribution of global resources, the smaller the country, the more likely it will be that its natural resources are severely limited. If, in addition, it is located in the tropics, then all of the basic difficulties of geographical determinism are multiplied and exaggerated.

Sometimes the deterministic approach is also expressed in cultural terms—in terms of the nature of the societies that occupy these land spaces. The societies and the institutions are accordingly seen as either stagnant, traditional, and more or less uniform; or else are characterized as heterogeneous with change encapsulated in the "modern" sector. Thus theories of dualism, of the lack of "n" achievement, or of the failure of the Protestant ethic to develop, are all used to explain the development and persistence of underdevelopment or to reinforce other so-called economic interpretations. When applied to small societies these difficulties are compounded, since the smaller population base constitutes a severe limitation on the probability of there being a large number of innovators, entrepreneurs, and achievers thrown up by the society. It also maximizes the possibility of a strong interaction between interpersonal and intercommunal conflict.

One can see clearly the thrust of such reasoning. If there are certain qualities, innate or otherwise, of an individual and social nature which can be termed either consistent with development (and hence favorable), or inconsistent (and hence unfavorable), then the favorable qualities will be seen as concentrated in the developed economies, and not only will the underdeveloped economies be seen as underdeveloped because of this skewed global distribution but also, given a random distribution of these qualities among the underdeveloped countries, then the smaller the population of any one area, the smaller its likelihood of achieving self-sustained material development.

While all these theories imply a certain "philosophical" resignation to the natural and enduring nature of poverty, the more pragmatic ones do combine this with a certain prescriptive content. These are the theories which explain underdevelopment in terms of "limiting factors." These limiting factors are to be found everywhere: in the general economic structure as well as in the demographic, cultural, political, and technological features of these societies. The most important feature of these constraints is their self-perpetuating nature. It is on this basis that a whole range of theories explaining underdevelopment in terms of vicious circles and low-level equilibrium traps has been derived. Underdeveloped countries are poor because they are too poor to buy riches. Pragmatic action must therefore initiate and undertake policies to remove or ease the limiting factors. Thus innumerable policies to improve the level of domestic savings, to attract foreign capital, to improve the efficiency of the market as resource allocator, etc., are propounded, and not surprisingly constitute the basis of much of the planning in underdeveloped economies. Sometimes these are phrased in terms of strategies and policies of "big-push," "minimum critical effort," "leading sectors," etc., the idea being to intervene decisively to break the self-reproducing cycle of poverty. If the economy is small, these arguments are expected to apply *a fortiori.* If a country is underdeveloped because of limiting factors, then its smallness constitutes a further limitation and dooms it to an even more enduring poverty.[4]

All this is of course familiar ground, and we do not propose to attempt in any way to cover it in detail again. Szentes's book contains one of the ablest and most recent detailed evaluations of these contributions.[5] Our purpose in referring to these theories here is simply to make two points which are important to the course of our argument. The first and more general is that despite the apparent diversity of these theoretical formulations, there is indeed a common methodological unity in that they all purport to explain underdevelopment as a phenomenon *independent* of the historical process. They are therefore fundamentally antihistorical theories, explaining underdevelopment in terms of innate characteristics of peoples and their environments, or in terms of self-perpetuating cycles of poverty. Given this line of reasoning, it follows that the economic policies and plans that have been derived and practiced on this basis are also not informed by any serious understanding of the underdevelopment process. We shall expand on this point in the following chapter, where we conclude this part of our study on the general framework of analysis with an examination of the dynamic characteristics of the growth of those small and apparently "successful" neocolonial states.

It is important to fully understand at this stage *that it is this absence of historical understanding and awareness*—rather than the usual petty-fogging criticisms, which refer to failings in the constructed "models" as regards the misspecification of functions, the overstatement of the role of capital, or any other partial weakness of these theories and their policy prescriptions—that constitutes their fundamental weakness. It follows that the correct starting point of any "economic" strategy aimed at transforming the mode of production of a neocolonial economy to that of socialism has to be deeply informed by a thorough knowledge of the historical process of underdevelopment. In particular, it must take account of the way that this process unfolds within the constraints of a small nation state.

It is indeed quite fortunate for us that, despite their indicated limitations in the area of prescription and the practical difficulties this has given rise to in unifying radical political theory and economic theory *qua* material theory, a number of excellent historical studies of underdevelopment cover much of the basic ground. This frees us for the task of extending these analyses in the areas appropriate to our modal-type society where relevant to the task we have set ourselves.[6] As we shall come to see, some of these extensions, particularly our interpretation of underdevelopment in the small neocolonial economy, are crucial to the economic analysis and policy prescriptions which follow in the second part of this book.

The second point we wish to make clear is that despite its obvious methodological limitations, bourgeois theory has nevertheless managed to partially infect the radical analysis of these societies and the radical perception of the potentialities of their productive forces. This point can only be developed fully as the analysis proceeds, but the evidence is striking *that much of the radical view of the small underdeveloped economy and its material prospects is little more than an uncritical acceptance of inane and arrogant imperialist views of the material capacities of these societies.*

Confused notions of economies of scale, resource endowment, demand, the capital goods sector, technological capacity, and so on, abound in the radical literature. Yet all these arguments, as well as others like them, as we shall observe in this study, have no real grounding in the material and historical conditions of these societies. Instead of clear analysis, we have a tendency to rationalize and romanticize the great virtues of poverty. As a consequence, the struggle for socialism is thought to be, and has even been analytically considered, distinct from the struggle to master and conquer the material environment, to integrate this environment with society on society's own terms, and to transform the mode of production. This failure, particularly of those radical theorists who live within these societies, is a by-product of two factors. One is that underdevelopment, smallness, poverty, and dependence usually combine to make the material environment in general seem a terrifying reality; and the other is the internalization within these societies of imperial views of themselves and their capabilities.

Underdevelopment and Dependent Economic Structures

A number of empirical and historical-analytical studies, by both Marxists and non-Marxists, have marshalled overwhelming evidence to establish that, as an observable dynamic, the contradiction which has given rise to the reality of the development of underdevelopment in Third World societies is the dialectical process of the internationalization of the capitalist system.[7] Historically, the dynamic expansion of capitalism as an international system has revealed itself in a number of concrete ways.

In the first place, in the underdeveloped economies it has been observed in the dominance of foreign ownership over their local means of production and the complementary forms of dependence, which initially sustained this and which by now have become, in differing degrees among different states, *functionally autonomous.* By *functionally autonomous* we mean independent of the juridical fact of legal ownership of the means of production. The dynamics of functional autonomy exist in all the previously colonized underdeveloped economies as the means whereby social and political relations—as well as cultural and psychological attitudes—having developed around the productive forces of colonialism, alien settlement, and conquest, are reproduced during the present phase of "flag" independence. These dialectical interactions between the previous historical phase and the present do not operate with similar intensities in every underdeveloped society. In some, "flag" independence was achieved much earlier than in others. Similarly, in some the colonial societies have started almost from scratch because of the colonial policies of virtual elimination of the indigenous population (e.g., the Caribbean and much of Latin America) while in others (e.g., most of Africa and Asia) a long and resilient indigenous historical tradition existed before colonialism and managed to survive the devastation of colonial plunder.

These factors obviously give rise to diversity. However, other things being equal, it would seem plausible to expect that in the small neocolonial economy the extent of the functional autonomy of dependence will be greater—if only because, as a by-product of specialization on a world scale, the degree of integration and dependence of these economies on international capitalism is usually greater. As a consequence the strength of indigenous social, cultural, political, and economic forces vis-à-vis international capitalism is vastly inferior.

For the purposes of our analysis, it would seem that the forms of economic dependency which are most important to the economic structure, which are most likely to survive revolutionary changes in political structures, and which succeed in eliminating foreign ownership of the major means of production are: (1) the reliance on foreign technology, (2) the critical role foreign decision-making plays in domestic employment, output, and income generation, and (3) the persistent income drains which occur because surpluses obtained locally are being transferred to the owners of capital, technology, and managerial skills in metropolitan countries.

These points are readily observable if one examines not only the economies of a random selection of these countries but also the present economic situation of both Cuba and Tanzania—the two countries which seem to have gone furthest toward institutionalizing socialism.

There are, of course, psychological and cultural manifestations of dependence, which are also likely to be *functionally autonomous.* Colonialism, as is well known, did not rely exclusively on the direct and continuous use of overt violence to maintain its rule. The development of social forces and the whole institutional superstructure which grew around the productive base of colonialism survived because they functioned so as to ensure that the momentum of colonial rule was *internalized* within these social systems. In this situation, the formal abandonment of colonialism does not stop—although it does impede—the internal dynamics of dependency. Again, all this is familiar ground. The real point is that not least among these social forces which can inhibit the thoroughgoing nature of any political and social revolution *is the almost universal perception of size, and the limited psychological freedom this seems to permit, in comprehending the people's capacity to master and to bring their environment into the service of society.* A close study of economic strategy and policy in a country as poor as Tanzania seems to testify amply to the grim truth of this proposition.[8]

Combining these strands of our analysis, it is therefore not surprising that the dependent economic structure of these states takes on particular features, over and above such underdevelopment characteristics as heavy reliance on agriculture, industrial underdevelopment, low labor productivity, etc. Typically, these features of underdevelopment have been combined in such a way that export coefficients (i.e., the ratio of the value of export sales to net material product or national income) are high, usually ranging between 0.30 and 0.70. This indicates in general that structural integration and dependence on capitalism have resulted in a very high degree of specialization of output marketed as export sales. Sometimes this specialization was induced, as when the indigenous subsistence economy of Africa was brought within the orbit of international capitalism after colonial conquest. At other times it has been the direct result of capitalism going abroad, as in the Caribbean and Latin America where the indigenous society was destroyed and the productive forces brought directly into the capitalist division of labor on a global scale.

In neoclassical economics this specialization of small economies has usually been interpreted as an exclusive and direct function of size. If specialization on a global scale was to be efficient, it was then argued, a small country had to husband its limited resources to produce a large volume of output in order to put itself in a position to reap economies of scale. To be able to do so, it had to specialize its production for sale in the international, and not the national, market:

> It has been frequently alleged that small nations generally have the following three characteristics when compared with larger nations: (a) a high ratio of international trade to national product, (b) a high commodity concentration in their export trade, and (c) a high geographic concentration in their export trade. It is also sometimes alleged that they should have a relatively low commodity concentration in their import trade. The essential principle of international trade is that each country specializes in the production, but not generally in the consumption, of the goods in which it enjoys a comparative advantage. Small nations specialize in the production and export of a more limited range of products, it is contended, and hence may be expected to import a greater variety of goods which are not produced domestically.[9]

It is not surprising that further empirical analysis along these lines has found that a comparison of both small and large countries shows that there is no statistical significance to the effect of size as a determining factor in observed variations in the degree of concentration of import trade. Nor has it been found, as is sometimes argued, that the geographical concentration of a small country's export trade reflects the fact that any one large country to which it sells would be able to absorb a high proportion of its output, leaving little scope for market diversification. The trade structures of these countries cannot be explained outside of the specific historical processes of colonialism. Size is the context, not the cause, of economic specialization. Trade ties, when measured in terms of market concentration, are above all else a reflection of which nation happened to be the dominant colonizing power vis-à-vis the country in question.

Moreover, the much-referred-to export dependency of the economic structure of these countries is not, and indeed cannot be, interpreted as a uni-dimensional phenomenon (i.e., it cannot be interpreted *simply* as a measure of the high proportion of domestic output which is exported, qualified by the degree of its market concentration). To be meaningful, measures of export dependency must also take into account the simultaneously occurring and compounding influences of: (1) the concentration of production for exports on primary output—that is, on either raw materials, simply processed, or more recently, as we shall analyze in the next chapter, on the assembly and re-export of knocked-down imported products; (2) the further concentration of this export production on a more or less narrow range of primary commodities; and (3) the further fact that sales in these narrow metropolitan markets, particularly of agricultural commodities, are unstable—that is, they are characterized by frequent imbalances between the rate of growth of overseas demand and domestic supply.

For the small neocolonial economy, the result of the present conjuncture of production relations and productive forces is to create an economic structure in which the generative impact on the domestic economy of the overseas sale of its domestic production is minimal in relation to the ratio of the value of these sales to total output. This does not mean—as it does in the radical literature where this feature is frequently exaggerated—that it is correct to argue that there is no "carry-over" from the export sector to the national economy. There is, indeed, in the form of wage payments, government taxes, and so on. Moreover, what is truly significant is that the carry-over is *often substantial, relative to the surplus needed to satisfy those domestic social classes which benefit from this dependent structure.* The real nature of the carry-over problem, however, lies in the fact that, despite the varying income shares obtained by the dependent countries from this pattern of integration into international capitalism, *relative* to the strategic role these sectors play in the economic process there has been and will continue to be insufficient carry-over, by way of the normal economic (and political) processes, to facilitate successful economic transformation. Thus, given the existing carry-over mechanisms and the social classes which principally benefit from the income generated in the export sector, trade has become not simply evidence of structural imbalance, but also serves to support those relations of production which can only exist through the systematic reinforcement of structural imbalance.[10]

Given the incapacity of the existing institutional arrangements to absorb and redirect the surplus in a way consistent with the requirements of transformation, it follows that, with so much of national output highly specialized and dependent on international capitalism, the rate of domestic accumulation and the transfer of technology from the capitalist center to these states will be highly dependent on the pattern and rate of foreign capital inflow. Historically, this has created a noticeable degree of what has been termed technological dualism (i.e., where the plantation, estate, and mining sectors have usually employed so-called best-practice technology, technology which is unrelated to domestic resource availability and is simply transferred from the industrialized capitalist countries to the local economy). Because such technology is adapted in these industrialized capitalist countries to their needs, and in particular to their tendencies to long-run labor shortages, it is frequently found that when operating within the local economy these firms have enjoyed low labor-cost/total-income ratios. These ratios are of course the result of a complex and dynamic relationship, made more complex by the fact that under the impetus of competition and the search for profit, there is a further self-reinforcing bias in favor of substituting machinery for labor power in order to contain costs and raise labor productivity. One important result for the structure of these economies is that these firms are well situated to pay wage rates on the local market which are considerably out of line with the "real" social costs of labor. The labor market is therefore not integrated but is divided in such a way that the prosperity of the high wages sector becomes the key factor in determining labor's share of national output.

This capitalist division of the labor market between the so-called modern sector and the reserve army of the unemployed and the peasants has given rise to the frequent allegations that a "labor aristocracy" has been or is in the process of being created.[11] From the point of view of the worker/peasant alliance, this raises issues important to the dynamics of their mutual relationship, as well as to the functioning of the bureaucracy under what, given the inevitable initial shortage of skills, is most likely to be its continuing petty-bourgeois leadership. While for the purposes of this study we have assumed the firm entrenchment of such a worker/peasant alliance, in order to focus at this stage on the struggle to cope with the development of productive forces and to transform the economic structure, we shall put off the discussion of the very important problems this raises in regard to these interactions until the last part of this book. Suffice it to state here that we regard the notion of, and indeed any significant development of, a "labor aristocracy" as strongly inimical to the real possibilities of constructing socialism in a small underdeveloped neocolonial economy.

Fortunately, this problem may not be as serious as it appears, for a number of reasons. In the first place, in comparative terms the members of this so-called "labor aristocracy" are nowhere as well off as the average paid worker in the metropolitan countries from which the capital that employs them emanates. In terms of absolute income levels, they can hardly be said to be particularly flourishing and prosperous—although in some economies (e.g., the oil-dominated economies) there can be pockets of very high wage incomes. Secondly, it must be recognized that proletarian struggle, which takes the form of organized labor movements operating in anarchic and distorted market systems such as those which still characterize these economies, constitutes part of the *national* struggle to retain domestic income, *no matter how inequitable is the resultant distribution of retained income.* Finally, while it is true that there will always be an incipient differentiation of wage income, even here the levels actually reached in the various neocolonial economies vary considerably. In some economies (e.g., Tanzania) wage employment in the high wage manufacturing sector is a very minute proportion of the total labor force, which up to now has remained predominantly rural.

Before leaving this point, it is worth noting by way of conclusion that we are not overlooking the very considerable prevailing inequities of domestic income distribution in these economies. On the contrary, we fully acknowledge that they exist. They are most strikingly manifest in the rapid growth and high level of urban unemployment, in some instances encompassing as much as one-quarter of the labor force. Often, as for example in Latin America, where urban unemployment has reached such high levels, it constitutes one of the most sensitive areas of social and political development. The urban ghetto becomes not only the physical locale of the unemployed, but a complex institutional framework, which all too frequently serves as the social formation for converting the peasant into a proletarian worker. In light of the relative infancy and the other limitations of the industrialization process in these countries, the strains and tensions located here are inevitably considerable. The conclusion follows that the economic structures of these countries, based as they ultimately must be on labor power, are both fractured and fragile. It is their awareness of this basic fragility which accounts for the increasingly repressive attitudes of their various local administrations, despite the fact that they call themselves "governments of the people."

Underdevelopment in the Small Economy: The Material Dynamic

The historical evidence shows that by the middle of the eighteenth century many of the economic preconditions of capitalism—the spread of money economy, the primitive accumulation of commercial capital, the level of technology, the network of trade, and so on—had generally developed to such a point over large parts of the globe that, although the social conditions conducive to the birth of industrial capitalism gave Europe an early lead, this lead was not of truly decisive proportions. It was rather made decisive and indisputable only by the developments which preceded and accompanied the development of Europe—plunder, slavery, and colonial conquest.

The establishment of colonial territories (e.g., British India) was a formal expression of the internalization, within the system of industrial expansion in Western Europe, of the development-underdevelopment dynamic of capitalism on a world scale. In other words, European development generated the underdevelopment of the rest of the world by destroying those indigenous social forces which otherwise might have led to the transformation of their precapitalist modes of production. In their place they offered trade (i.e., participation in the global division of labor as providers of raw materials and consumers of manufacturing output). This trade, reinforced by politically directed violence, destroyed and put into disarray the existing relations of production within these countries. The consequence was that European-directed relations of production took over. Naturally, these were designed to bring the domestic productive forces into the service of the industrial bourgeoisie of Europe. The ultimate consequence of these developments was that *the productive forces of these countries were torn loose from their roots in the domestic market.* Thereafter, production became increasingly divergent from, and unresponsive to, the needs of the local people.

Our attempt to develop the historical analysis in the context of our modal-type of society has brought us to the point where we can advance the major proposition which underlies the strategy developed in Part 2 of this book. Interpreting the historical evidence, it suggests that there is a crucial feature in the combination of smallness and underdevelopment. When dynamically applied and expressed in terms of objective, material phenomena, this consists of the fact that the conjunction of production relations and productive forces is of such a character that the measure of structural dependence, underdevelopment, and the economic backwardness of the process of production which is important above all others is *on the one hand, the lack of an organic link, rooted in an indigenous science and technology, between the pattern and growth of domestic resource use and the pattern and growth of domestic demand, and, on the other, the divergence between domestic demand and the needs of the broad mass of the population.* This interpretation has both quantitative and qualitative dimensions.[12] Together they demonstrate that the crucial elements in the functioning of an economic system *qua* economic system (i.e., the linkages between: labor-resources-technology-production-demand-needs) are of such a character and are organized in such a way that these communities have internalized through their social relations of production and the use of their productive forces, a pattern of consumption that does not represent the needs of the community and a pattern of production not oriented to either domestic consumption or domestic needs.

This observation is well supported by Rodney's study of African history:

> Europe exported to Africa goods which were already being produced and used in Europe itself—Dutch linen, Spanish iron, English pewter, Portuguese wines, French brandy, Venetian glass beads, German muskets, etc. . . . the overall range of trade goods which left the European ports of Hamburg, Copenhagen, and Liverpool *was determined almost exclusively by the pattern of production and consumption within Europe.* From the beginning,

> Europe assumed the power to make decisions within the international trading system . . . *Above all European decision-making power was exercised in selecting what Africa should export—in accordance with European needs.*[13]

While a correct interpretation of the historical data and a correct focus on the central mechanisms of underdevelopment as we present them here are crucial to the development and design of an appropriate economic strategy, it does not follow that such familiar economic indices as per capita income, or social indices related to the standard of living, convey no significance. On the contrary, used with their usual limitations and cautions, such notions are of immense usefulness in gauging the prevailing levels of operation of the productive forces and in the planning of transformation. What the interpretation presented here really seeks to convey is not a simple index for measuring underdevelopment, but an interpretation of the material dynamics of developing underdevelopment in small economies such as Cuba and Tanzania which, in the absence of an indigenous technology, centers on the process of a dynamic divergence between domestic resources and domestic demand.

To be sure, this divergence, as we have seen, has been historically created. Tendencies toward this initially developed also in the larger colonial areas, but by and large this process has not developed to the same extreme, largely because the national market of these countries constituted an important area of exploitation in itself, to the extent that domestic production could be organized to do this. The early European capitalists certainly recognized this. But, more importantly, the existence of this market has given an opportunity for the rise and persistence of indigenous capitalist sectors in some of the larger ex-colonial areas (e.g., India), and this has progressed to such an extent that today, with the aid of the state, they are seeking to establish themselves as a class capable of challenging capitalism from abroad and to generate an indigenous capitalist development of productive forces.[14] In the smaller economies such developments have not, and indeed could not have, taken root to this extent.

There were no internal imperatives in terms of market size to justify the capitalist development of indigenous production for the local market. Integration into capitalism was therefore so complete that the perspective for profitable opportunities in production, which precluded all other opportunities, was that of the capitalist of the center countries. What has also been equally important, as we shall observe, is that the coming of "flag" independence has not been sufficient to alter decisively these basic features of the economic situation. Thus, unlike in some of the larger economies, there is no *genuine* alternative confronting these countries in the sense that development of their productive forces could take place *either* through the development of indigenous capitalism or through socialism. The only alternatives for the small underdeveloped economy are the perpetuation of the neocolonial mode or the development of their productive forces under socialist production relations.

Now, historically these divergences have been made manifest through different institutional forms of resource ownership, resource use, income creation, and demand formation. These have varied over time, both among states and within states. But given the relative smallness of these societies, the key aspect of the institutional variability has been its *totality*. By *totality* we mean the degree of necessary control of political, social, cultural, and psychological development which each institution engaged in economic exploitation presupposes in order to function *qua* institution. Thus we have had exploitation and underdevelopment, organized through such slave institutions as the plantation, the modern multinational corporation, direct colonial rule (i.e., the administration of production Crown Colony style), as well as through alliances with "independent" client states and the management of their state capitalist enterprises. While in each case the material dynamic has been the same, the cultural and psychological dimensions of dependence have differed to some degree. And it is to these differences we must turn in seeking to explain some of the surface contradictions among the Third World societies.

Underdevelopment: Further Dynamics

While the features examined above have historically characterized the process of underdevelopment, in designing strategies and policies for socialist transformation it is essential to take into account those further dynamic changes which are intrinsic to the present international economy and whose influence will be increasingly important in the near future (i.e., during the period when transformation is most likely to be attempted). In order to complete this discussion of the historical forces which underlie the strategy for transforming the mode of production in the small underdeveloped economies, it is therefore necessary to attend to two further tasks. The first of these is to highlight briefly those international aspects of the future development of the neocolonial mode of production which are crucial to our planning strategy. The second is to indicate certain priorities of action which are needed to establish the framework of planning we consider necessary. These tasks are attempted in this and the next section.

The first of the features of the international economy relates to the development of technology. When interpreting the material base of underdevelopment, we have advanced the view that indigenous technology is the basis for an organic integration of domestic production and demand structures. Recent developments indicate that the dynamic processes of technological dependence are leading to newer patterns in the global distribution of capitalist technology. Of most immediate and striking importance is the fact that the resources devoted to technology by governments, the military, and private firms are increasing at a very rapid rate. Inevitably this has meant that the gap in technology between the capitalist states and the periphery—where resources invested in technology are not increasing at the same rate and with the same success—is widening at a faster rate than even the much heralded gap in average incomes and levels of living.

As the Hungarian economist Bognár has noted:

> Among the long-range factors of economic growth, *education, vocational training, and scientific inquiry* are decisive. Unfortunately, qualified labor and science are even less equally distributed in our world than incomes or production . . . only 5 percent of the scientific capacity relevant for the development of economic life can be found in the developing countries whereas 95 percent is concentrated in thirty advanced countries.[15]

This distribution of technological capacity has to be measured against the fact that the former set of countries account for approximately 70 percent of the world's population, 56 percent of its land area, 20 percent of its income, 11 percent of its industrial output, and 17 percent of its foreign trade.

Such developments have created several inevitably devastating by-products of polarized growth and dependence. One of the most crucial of these is the so-called brain-drain (i.e., the transfer of skilled personnel from the periphery to the center).[16] This process is often heightened in the small economies where the "limited opportunities" for scientific inquiry and for "proper monetary rewards" are offered as behavioral rationalizations. Unfortunately, the fundamental implications of this phenomenon are not always as fully understood as they should be.

To take one example: It is commonplace—the "green revolution" notwithstanding—for scientists and others to be even more strident than in the past in their warnings of overpopulation. Almost incongruously this has been occurring at the same time when man has started to colonize beyond his planet. The radical response to this situation has been mainly to assert that overpopulation is a demographic concept, and that population growth should be relative not simply to known resources, but to resource potential and the pattern of distribution of goods, both within and between states. While this is true, if we reflect a bit we can see that there is an even greater congruity, a super-congruity as it were, in the statement. That is: the technological resources of those societies which have put man on the moon *are presently not available* to the countries with the highest population masses relative to present levels of resource exploitation *and will not be available, at least in time, through any normal trickle-down processes* to these countries. The super-congruity therefore lies in the reality, not the appearance, of the contradiction.

What this little digression indicates is that *extensive* reliance on the import of technology does not mean *free access* to the marketplace of technology. If technology is basically a monopoly of the capitalist center, it follows from the dictates of the profit motive that its distribution from the capitalist center must inevitably follow certain market norms. Among these are the need to balance the distribution of technology (i.e., the gains from its use) in order to be assured that the monopoly is maintained, not in a static sense, but dynamically, through concentrating on the really strategic areas of technological leadership as they emerge. Thus the shifting pattern of resource exploitation by the metropolitan countries of the economies of the periphery (particularly from primary production to light manufactures) reflects a shift in the technological dependence of the periphery to the newer areas of computer and communications technology, etc., and the willingness of the center countries to relinquish, at a price and for restricted uses, the technology of the light manufacturing of certain mass consumption goods. Unless this is properly understood we cannot grasp the full complexities of technological dependence.

A further consequence of this global pattern of technological growth, which as we have seen is predominantly a response to the *needs* of capitalism, is that it has been accompanied by a progressive diminution of the significance of traditional raw materials. This has been manifested in three different areas. First, there has been the widely observed growth in the development and use of synthetics (e.g., rubber, textiles, insecticides, etc.). Second, there has been a decided improvement in the final product yield of traditional raw materials. Thus the proportion of raw material input per unit of final output has been decreasing. Sometimes these two factors have operated simultaneously, compounding each other on the export earning capacity of the primary exporters. The third form of technological change has been the development of a technology that allows for the economic use of more and more marginal quality inputs to produce a final output. Whereas one would have expected that in general this would strengthen and improve the demand for raw materials from traditional sources, it has in fact (as in the case of iron ore) stimulated the use of the marginal raw material resources available within the industrialized capitalist countries themselves to the detriment of the periphery.

To cap the whole situation, when technical progress has been centered on the products of the primary producers this has tended to be reflected in a fall in prices (i.e., in favor of the consumers), in contrast to the situation in industrial countries, where technical gains are more generally distributed in favor of the producers rather than the consumers of the product. This situation has been widely observed in the literature and it reflects a number of forces at work. Not least of these are the greater monopolistic elements to be found in the production and exchange of manufactured goods as compared with primary products, and the institutional mechanisms in the industrial countries that favor wages relatively more than in the primary-producing countries. Again, these developments cannot be properly understood unless the main push toward technological advance is seen as a requirement of capitalism.

Given these forces, it is to be expected that the smaller economies would be even more disadvantaged in the process. The resources they can command in their anarchic productive arrangements do not allow for any effective challenge to this situation. It follows that a central component of the material struggle at home must be the development of an indigenous technology. But to achieve this, technology has to be seen as a response to certain social forces, and to the production and consumption relationships to which they give rise. We shall deal with these issues at length in Part 2.

The second dynamic feature, whose economic and other implications for the transition period are very important and have not yet been adequately analyzed in the literature, is the changing pattern of political and economic relationships among capitalist states. The most striking of these is the present process of rationalization of the restrictive features of nation states during the present period of capitalist expansion. This may be clearly observed in the growth of such integration and common-market agreements as the European Economic Community. A number of studies, particularly those made by Chenery in the early 1960s, have highlighted the impact of size, income, and resource endowment on the pattern and levels of industrialization of capitalist states.[17] From these it would appear that given the establishment of a capitalist industrial economy, and barring war and social collapse, the larger the market and the more diverse the resource base it can command, the greater will be its long-run growth momentum. From this it would seem that the search for integration in Europe is both an economic and a political response to the centralization of, and the competition from, the continental economy of the United States, and, to a lesser extent at the moment, to the development and consolidation of economic relationships among socialist countries.

This present process of rationalizing and widening the political and hence market limits of the relatively "small" industrialized capitalist economies of Western Europe through integration schemes which seek to widen the base area of capitalism has basic and fundamental implications. It seems to us almost certain that such developments will lead to a considerable upsurge of West European production and productivity as cartelization and market sharing are allowed to extend beyond the limits of each nation state in Western Europe. But, paralleling this upsurge in output, it must be reckoned that there will be a reduced sensitivity of Western Europe to trade—in particular, to trade with the underdeveloped economies. This follows not only because the larger economy would make neomercantilist and autarkic policies more efficient under capitalism, but because of the same long-run factors (such as the growth of substitutes, changing consumption habits, etc.) that have been leading industrialized economies to trade more with each other than with the underdeveloped economies. Given this juxtaposition of a fast-growing and dynamic regional market with tendencies toward a lowering of the income elasticity of demand for the output of the products of the underdeveloped countries, the trade bargaining position of Western Europe will be enhanced beyond its already excessive limits. This is almost certain to induce a scramble for association with Europe, particularly by the smaller undeveloped economies.

We can already see this process at work in such motley trading arrangements as the Lagos Agreement, the Yaounde Treaty, the Arusha Agreement, and the proposed associations that may be expected to follow as Britain's ex-colonies negotiate to keep their links after its recent membership in the European Common Market. A close analysis of these agreements shows that the basic strategies of these countries are both defensive (i.e., seeking to avoid exclusion from the Common Market's market or to prevent some other country that has a relationship with the Common Market and that produces products competitive with one's own from doing so) and opportunistic (i.e., aiming at carving out a special preferential access within what seems to be a rapidly growing market). There will no doubt be added to these naive efforts to try to exploit such political and economic contradictions as will arise between Western Europe, the United States, and Japan. As most of these developments will occur over the next few decades, it is important, when considering the prospects for the small underdeveloped economy in transition to socialism, to bear in mind that all these conflicts of national and regional capitalisms will in fact be taking place within the capitalist framework. The lesser regional and national capitalisms may disappear, but, short of nuclear war, higher stages of capitalistic organization and efficiency, and hence a greater capacity for exploitation, will be achieved in the process.

In other words, we might conclude that the West European Common Market is essentially a reflection of the tendency of the capitalist mode to transcend national forms. It is a direct correlate of the growth of global monopolies, the spread of multinational corporate enterprise, and the worldwide consolidation of national "capitals." In this fundamental sense these tendencies are inherent to the growth of capitalism and derive from its tendencies to reproduce the objective socialization of global production—tendencies which historically have contradictorily been supported by the strengthening of the bourgeois state.

There has recently been a tendency among the smaller underdeveloped economies to seek integration arrangements with each other, largely in imitation of developments within Western Europe. Thus we have a proliferation of such groupings as the Caribbean Free Trade Association, the East African Common Market, the Central American Common Market, and the Latin American Free Trade Association. We shall in the course of this study refer to these developments from time to time.[18] It is obvious that one way to overcome the limitations of size is to struggle politically in order to expand the geographical area of common political and economic action. But, as we shall argue, if this takes place *without* the explicit aim of transforming the production structures, then such arrangements will merely expand the permissive area of exchange (i.e., enlarge the market for neocolonial penetration) and increase the opportunities for a further deepening of the underdevelopment process—without even the compensating possibilities of developing a large national industrial structure or a capitalist class. Unless the geographical area of integration results in an effectively unified economy of considerable size—a prospect which appears very unlikely in the near future—the momentum created by the impact of imperialist rivalry and the achievement of national independence will lead toward the effective disintegration, rather than effective integration, of many of these states. Pakistan and Bangladesh are the most recent and spectacular examples.

The third and final factor we shall refer to at this stage is the growth of the socialist group of countries. We cannot pretend to discuss all the ramifications of these developments here, but it is useful to note that one important impact of these developments has been to speed up the growth of "flag" independence and to reinforce the tendencies toward neocolonial and neoimperialist methods of controlling the economic resources of the capitalist periphery. If physical occupation of territory can provoke a military confrontation that could lead to suicidal nuclear war, and if unrestricted rights of establishment to metropolitan capital are no longer politically acceptable, then imperialist penetration through the less overt methods of "aid," "technical assistance," or "partnership and management arrangements" *become more necessary, if not more profitable.* Initially, most of the aid and technical personnel were almost exclusively supplied on a bilateral basis, but recently there have been tendencies for this aid to be provided through multilateral agencies and their accompanying experts and technical assistance personnel. This difference, although largely an illusory one, is indicative of the nature of political realities. In general, the multilateralization of aid has meant the same sorts of projects, fitted into the same structures, staffed by the same experts, using the materials and technology of the same major donors.[19] The change in approach is therefore a stratagem which aims at minimizing the dangers of a purely nationalist reaction, since in many of these countries the colonial administrators have only formally taken leave in recent times, and sensitivity, if not outright suspicion, of expatriate personnel runs very high.

The dynamic consequences of the growth of socialism in some countries have been not only to induce a shift in the way capitalism maintains economic control of the periphery, but also, as a consequence of the very existence of a rapidly industrializing group of socialist countries, to increase the trading and economic alternatives of the state in transition. The alternatives to disengagement from international capitalism are therefore a drive to dynamic self-sufficiency, economic integration with the socialist group of countries, integration with other Third World countries, or some planned combination of these alternatives. In this sense, there is a fundamental widening of the options to be derived from trade.

The Political Priorities of Planning

In this the final section of the chapter we shall indicate in a very broad and general way the sort of priorities of political action which we consider to be absolutely necessary if the state is to be able to establish the planning framework with which to implement the strategy of economic transformation, as we shall be presenting it in Part 2 of this book.

In the typical small underdeveloped economy, what is presently represented as economic planning constitutes at best an informed forecasting of the major trends in the economy so as to be able to anticipate occurrences over which it is well known that the planners can, and indeed will, exercise little or no control. This situation reflects clear and definite ideological preferences. The ideology of development is frequently one in which "too much control" of the economy is considered "inefficient" and undesirable, and inconsistent with the "free" development of the market. Planning seeks to aid market development until a stage is reached where the market alone is capable of generating efficient incentives to competition and consequent changes in productive structure, capacity, and output. In this situation it is assumed that the prices in these markets will become efficient indicators of resource scarcities and consumer preferences. It is through this mechanism, therefore, that balances between supply and demand will be maintained. Planning is also rationalized as an attempt to support the development of an indigenous industrial capitalist class.

In truth, planning in these societies cannot be justified either in terms of complementing the market and correcting its deficiencies, or of promoting the growth of a genuine indigenous industrial capitalism. In the first instance, the indigenous industrial capitalist class whose situation this planning seeks to improve is virtually nonexistent. Second, the neoclassical theories on which such planning activities are based presuppose that the economic system functions with certain stabilities and regularities to permit reasonably accurate forecasting. But, given the smallness of these economies, their patterns of integration into the international capitalist economy, their excessive dependence on receiving impulses integral to the capitalist center in order for their output and employment to grow, and, finally, given the absence of a comprehensive planning capability, the assumed stabilities and regularities of these economic processes do not obtain. Consider in this regard the key relationships of the Keynesian macroeconomic short-period income, output, and employment-regulating mechanisms, on which short-period planning is all too frequently based. In these economies, the level of domestic investment does not depend on the rate of interest and the marginal efficiencies of capital, as these theories would have us believe. Given the high ratio of foreign to domestic finance in capital formation (both in the public and the private sectors), the level and rate of accumulation becomes highly dependent on the volume of foreign capital inflows. Indeed, it is not even reasonable to pretend that the rate of interest is an independently determined index of capital scarcity in the local economy. Given the dependence of the financial systems of these countries on multinational financial institutions and, as is frequently the case, on some one or other metropolitan monetary standard for both their external and internal monetary regulation, the institutional rates of interest which prevail have come to reflect these relationships much more than the supposed balance of capital availabilities and demand at home. The same sort of phenomenon is clearly evident if we also take into account that the level and variability of employment and the size of the wages fund are more a function of the foreign demand for domestic primary output than of the domestic wage rate or, for that matter, the rate of technical innovation at home.

Now it is obvious that for purposes of designing an economic strategy to achieve the development of productive forces and the transformation of the structure of production of the typical small underdeveloped economy during the present neocolonial phase, planning of this kind is worse than useless. What is needed instead is a more comprehensive type of planning, directed toward the *creation of new conditions of economic life and new processes to be effectively and directly determined by the planning authorities.* Planning has therefore to be an *active* process, clearly differentiable from the processes and mechanisms which operate presently. Economic relationships and patterns of economic behavior, accepted by these economies and their existing planning authorities as parameters, are, under the conditions of comprehensive planning, instruments of policy. Indeed, even when it is necessary in the process of planning for recourse to be made to indirect techniques of economic control and plan implementation, this should not entail altering the qualitatively different nature of the process of planning as we have envisaged it here.

There are certain basic features of such planning which it would be useful to highlight at this stage because they permeate the vision of economic processes as presented in the rest of the book. First, let us take comprehensive planning of the kind we assume as capable of replacing the market mechanism. Where they do continue to exist, market mechanisms are expected to perform limited and auxiliary functions to the central process of planning. Thus the level of surplus accumulation, the allocation and coordination of investments, the level and pattern of consumption, wage payments, the balancing of overall supply and demand, are all to be consciously planned activities and not the consequences of the operations of the market. Such comprehensive planning of course has other dimensions. One of them is that insofar as it is an active process it ensures that there is no fundamental division or separation between planners and implementors. When planning is an active process, performed on a comprehensive scale, plan preparation and plan implementation, even if they are conceptually different activities, are nonetheless integrated into the same units of action.

Such interactions between planners and implementors ensure the achievement of the fundamental preconditions for the technical solution of the problems of target setting, of achieving consistency in plans, of introducing devices to maintain efficiencies, and of optimizing output sequences.

The administrative structures, the various planning levels which are established to cope with these activities, and the use of continuous planning horizons which they must necessarily operate, have to be organized and structured in such a way that they progressively constitute an *active iterative process* which substitutes for the market in achieving consistency, feasibility, and the efficient testing of plans. In this regard, comprehensive planning achieves a further dimension which is, as it were, a by-product of its own comprehensiveness—within its own machinery are to be found the mechanisms for coping with problems of integrating the macro-formulation and micro-implementation of economic plans at the level of projects.

Comprehensive planning on this basis is directed not only to production, as is generally envisaged in discussions of this sort, but, as we shall see later, to consumption as well. If the planners are the implementors, then the simultaneous solution of the overall supply-demand balance equations is achieved.[20] This has two important consequences. First, the level of demand is not a constraint on output. Given the available technology, anything can be produced, irrespective of scale considerations, and any level of output can be achieved. The dominant constraints on output decisions are the level and rate of accumulation that are both possible and desirable. This removal of the demand constraint allows us, in a sense, to wipe the economic slate clean and to envisage economic processes as those in which the establishment of new activities (which is one of the principal purposes of planning) is guided by the requirements of economic transformation.

It is not to be presumed from this removal of demand as the binding constraint on output that output can therefore be raised without limit. The rate of accumulation is determined by that proportion of output which it is planned to withhold from consumption. In contrast to what happens in a market economy, this is a centrally planned decision and thus does not reflect either the level of profits or the rate of interest, or even the level and directions of foreign economic flows. In practice, however, such decisions are usually bound by several constraints. Since, other things being equal, accumulation is an alternative to consumption, the planned level of accumulation has to take into account both the levels of consumption desired in the society and, given the levels of poverty which generally prevail, the effect on health and work incentives.

Second, given the comprehensive planning approach, the labor surplus problem can, and frequently does, become one of severe labor shortages. This follows because comprehensive planning by definition aims at the full use of existing resources, in particular labor, at all times. In other words, in planning one begins by using what one has as fully as possible. As a consequence, the rate of accumulation has in practice pretty quickly come up against the constraints of labor availability. However, given the substantial reserve army of unemployed and underemployed to be found in the typical small underdeveloped economy, this constraint seems unlikely to be as crucial as it had been in some other socialist economies.

In addition, the level and rate of surplus accumulation are bound either by the domestic availabilities of those material and physical resources that are to be used in the proposed projects, or in situations where imports can act as substitutes by the availability of foreign exchange.[21] Furthermore, while the labor constraint is unlikely to be initially a very stringent one because of the prevailing levels of unemployment and underemployment, it must be realized that the effective use of this labor requires an adequate supply of wage goods. This factor therefore places a heavy burden on domestic food supplies, which in turn creates pressures on both surplus accumulation and the use of foreign exchange. Finally, although in general these economies are likely to have a labor surplus, there are also severe bottlenecks in the availability of skilled personnel, and these can only be eased by the rapid development of adequate training facilities.

From all this we can see that the removal of the demand constraint on output makes, as the only *real and ultimate determinant* of what ought to be produced, the social costs the societies are prepared to pay.

The second of the major consequences which follow from simultaneous supply-demand planning is that important sources of inefficiencies, and the social costs of growth these give rise to in the market economies, are removed. In the usual market-economy process, growth takes place by way of attempts to balance, through time, a demand-supply disequilibrium. The level of aggregate production is planned in anticipation of a level of market growth over which the producers have no control. Invariably plans do not materialize, and the resulting fluctuations in economic activity are a reflection of the way the economic system is organized. These fluctuations, which characterize all market economies, are not only the product of an internally determined disproportionality of aggregate supply and demand, but, given the interrelationships of these economies, are also easily and readily transmitted internationally. In view of their high export ratios, their high marginal and average propensities to import, and the high foreign to domestic ratio in domestic investment, the small underdeveloped economies are particularly exposed to these internationally transmitted trade cycles. Not only are the social costs of operating these systems considerable, but, given the dynamic divergence between domestic resource use and domestic demand and the dependence on imported technology and capital, the anarchy which characterizes economic systems under capitalism is heavily compounded in the economies we are here considering.

The purpose of the preceding discussion has been primarily to indicate the broad analytical foundations on which the basic strategies we employ have been developed. These foundations clearly suggest that, in the broadest terms, the fundamental strategy must be one aimed at severing the traditional and newer links with international capitalism which maintain these economies as appendages of the center countries. It also suggests that given the present and growing disparities of economic wealth, it is necessary to husband resources and employ strategies of disengagement *at those points where they are most essential.*

Two priorities of political action immediately follow from this. The first is to secure complete local state-ownership of all the dominant means of production. If the country is politically constrained to pay compensation, then it is necessary to go to great political lengths to base this compensation on a historical evaluation of the social costs of—as against the private incomes generated by—the foreign ownership of these resources. *The importance of being able to effect the return of the people's resources by means of direct expropriation, with social cost and not political blackmail as the basis of compensation, cannot be overestimated.* The costs of alternative procedures run very high, particularly if, as is often the case after so-called nationalization, the transfer of resources from foreign to local ownership, by virtue of that very fact and of the "legal" premises on which it is based, generates a "legal" claim on future resource flows based on replacement costs or on the earning capacity of the enterprise. This not only reduces the available surplus in the future, but also tends to reduce considerably the flexibility of the remaining surplus. This follows because in many of these small economies the areas of economic activity under foreign domination are large, and the absolute size of the minimum capital funds needed for reinvestment in order to maintain normal growth is large relative to total domestic surplus generated domestically. It is therefore a clear priority of political action to seek to avoid ransoming future surpluses as compensation to capitalism.

The second priority, which really derives from the first, is the complementary need for decisive intervention by the state in foreign trade. This allows for rational management of external economic relations by permitting the rapid establishment of communications and exchange arrangements (e.g., with other Third World countries and the socialist bloc) which break the monopoly of vertical metropolitan links. It also allows for the rational management of foreign exchange, and for control over the distribution of imported goods, particularly consumer goods. Above all, it helps to consolidate state control over the economy and therefore facilitates the pursuit of the struggle for disengagement from capitalism.

Since these priorities are by no means novel, it is pertinent to note why they are re-stated here. This has been done to make clear *why* these priorities are chosen and *how* their formal acceptance as priorities must be linked to their *content* and *methods* of operation and implementation, as will be discussed in the second part of this book. It is also important to note, as we shall examine in the next chapter, that many Third World states deny the priority of these actions and yet claim significant success for their own approaches to eliminating poverty and unemployment and thus for their *long-run* prospects of disengaging from international capitalism! Again, we must analyze and try to understand the form, content, methods, and consequences of these alternative strategies and not simply dismiss them out of hand, as is wont to be the radical reaction.

Before doing so, a couple of observations of relevance to the later argument are worth noting. The overriding reason for advocating that the small underdeveloped economy should galvanize political action and marshal limited resources in order to transform the commanding resources to the state sector is simply that despite its widely publicized and genuinely feared capacity to manipulate state enterprises, partnerships, etc., international capitalism *optimally* prefers ownership as the basis of control. The implications of this are that other forms of control are theoretically second best. This does not deny that in actual practice there is evidence that these other forms of control can yield, and indeed often have yielded, better profits for the metropolitan countries, but potentially this can be overcome with experience, if the theoretical sub-optimality of these other approaches are appreciated and the momentum toward socialism clearly established.

This preference for ownership as a means of control should not be surprising. The fact of ownership (i.e., the uncontested property interest in the major means of production) *guarantees* control over the products. It is, therefore, to be preferred over a form of control which is exercised over the means of production, but which resides in the management and/or distribution and/or exchange of the product. It is for this reason that such devices as management contracts, the new hallmark of neocolonialism, can be considered theoretically, and thus potentially in practice as well, to be inferior to direct foreign ownership of domestic resources. In practice, the present theoretical significance of this point may be limited insofar as the evidence currently suggests improved surplus and income drains under these neocolonial economic arrangements. But the theoretical sub-optimality of these approaches to control is itself a function of whether or not serious efforts are being made to disengage from capitalism and to establish socialist production relations. As we shall see in the next chapter, where these arrangements are supportive of local capitalist development, the consequence is mainly to deepen the underdevelopment process.

Notes

1. V. I. Lenin, *Selected Works*, vol. 1, pp. 598-99 (emphasis in the original).
2. A. Emmanuel, *Unequal Exchange*, pp. 123-24, 375-76 (emphasis in the original).
3. Ibid., p. 129. With the usual widespread tendency to dismiss the small countries, he states (pp. 156-157): "It would be foolish to suppose that a wage increase amounting to a few French-African-Community francs per hour in a country so small as Gabon, or the Central African Republic, would suffice to start a movement there by international capital looking for somewhere to be invested."
4. For a representative sample of the literature see D. H. K. Lee, *Climate and Economic Development in the Tropics*; P. Gourou, *The Tropical World: Its Social and Economic Conditions and Its Future Status;* J. H. Boeke, *Economics and Economic Policy of Dual Soci-*

eties; D. McClelland, *The Achieving Society;* E. Hagen, *The Theory of Social Change: How Economic Growth Begins;* R. Nurske, *Problems of Capital Formation in Underdeveloped Countries;* Sir W. A. Lewis, *The Theory of Economic Growth.*

5. See T. Szentes, *The Political Economy of Underdevelopment.*
6. A. G. Frank's book, *Capitalism and Underdevelopment in Latin America,* is already well known. A recent and quite outstanding analysis of Africa is W. Rodney, *How Europe Underdeveloped Africa.*
7. In addition to the texts cited earlier, particularly Rodney's and Frank's texts cited in the previous footnote, see P. Jalée, *The Pillage of the Third World;* J. Rweyemamu, "International Trade and Developing Countries"; H. Magdoff, *The Age of Imperialism;* G. Beckford, *Persistent Poverty;* E. Williams, *Capitalism and Slavery;* K. Nkrumah, *Neo-Colonialism, The Last Stage of Imperialism;* G. Myrdal, *Economic Theory and Underdeveloped Regions;* D. Seers, "The Stages of Growth of a Primary Producer in the Middle of the Twentieth Century."
8. An earlier draft of this study incorporated an analysis of Tanzania which highlights these conclusions. It was presented at a seminar of the Economic Research Bureau, University of Dar-es-Salaam, in November 1972.
9. P. J. Lloyd, *International Trade Problems of Small Nations,* p. 14.
10. For a contrasting view which extols the potential virtues of primary commodity export trade, see G. M. Meier, *International Economics of Development.*
11. See G. Arrighi, "International Corporations, Labor Aristocracies, and Economic Development in Tropical Africa."
12. In Chapter 4 the precise economic interpretation of this concept is provided. In the chapter immediately following this, we shall examine some of the contemporary features of this process under the impact of recent industrialization.
13. Rodney, *How Europe Underdeveloped Africa,* p. 86 (our emphasis).
14. We should also of course take into account other factors in the rise of the local capitalist classes in the larger countries, such as the impact of two world wars and the weakening of colonial relations this has entailed. In many parts of the underdeveloped world (e.g., Latin America), this was a period of considerable industrial growth of a kind.
15. J. Bognár, *Economic Policy and Planning in Developing Countries,* pp. 46-47 (emphasis in the original). See also F. Harbison and C. A.

Myers, *Education, Manpower and Economic Growth;* and Szentes, *The Political Economy of Underdevelopment.*

16. One of the ironic contradictions of capitalism in this respect is its institutionalized racism—see the immigration laws of Britain or the United States. This more than any other single factor has probably impeded the flow of skilled people from the periphery to the center.
17. See H. Chenery, "Patterns of Industrial Growth"; and H. Chenery and L. Taylor, "Development Patterns Among Countries and Over Time."
18. See in particular the first part of Chapter 9, and Chapter 3.
19. For recent discussion of some of these developments and of the way aid has been used to "avert disruptive crises," see T. Hayter, *Aid as Imperialism.*
20. The level of achievement of balance of demand and supply in specific product lines will of course reflect the general levels of efficiencies at the micro-level, but overall balance in the aggregate sense is quite easily achieved.
21. The significance of this will be brought out fully in Chapter 7.

3

Underdevelopment, Dependence, and Growth: The Experience of the "High-Growth" Economies Under Capitalism

In the previous chapter we sought to analyze the manner in which the relations of production, historically formed in the context of capitalism and neocolonialism, have given rise to the present widespread underdevelopment of productive forces and to the sustained reproduction of dependent economic structures. The particular material manifestations of these in the small economy were indicated. To round off the discussion of the first part of this study, it remains for us to examine the recent efforts of these states to develop capitalist or other nonsocialist production relations in order to generate a basis for overcoming poverty and underdevelopment. In the present chapter, we shall examine these efforts from the point of view of what have been called the most "successful" states (i.e., those with the highest annual per capita income increases). Since these account for only a very small minority of the total number of such countries, we shall be in effect deliberately putting the most favorable construction on the general achievements of these approaches to economic transformation.

There are four basic objectives in pursuing this analysis. In the first place, we shall try to extend the analytical framework of our interpretation of underdevelopment of the small economy to encompass the recent experience of these "high growth" economies. On this basis, we shall then attempt to indicate the general limits which constrain the capacity of such growth to transform the mode of production of these states. Third, we hope that our analysis will also serve to underline the great urgency with which we regard the need for a critical consideration of the alternative strategies outlined in the second part of this book. Finally, we will also seek to emphasize the fundamental importance of the fact that intervention through state ownership is not, and indeed cannot by itself be, sufficient to guarantee the obliteration of dependency linkages within the international capitalist system so as to initiate autonomous development. Often in examining the experiences of the small underdeveloped economies attempting to "construct socialism" (e.g., Tanzania), one gets the strong impression of a failure to recognize the extent to which a developmental strategy that divorces the *juridical and formal* ownership of the means of production from the *content and methods* of such production must, by the very nature of the social organizations thereby created, undermine the processes of socialist transformation.

High-Growth States

When considering the experiences of such small states as Puerto Rico, Taiwan, Singapore, and the Ivory Coast which have achieved high rates of growth of per capita product over the last decade or so, neoclassical economists have generally been highly enthusiastic over the future growth potential of the neocolonial mode of production. They have argued that those skeptical theorists both inside and outside their ranks have seriously underestimated the benefits of international trade and the dynamic contributions the multinational corporations can make to small economies through their mechanisms for transferring technology, capital, and skills in management, design, and marketing. It follows by implication from this argument that, in the present neocolonial phase, a small underdeveloped economy can transform its economic structure by relying on the development of an indigenous capitalism, initially spawned through partnership with multinational firms and guided by the state. Coincidentally (!)—to those who have traveled through the capital cities of these adjacent countries—all of the small underdeveloped economies attempting to construct a socialist system are geographically juxtaposed to one or other of these outstanding "high-growth" economies. Thus we have North and South Korea, Tanzania and Zambia and Kenya, and Cuba and Puerto Rico and Jamaica, all exhibiting marked contrasts within a limited geographical area. To those who have traveled through these adjacent countries, the apparent contrast is indeed a striking one.

A comparison of the most popular, and probably most misleading, index of the level of development (i.e., per capita product) shows that a few of the small underdeveloped economies, following capitalist or so-called pragmatic nonsocialist strategies of economic development, have recorded considerably higher rates of growth of per capita product than those countries which are more ostensibly socialist in their approach to development and to the transformation of the mode of production. Some of these data are shown in Table 1, below.

As can be seen, with the exception of North Korea (whose performance is somewhat less than that of the South) the recorded growth of per capita product of those economies pursuing socialist strategies has been very small. In Tanzania over the period 1960-1969 the growth of per capita product has only been 1.6 percent per annum, while in the case of Cuba negative growth rates have been recorded. By contrast, the small economies pursuing capitalism listed in Table 1 have all attained impressive growth rates of per capita product.

Table 1
Average Annual Growth Rates of GNP per capita, 1960-1969

"High-growth" economies with capitalist and "nonsocialist" economic strategies.	
Taiwan	6.3 percent
Puerto Rico	6.0 percent
Zambia	5.4 percent
Hong Kong	8.7 percent
Greece	6.2 percent
South Korea	6.4 percent
Israel	5.3 percent
Singapore	4.5 percent
Ivory Coast	4.7 percent
Panama	4.8 percent
Jamaica	3.0 percent
Trinidad and Tobago	3.8 percent
Economies with "socialist" economic strategies.	
Tanzania	1.6 percent
Cuba*	-3.2 percent
North Korea*	5.9 percent

Source: Finance and Development Quarterly, no. 1 (1972). Based on the sixth edition of the *World Bank Atlas.*

* As indicated by the sources, net material product has been converted into GNP at factor cost. This allows a wide margin for error, which is increased when conversion of GNP is then made into U.S. dollars.

There are four responses radicals can make to this situation. The first is that the sample of "nonsocialist" economies is not representative. The second is of a purely technical nature and centers on the problems of converting prices in a transitional socialist economy to an international standard of value, and, in the case of Cuba, of equating net material product to gross national product at factor cost. As the United Nations source indicates, there is a wide margin of possible error involved in making such calculations, if only because one of the characteristics of a transitional state is the deliberate disruption of the price mechanism from the way it functions under the "market" system. If the deficiencies of the statistical series for the earlier years—when such facilities for gathering economic statistics were very rudimentary—are added to this, the data used become in most cases little better than informed guesses.

The third response is to point out the political and social consequences of the policies being pursued in the "successful" countries. From the list of countries shown in Table 1, it can be seen that many of these states (e.g., Hong Kong, Taiwan, Puerto Rico, Panama, Israel) are patron states of international capitalism, "enjoying" the benefits of strategic access to capitalist markets and investments in the major capitalist countries. In some cases (e.g., Singapore and Taiwan), the growth has in no small measure been achieved at the expense of aiding and abetting in the destruction of other small states, as their economic roles in the war in Indochina clearly demonstrate. This can be contrasted with the socialist countries, where, even if per capita product is not rising rapidly, basic structural adjustments in the relations of production are being attempted. By their very nature these cannot always bear immediate fruit. Indeed, these countries have all been locked in strong conflict with the external forces of international capitalism, as in the war between North and South Korea, the blockade of Cuba, and the Portuguese harassment of southern Tanzania. Under such circumstances, any economic progress is a remarkable achievement.

To most radical economists these arguments would be sufficiently conclusive for them to dismiss the achievements represented here as atypical and not generally indicative of future economic experience. While there is a great deal of justification for this view and, by extension, for the implied argument that most people, if they understood it, would find the price of such growth unacceptable, surely the problem still remains one of examining the nature of the growth these societies have been paying for. This is all the more important since, despite the technical objections that might be raised over the measurement of the course and trend in gross national product, in general the data do give added credence to the impression that some small states have achieved high rates of growth in incomes, exports, and industry while pursuing capitalist and nonsocialist development strategies. At the same time, the socialist states, with the exception of North Korea, have been having severe difficulties in coping with underdevelopment and transforming their dependent modes of production.

While these difficulties are not to be measured by the disparities in per capita product, since the rates of growth of this index mask real difficulties in the "successful" states, it does seem reasonable that, over and above the preceding responses, there be an attempt to evaluate the performance of these countries. Particularly their economic strategies and their approaches to the central problems of resource ownership, resource use, production, technology, and consumption should be examined in order to observe those effects, apart from the high per capita product increases, which this type of growth has had on the dynamics of underdevelopment, as described in the previous chapter.

A useful way of beginning our examination of the performances of these countries is to make a simple, nonexclusive categorization of their basic policies and strategies for promoting local resource control and ownership as an indicator of the relations of production which they aspire to create.

Before we proceed further with this, it should be noted

that despite the different degrees of importance which, as we shall see, these various policies attach to the freedom of private ownership of property and the freedom of markets, they are all fundamentally characterized by the deliberate intention of using the state apparatus as a principal instrument of developing a strong class formation, capable of assuming the responsibility of raising the level of development of the productive forces. Traditionally, in the context of highly developed class societies, socialist analysis correctly interprets the state apparatus as the *object* of class conquest and the *instrument* of class rule. In the historical situation that prevails in these countries, it is more correct to argue that the state has become, as it were, an *instrument of class creation.* This observation highlights the crucial difficulties which are posed for a socialist analysis of the state by the existence in these societies of what is often only a very immature industrial working force, and an underdeveloped local bourgeoisie. This results in at least two very important dimensions being attached to the "instrumentality" of the state. One is, of course, its well-known instability and easy susceptibility to even very narrow changes in alignments among the petty-bourgeois elements which presently dominate the state machinery. The other is its illusory appearance of being *independent* (i.e., in effect "beyond class") both vis-à-vis the international capitalist order and local class formations.[1]

Returning to our proposed classification, on the question of ownership of the means of production we can identify four basic strategies which are being pursued by these countries. All fall far short of socialization—or even nationalization—of the means of production. Precisely because of this, it is frequently argued that these strategies maximize international capitalistic participation in the national economy, while at the same time allowing for actions by the state to minimize the harmful consequences of this. Given this "positive" role assigned to the state, it is sometimes further argued that these policies are pragmatic attempts to increase the long-run capacity of the country to transform itself by building up an infrastructure of material production and the requisite skills. These strategies may be categorized as:

1. Localization of senior management and administrative staff (e.g., Africanization).

2. Requiring foreign firms to localize their ownership by raising a substantial part of their capital requirements from the domestic capital market through the issue of local equities.

3. State participation through the establishment of national institutions to compete with foreign enterprises in these areas of activity.

4. State participation in the ownership structure of foreign capitalist firms through a majority share of ownership.

We shall examine each of these in turn, although it should be understood that in actual practice states do not rely on one or another strategy in isolation. It is usual to find a combination of these policies being pursued.

Localization of Management

In almost all of the small underdeveloped economies, a great deal of state activity continues to be directed toward publicizing and pressuring foreign-owned companies to allow participation by nationals in the higher levels of management and decision-making. This strategy, which is based in those nationalist forces which were the mainstay of the struggle for constitutional independence, seeks to find attractive employment outlets for local skilled personnel while at the same time claiming that such an infusion of indigenous people into key management positions will serve to localize these companies in their operations and decision-making. Inasmuch as such localization is seen as operating to dramatically offset one of the major means of perpetuating dependency, it is not infrequent to find that progress is simply measured in terms of the number of foreigners whose jobs have been taken over by local personnel—and, judging from the propaganda claims all around, this progress has in recent years been quite considerable.

There are of course a number of very serious limitations to the effectiveness of this approach, two of which we can single out as being the most fundamental. In the first instance, while in some countries this policy is undoubtedly a logical extension of the dismantling of the administrative apparatus which began during the struggle for constitutional independence, it nevertheless seriously underestimates the social power of these institutions and their almost total control over individual lives. Pursuing such a policy in the context of a drive to establish an indigenous capitalist class can contribute very little to the struggle to transform the mode of production because the local persons, when appointed to positions in these companies, inevitably move into particular institutional structures which in turn have developed their own particular ethos, values, life-styles, and ways of doing things, all in direct relation to the imperatives of exploiting local resources for the benefit of metropolitan capital. These nationals, therefore, function in an institutional situation where there are strong historically built-in pressures to conform to the patterns of behavior of the enterprises. The pressures inevitably continue as long as the individual is a functioning part of the corporate entity.

But as this socialization process continues, it becomes evident that instead of the company becoming more and more national in its outlook, character, and purpose, it is in fact the nationals who are becoming more and more integrated into this foreign system and who usually end up as extensions of the exploiting corporation. In this conflict between effective localization and integration into the existing company system the enterprises are indirectly aided by the very public policies which seek to encourage capitalism. Thus these policies create a contradictory situation in which it is easy for the national bourgeoisie, which they themselves seek to create, to become effectively denationalized in practice, since it is required to operate as a peripheral force to international capitalism.

It is their confidence in and reliance on this acculturation process that have encouraged many of these multinational corporations not to resist pressures for localization, but instead to appear to eagerly welcome nationals into their operations. It is by now a well-accepted part of the corporate strategy to acquire a "national" image this way, knowing full well that this will hardly endanger the true nationality of the corporation. If one lives in these societies, proof of this can be readily seen from the striking frequency with which the news media refer to these various promotions and appointments, made to very public positions, so as to maximize their publicity value. Thus we have a pattern of appointments to directorships, either on boards with little authority or on boards which do have authority but where the local appointments are in a minority; of appointments to public relations offices; and, of increasing strategic importance, of local appointments as personnel officers. The latter has the additional advantage of being able to divert workers' hostility by "hiding" the true identity of the enterprise. Whatever the particular stratagem employed, these companies seek, as indeed they must, to undermine the significance of this strategy to nationalize their operations. They naturally hope to be able to exploit the dynamics of cultural and psychological dependence. In small economies, the sheer weight and power of international capitalism are in their favor, and it is correspondingly difficult for their entrenchment to be overcome in this way.

The second weakness of this strategy arises from the technique of organizational substitution which has been facilitated by the technological possibilities of virtually instant communication. This process permits the companies to let nationals nominally fill managerial positions while at the same time depriving these positions of any decision-making significance by referring to the head office decisions that would normally and routinely be made locally if the head office had the uncontrolled and uncontested right to appoint management. Of course, insofar as the previous argument holds (i.e., that local management is acculturated to the values of the enterprise and is also assumed by the head office to be efficient), the need for this form of organizational substitution is diminished. The degree of substitution can be seen as a useful gauge of the importance of cultural and psychological dependence in the development of the local managerial class.

The beneficiaries of the nationalist pressures on the corporations, who have been aptly called the *nizer* class, are supposed to constitute the embryo of an indigenous capitalist class.[2] They are supposed to acquire from their jobs and their positions in the multinational firms the technical and managerial skills which will enable them to play a pioneering and innovative role in the transformation of their economies. But, being dependent on the multinational corporations and on local nationalist sentiment to ensure their mobility, it is not clear where they are going to get the capital for indigenously owned enterprises, even should they acquire the necessary entrepreneurial capabilities. Some therefore engage in petty businesses, mainly housing and land speculation, as sidelines, but it is clear that the returns are marginal to the capital needs of the society. The class remains at present *objectively* very much a dependent offshoot of the multinational firm and probably will become little more than a further agency for internalizing the dependency characteristics of the society.

Local Share Issues

The second strategy (i.e., issuing local equities in order to ensure local private participation in the ownership of the enterprises) also contains a number of fundamental limitations. First, practice has shown that when compelled to incorporate locally these companies have managed to issue shares in such quantities, and in such a way, as to avoid putting any real control of their companies into jeopardy.

They are often encouraged in this by generous timetables set by the local governments for achieving stated levels of local private participation in their activities. The governments argue that these generous timetables are necessary to minimize disruptions of the local capital market. Second, this device is strongly reinforced by the tendency for these shares to be taken up by other similarly "local" enterprises (e.g., a financial company that has been previously localized in a similar fashion, or by a particular group of local businessmen who specialize in the "partnering" of local and foreign capital).

A third difficulty with this strategy derives from the familiar strategem employed by the companies of making the local share issues raise sufficient funds from the local capital market to finance the physical construction costs of the enterprise, while "exchanging" the remainder of the shares for patent rights, technical services, etc., from the parent firm. Furthermore, where the enterprise is already a long-established and going concern, the issuance of local shares to enable participation in this way simply provides the firm with funds that it may then choose to invest elsewhere, particularly if the fear of local incursion into its control is taken seriously. In the context of this strategy of issuing local shares, where foreign capital comes, woos local capital, uses it, and controls it for foreign ends, it becomes impossible to sustain the claims made for private international capitalism by its supporters regarding its ability to augment national resources.

This clamor to issue shares on the local market is often directed toward foreign-owned enterprises. At the same time, there remain many locally owned firms that are not very "public" in their ownership structures and that remain in the firm and uncontested grip of particular families and business cliques. While, in terms of capital employed, these are of minor importance compared to their foreign counterparts, this failure to implement positive policies aimed at diluting their ownership structures serves to emphasize that the strategy is based on the creation of a new local capitalist class to replace the foreign capitalists within their enterprises and does not in any way seek to contest the legitimacy of the capitalist structure itself.

The Local State-Owned Competitor

The third approach to the issue of resource ownership and control has been the strategy of establishing local state-owned institutions in order to have them compete with their foreign-owned counterpart institutions. A great deal of this effort is purely symbolic, a token recognition of the issues at stake. But in societies where symbols can, and often do, reflect dependency relationships, one cannot dismiss symbolic gestures out of hand, for they are frequently of great psychological significance. Nevertheless, both the waste involved in duplication and the very futility of seeking to miniaturize a multinational corporation through peaceful competition within the framework of capitalist rules, indicate a basic unwillingness and/or political incapacity to tackle the real problems.

Over and above its purely symbolic efficacy it is sometimes claimed that whether or not the state-owned enterprise remains small in its turnover relative to the total size of the local market for the particular product, it can have a qualitative impact on the system far beyond its size. This derives from the extent to which the very fact of its existence forces the multinational corporation to become sensitized to local needs.

There is a grain of truth in this. But often this sensitization is confined to such marginal responses as taking on more local personnel, advertising with local people, and in general more closely designing marketing strategy to fit the local situation. One can note here by simple observation the similarity in "local" advertisements in, say, West Africa and the Caribbean on the one hand, and the similarities and differences between these and standard corporate advertising in Euro-America on the other. While this sensitization can readily be seen in these crude corporate adaptations, of equal importance to the whole process is the fact that the state-owned institutions *also* become sensitized to the market as created by the multinational firms. The oldest rule of competition against established rivals is to make your own products more and more similar to theirs. Thus over time the local institution narrows the differences between its product and that of its competitors. As this process continues, the same culturally dependent characteristics that lead to the self-contempt of local efforts operate against the local institution and *any* differentiation of product is looked on as a manifestation of local inferiority. As a consequence, in the absence of further regulations to support the enterprise even nationalist sentiment is soon unable to win support, for the foreign firms too are going "local" and "buy local" campaigns no longer have any special meaning.

Throughout all this there is a genuine uncertainty, indecision and ambiguity attached to the roles of those who run these government enterprises. To accumulate private capital while working in a state-owned institution is never an easy task. Alternatively, to support the growth of their enterprises through support for the expansion of state capitalism also proves difficult because of conflicts with private capitalist interests. Caught in this trap, the hopes of an emergent capitalist class are doomed.

Majority State Participation

The final strategy, that of the state being the majority shareholder (i.e., the 51 percent formula), is the most common among the progressively inclined underdeveloped economies. While the national struggle to contain the multinational firm is implicitly anti-imperialist, when pursued in the context of generating an indigenous capitalism there are at least three basic reasons why this policy is incapable of leading to effective control of local resources.

First, given an absence of local confidence regarding that

knowledge of the technical, marketing, and managerial processes of the firm, such participation in ownership has been frequently counteracted by the practice of simultaneously entering into management contracts with foreign capitalists. To the extent that this practice prevails, it is possible for these arrangements not to diminish the power of foreign decision-making in these enterprises. Moreover, when pursued in the context of generating a local capitalist class, this policy also does not provide a dynamic basis for phasing out these foreign decision-makers.

Second, experience has shown that contracts made for these services often constitute a significant income drain. It has been observed that in Tanzania, where there is a socialist program for phasing out this foreign dependence, management contracts have been concluded on such bases as the total rate of sales (turnover) of the firm! Since such expenses are prior to profits, we find firms having persistent commercial losses forced to carry the income drain of foreign management contract payments. In other instances, either full profit repatriation is guaranteed or the state implicitly, or occasionally explicitly, accepts the obligation to "manage" and "stabilize" the labor situation. All these in effect provide these firms with guarantees they never would have had in the absence of state regulation.[3]

The third fundamental weakness of this strategy lies in a basic misunderstanding of what a multinational corporation, and particularly an exporting corporation, represents locally:

> It is essentially a plant. It is not a firm. It is true that there are titles such as Directors, Managers, Managing Directors, etc. But the local expression . . . makes no decision as regards prices . . . output . . . levels of investment, or the markets. All these are done at the head office, where decisions which normally define a firm are made. The apparatus which exists locally is just a participation in a multi-plant firm. Therefore, when we seek meaningful participation, it is not simply to acquire a share in the local apparatus, but to ensure that inroads are made into the decision-making centers which exist in the North Atlantic.[4]

If this point is not fully grasped and if the thrust of state policy is confined simply to legal ownership of part of the expatriate enterprise, there will inevitably be little change in the content and methods of production.

At this stage it would be useful to examine some of the implications of the typical agreements these countries enter into with foreign companies. As a general rule, a close examination of these agreements shows that they entail a considerable tendency toward monopolistic restrictions in favor of the multinational firms.[5] In the first place, it is quite frequently found that these arrangements explicitly require both the government and the locally operating enterprise to observe restrictions on the export of the locally produced product. An important by-product of international patenting laws, which give to the patent owners considerable rights over the determination of the sale of their invention, is that companies are able to use this monopoly to specify the areas in which the government and the locally operating enterprise can sell their output as licensees. The contracts closely specify the areas of possible sale and the usual practice is to restrict quite closely the rights of the local enterprise to export the product under license.

One consequence of such contracts is to reinforce the bias against developing an industrial export capacity in these countries. Another is to reinforce the country's dependence on the technology of a particular firm. It is usually argued that these arrangements encourage the transfer of technology from the multinational firm to the local economy, but given the context of agreements with the locally established subsidiary in which this technological transfer must normally take place, a number of serious issues arise. In the situation where consumer goods are imported, the dependence on a *particular supplier* is less acute. It is true that "brand loyalties" and other attachments to a particular commodity may be strong, but in general it can be assumed that sources of imports of consumer goods can readily be shifted should this seem necessary. What is of crucial importance is that reliance on the assembly and fabrications of consumer goods from the industrial capitalist countries can to a large extent pre-empt the shape of the future intermediate and capital goods industries which serve the consumer sector.

Where the agreements relate to technology (i.e., to the ultimate establishment of a locally based cycle of production), the possibilities of dependence on a particular supplier are more acute. Agreements covering the use of technology are generally of a long-term nature. They tend not only to cover current operations and the installation of the purchased machinery, but in addition to include routine provisions covering the renewal of patents and licenses, consultation fees, technical services, and the terms under which further innovations in the particular production cycle can be purchased. As a result, the commitment which has been entered into is de facto of a long-term nature, extending dependence on technological change in the capitalist countries.

These legal restrictions are frequently supported by the tendency for most Third World countries to have almost identical patent laws and to be members of the International Union for the Protection of Industrial Property. Indeed, these practices are virtually *sine qua non* for attracting foreign private capital. The result is to put a tight ring around efforts to circumvent these restrictive arrangements: if one country sought to abrogate the legal conditions and tried to export a product, the multinational company would still be protected by the fact that they would continue to apply to the *importing* countries. Simply renouncing these laws *and* hoping to continue to function in the international capitalist market is therefore not possible.

Restrictions on exports are usually combined with monopolistic clauses governing the sources of purchases of raw materials, machinery, spare parts, etc. This practice has been rationalized as necessary to protect and maintain the quality of the products produced under the brand name. Again, this serves to strengthen the dependence of the local subsidiary on foreign technology and specifically on that of the parent or associated company. By limiting the scope of purchase of inputs and capital equipment, the options even *within* the capitalist world are therefore severely constricted. This is further seen in the prevalent practice of discriminatory pricing, favoring those customers whose dependence is greater.

Finally, these agreements, where they do allow for export of the locally produced commodity, vest the sole rights of marketing in the parent company. This is rationalized on the basis of the need to maintain the image and marketable quality of the products produced under license. When it is also taken into account that the parent company possesses a worldwide and well-established marketing and sales network that far exceeds the scope of anything the local company could hope to duplicate, the case for this marketing dependence seems overwhelming. As would be expected, a commission charge is levied for services provided in making these sales.

From this brief review of the broad strategies for achieving resource ownership, it is readily apparent that these policies are not capable of yielding any significant changes in the structure of production relations. The use of the state as a deliberate instrument of class creation has not been successful. Even in countries where the number of persons who benefit from these policies is significant, they have been incapable of mobilizing enough capital to give these groups a material base for further self-reproduction. As a class, they reflect the weaknesses of the state that has tried to create them, remaining dependent and peripheral vis-à-vis the main sources of capitalist economic activity (i.e., the ownership of capital and the knowledge of technical processes). If anything is distinctive about them, it is the new way in which the classes, which have historically acted as agents for internalizing dependency, are now being created. We can conclude that the basic weakness of the strategies examined here is that they all derive from the poverty of historical understanding which guides them.

Patterns of Economic Change in the "High-Growth"

Given the difficulty encountered by these strategies in establishing new patterns of production relations outside of the dependency and underdevelopment ones which prevail, the question which remains is what has been their impact on the search for economic transformation? Despite impressions to the contrary, the high rates of growth of per capita product (as indicated in Table 1) cannot be exclusively, or even largely, attributed to the strategies of resource ownership and control. Nor can these rates be attributed to the tariffs and other forms of protection which have been erected to induce foreign and domestic investment.[6] As we already know, other states have pursued similar strategies with much less dramatic results in the rate of per capita product increases.

Two overriding considerations have guided the growth of the states listed in Table 1. One is that their attractiveness to foreign capital, and their preferred access to capitalist markets, cannot be separated from the special political and strategic positions which they hold as a result of wars waged by the capitalist countries against movements of national liberation in other Third World states, particularly in Indochina. The second consideration has been the role of discovery and use of primary materials, such as bauxite, oil, and copper, which have contributed to the rapid growth in Jamaica, Trinidad, and Zambia.[7] The boom conditions which the markets for these products have enjoyed over much of the period cannot be divorced from the impact of war and its aftermath. In addition, tourism has been a very special factor in these growth experiences. As client-states, they have enjoyed special advantages in this regard.

Instead of pursuing the argument as to which factors have contributed most to the observed growth, it seems more important to attempt at this point to draw some major and general inferences from these performances and in this way to indicate the ways in which the countries have failed to deal with the basic problems of transformation.

One striking characteristic of these high-growth performances has been that the pattern of industrialization that has emerged is heavily confined to terminal activities. This can be observed in the extent to which domestic production has concentrated on the traditional sectors, on mining, and on the simple processing of primary materials for export. In addition to a focus on the traditional simple processing of primary materials for export, there has also been a growth in the much-vaunted "modern" sector characterized by the rapid establishment of industries for the assembly of consumer products imported in a prefabricated condition.

While the traditional primary exports are therefore geared to overseas consumption and the needs of industrial capitalism, the domestic assembly of consumer goods is geared to the small high-income sector within these economies. As a consequence of the heavy reliance of the latter set of industrial establishments on imported inputs, the local value-added component of these activities has in practice tended to be quite minimal.[8] What else is to be expected of a country like Trinidad, where there are four "major" car assembly plants in operation, producing an annual output of just over 7,000 vehicles! The small volume of sales generally indicates the narrow range to which this industrialization caters. Since market size, as indicated by available individual purchasing power, is the major indicator of what is produced, the existing pattern of income distribution and demand—indeed the existing social system itself—is taken as given and the use of the community's resources is geared to reproducing this system. Given the poverty, unemployment, and inequitable distribution of income and wealth, it follows that such production bears little or no relationship to the needs of the broad mass of the population. The dynamic divergence between their needs and existing demand continues without significant modification.

On the other hand, the pattern of resource use which has accompanied this industrialization also shows no convergence between domestic resource use, production, and existing demand. From the point of view of our interpretation of underdevelopment in the small economy, this has meant that these achievements have not contributed to the structural transformation and elimination of their dependent economic structures. Where minerals and other primary products have been processed for export, the stimulus to production has been the needs of industrial capitalism and domestically retained income has been a small proportion of the value of the final product.[9] Where production has focussed on the simple assembly of imported consumer products, this has been geared to the needs of a small high-income group, and the bulk of the added value created by changes in demand for these products has accrued to the overseas suppliers of the local firms, usually the parent company or other associated enterprise.

Two of the crucial dimensions to such an industrialization process are that it inhibits both an indigenous technological effort and the development of a capital goods sector. A necessary condition for the development of an indigenous technological capacity is a capital goods sector geared to the exploitation of domestic resources. In the case of the small underdeveloped economies, the market incentives are clearly inadequate. Given the assumptions of the multinational corporations which invest in these economies about economies of scale and their implied levels of profitable maximum output, such forms of indigenous technological development can only appear as an indiscriminate duplication of capital goods sectors in the national markets within which they operate. The rational pursuit of profit on a multinational level means that resource availabilities and investments in plant technology have to be measured in terms of internationally traded availabilities and prices. From this standpoint, there is clearly little market inducement for the development of a local technological capacity. Investments in "research and development" are already made in the "home" territory of the company, where the centralization of these investments ensures certain obvious economies of scale which a small economy, with a small and limited local turnover, cannot achieve.

It follows that local resources, when they are brought into use, conform to the technological imperatives of the capitalist center which generates the needs for these resources. Local production, when it is geared to the local market, likewise conforms to the pattern of demand created by a social system that is distorted and inequitable and which itself is but the objective manifestation of underdevelopment. The vital relationships we discussed earlier (i.e., the linkages between domestic resources, domestic use, production, technology, demand, and needs) do not exist. The material structure of these economies remains untransformed, with the existing market incentives unable to generate a significant development of productive forces.

In the previous chapter, in connection with the idea of a "labor aristocracy," we indicated that for a complex of reasons the rate of return on capital employed in the import-substituting consumer goods industries has been very high. This has been accompanied by the use of a metropolitan-derived technology which has tended to be capital-intensive, reflecting its adaptation to the resource configuration in the capitalist center and the rising use of capital relative to labor in the competitive struggle there. The high rates of profit have been made possible more often than not by the extent to which these firms enjoy monopoly power. This monopoly power is in turn a product, on the one hand, of governmental controls on imports, which reduce competition from overseas suppliers and which are usually offered as an incentive for the establishment of local production facilities, and, on the other hand, of the technical requirements of the optimum size plant, which frequently requires longer runs than those made possible by the size of the local market.

This combination of technical considerations and public policy serves to make the monopoly almost "natural" to the small underdeveloped economy. Despite this, there are other elements in the overall situation that frequently reinforce this. Often it is found that these firms continue to obtain very generous tax incentives (such as income-tax rebates, accelerated depreciation, duty free imports, etc.) despite their high profitability rates. Furthermore, investigation also reveals that their intracompany purchases from the head office or other associated enterprises involve considerable duplicity: cases have been found of firms "purchasing" for domestic use machinery written off elsewhere. Or again, evidence is mounting of considerable overinvoicing of imported raw materials. Thus, measuring overinvoicing as the difference between the price paid by the country in question for its purchased inputs less the f.o.b. prices quoted in different markets, and expressing this figure as a percentage of these prices in different world markets, Vaitsos found that the weighted average of overpricing of seventeen selected Colombian firms was 155 percent in 1968. The rate of overinvoicing ranged from 1 percent to 483 percent.[10] Finally, it is quite often found that, when monopoly is fully secure, the firms have tended to relax their operating standards. Sometimes this is rationalized in terms of difficulties with the work force, but it would really seem to reflect the absence of a local standards bureau and effective consumer organizations and agencies.

There are a number of important consequences for the dynamics of the social system which follow from this high rate of return on capital employed. We have already observed that these firms can afford to be "generous," as they term it, in wage and other fringe-benefit payments. Just as they seek to suborn the new management elite, so they seek to suborn the loyalties of the working class and to win their commitment to the virtues of present industrial growth. It follows that if the tendency develops to treat these strata as an "aristocracy," then the ideological role and contribution of the working class will be seriously hampered. Indeed, conflicts have already been generated along these lines, and it has all too frequently been asserted that the workers are "exploiting" the peasants! That such developments profoundly undermine the potentialities of change goes without saying.

High rates of profit on small-scale local operations also reduce the incentives of firms to widen their markets, either through lower prices and the development of the mass selling techniques of their home country, or through the development of a genuine export capacity. In some of these countries (e.g., Singapore) assembly for re-export on a world scale (i.e., the entrepôt function) is highly developed in one or two individual product lines (e.g., cameras). But in general exports are only considered in terms of rationalizing plant capacity by sales to neighboring countries. This often rests upon initiatives in support of free trade areas, customs unions, etc.[11] This means that the industrialization process does not have the dynamic ability to break the bottleneck of foreign exchange earnings. Since industrialization does not lift the "export floor" of the country, foreign exchange earnings continue to depend heavily on primary raw material exports, foreign investment, and, more recently, tourism. Indeed, since these industrialization programs are forced to rely on a high import content and foreign exchange expenditure to purchase machinery, raw materials, technology, skilled personnel, and to provide for profit repatriation, the "import ceilings" of these countries are also not significantly lowered and in some cases have in fact been raised.

A number of studies of Latin America, in particular, support this conclusion and indicate quite strongly that industrialization has led to the worsening, rather than the expected improvement, of the foreign-exchange position of the country because of the high import intensity of import substitution.[12] It follows from these circumstances that the country's productive base does not allow for dynamic and profitable specialization in the international economy. Trade cannot play a crucial role in economic transformation; indeed, it continues to be a manifestation of, and a contributing factor toward, the structural dependence and underdevelopment of the economy.

These limitations of the industrialization program are also evident in the field of agriculture. To begin with, the industrialization process is not planned to promote (and is indeed incapable of promoting) any dynamic linkages with domestic agriculture. It is true that "local" foods are sold through some of the world's largest multinational food processing corporations, but often the "local" products, such as various vegetables, milk, and fruit juices, are simply imported as chemicals or dehydrated powders to be reconstituted locally. The result is that the growth in the consumption of high-protein food among the high-income elite is not organically related to the domestic production of such food, based on the use of domestic resources and technology. At the same time, insofar as the mass-consumption foods—mainly starches and carbohydrates—are concerned, these continue to be produced under traditional limitations as there is often no systematic effort to overthrow the structure of relations which exists on the land. The result is that although these wage goods are consumed in woefully inadequate amounts, the level of development means they cannot be supplied with local output. Wheat, maize, rice, and potatoes are all imported regularly to cover the deficit in food supplies.

Meanwhile, it is often the case that the prime agricultural land is tied up under the control of estates, plantations, and other latifundia, which specialize in the export of such traditional crops as sugar, cotton, coffee, bananas, etc. When domestic agriculture is linked to industry, it is confined to the simple processing of these export staples. Under these circumstances, agriculture also reflects the dynamic tendencies of divergence between domestic production and domestic demand, and between domestic consumption and the needs of the population as a whole. Agricultural resources, as in the other sectors of the economy, are therefore geared toward producing what is not consumed at home, while the dynamic component of domestic consumption of agricultural production is satisfied, under the aegis of multinational food processing firms, through imported and locally processed foods.

The traditional limitations of the agricultural sector are to be found in the predominant semi-feudal and other pre-capitalist land-holding relationships. These are usually compounded by the continuing use of ancient methods of production, without the benefits of the systematic application of indigenous science and technology to local ecological and environmental possibilities. Thus in Trinidad, despite the long existence of one of the world's most renowned tropical-agricultural research institutes (the Imperial College of Tropical Agriculture), almost all the research at that Institute has focussed on traditional export staples.[13] More recently the focus has shifted, under the encouragement of multinational drug companies in their search for new chemicals, to the chemical study of exotic tropical plants. As a result, this region is still unable to produce even one livestock animal bred and reared to the ecological requirements of the area and capable of producing cheap high-protein food on a mass scale.

Instead of developments along these lines, we find that these areas are characterized by the pressures of anarchic urban growth. Restrictions on land availability, combined with rapid population growth, have created an atmosphere of continuous speculation in land, rising land prices, and rent gouging. This has, needless to say, resulted in the growing dispossession of the peasantry. The landless peasants drift to the towns to pursue the illusion of a prosperity they are not yet aware that they cannot share. The ranks of the unemployed are swollen and the symptomatic manifestations of underdevelopment in the context of high growth can be seen everywhere.

The prevailing relations of production therefore reproduce themselves even in the context of high per capita product increases. This is so despite deliberate efforts to develop an indigenous capitalism which will shatter these relations. The attempts to woo foreign capital, with the hope that safeguards will prevent rampant exploitation, have generated a structure of production that is in no way fundamentally different from that of the colonial order. Consequently, the weaknesses highlighted here are not to be treated as isolated phenomena. They reflect the interconnected relationships of a social system where dependency relationships are reinforcing each other. Unless a comprehensive socialist strategy is adopted along the lines indicated in the second part of this book, there is no real possibility for these economies to develop beyond the misleading rises in per capita income, or indeed of even sustaining such advances on a long-term basis.

The much vaunted "pragmatic" strategies, as outlined above, have only succeeded in creating what are in effect enclaves—social, economic, and geographical—where international capitalism is located. The widespread growth of urban suburbs, in these countries, with their fancy houses (almost always made "burglar"-proof), is but a physical manifestation of the malformation of the city and the economy. Excessive unemployment, unbearable housing conditions, poor health and an environment of constant "crime" where every hunger pang inevitably leads to a "hustle" or a "choke and rob"—these are routine ways of existence and survival. The industrialization that has occurred has done little to liberate the social order.

Because of the rapid growth of the lumpenproletariat and the unemployed; because of the demoralization of the workers and the peasantry; and because of the existence of institutions which inculcate attitudes that facilitate the drain of skills, the flight of domestic capital to safe-houses abroad, the preferences of investors for speculative ventures in land, housing, and foreign exchange, these developments have not as yet generated a broadly based capacity to transform these societies. All that has so far been created is a group of "nizers." Of this group, those who are in business, with access to capital, gain little or no experience from an exposure to technology and production cycles. They remain in essence merchants, but instead of seeking licenses to import and distribute as was hitherto the case they now obtain licenses to "produce." As we have seen, such production is really disguised importation since the level of technology involved requires little more than the screwdrivers needed to assemble the knocked-down equipment.

It is not surprising that the governments of these territories are frequently forced to rely more and more on open repression and tyranny. This is of course respectably rationalized as the need to stabilize the social order, in the vain hope of winning the "race," as they call it, between revolution (i.e., their downfall) and development (i.e., the success of indigenous capitalism in spreading the benefits of growth)!

It is frequently felt that the crucial constraint on the government's capacity to stimulate the desired changes is the smallness of the national market. It is believed, correctly, that small national markets cannot generate sufficient incentives and inducements for the transformation of the neocolonial mode of production by private capitalism. The solution is increasingly sought in regional trade associations. Although we shall be taking up the discussion of this again in Chapter 9, it is useful at this stage to highlight a few of the dimensions of this strategy. The schemes behind these regional trade associations center on extending the market by widening the permissive area of "free" exchange. They concentrate on liberalizing trade in a given region and hence do not seek to integrate and transform regional ownership and the use of domestic resources, or to plan the region's consumption pattern. Because of the limited focus on widening the market, these associations have merely created a framework that allows the multinational firms to rationalize their plant capacity and thus monopolize the benefits of regional cooperation.

It often happens that, despite the national monopolies which have been created with the aid of national governments, the region can be served at a lower unit cost of production, and, other things being equal, with a higher profit per unit of output, if one plant is made to serve an entire region, instead of several duplicating plants. The improvement in the profit rate on each unit sale is of course measured by the change in unit cost of production relative to the change in the unit price of sales. The latter depends on the direction and amount of change of the weighted average of restrictions and monopoly power that the firm can command in the region as a whole, as compared with the weighted average unit price on sales before integration. The direction of this movement is not always certain. Sometimes it happens that, in exchange for the entire unified regional market, the firms have to trade off the level of fiscal and other incentives they can command. In other instances, licenses to produce might have already been given to more than one company in the territories to be integrated. Accordingly, the firms will have to negotiate and work out a basis for their competition and their ground rules for market sharing. In these arrangements they also frequently obtain government support, since no territory wants to see any impairment in the level of performance achieved by their industries before the union takes place.

Success in widening the market in this way operates as yet another dis-incentive to the attempt to widen their markets the hard way (i.e., by lowering unit prices, adopting mass selling techniques, or forging a genuine export capacity). The movement toward economic integration becomes but a simple extension of national import substitution to the regional level. It neither aims at, nor is it capable of, generating the market preconditions for spawning the growth of an indigenous capitalism.

Protection, Industrialization, and International Capitalism

Insofar as most of the industrialization which has occurred in these countries has been based on the dynamic exploitation of the national market through a program of import substitution, it follows that the level and pattern of protection in these countries is of some significance in evaluating governmental policies and their relationships to industrial development. Recently, a number of empirical studies from a neoclassical perspective have highlighted an important factor that has given rise to misleading and unwarranted evaluations of the industrialization process in these economies, and consequently to a number of spurious policy recommendations which are designed to "cure" some of the defects of the industrialization process. The rest of this section will be an attempt to put this work into perspective.

The important neoclassical discovery has been that the level of tariffs, quotas, and other protective arrangements which have been designed to attract investments from the multinational corporations in these countries frequently confer a very high level of effective protection. *Effective* protection is measured in terms of the differential between the domestic production cost per unit of the local product and the overseas supplier's cost of producing the imported equivalent. Whereas we find that the usual comparison of the heights of nominal tariffs is based on the measure of differences in final post-tariff prices of commodities, the implicit tariff measures differences in the levels of protection afforded to domestic value added. Often, this high level of effective protection is further reinforced by the frequent tendency toward overvalued foreign exchange rates. An overvalued foreign exchange rate reduces the competitiveness of exports by raising their price in terms of foreign currency and encourages importation of inputs to support simple fabrication processes domestically by reducing their price in terms of domestic currency. Insofar as the protection of local value added which is afforded by any given nominal tariff rate rises as the proportion of local value added falls, it is argued that the tariff must therefore drastically distort the development process in favor of the pattern of industrialization we have already observed. The large number of empirical studies which indicate much higher levels of effective protection than would be inferred from a casual inspection of the nominal tariff schedule is seen as proof of this assertion.

The effective protection rate P is calculated in terms of activities as:

$$P_j = \frac{t_j - a_{ij}\, t_i}{1 - a_{ij}}$$

where P_j is the effective protective rate for activity $_j$; t_j is the rate of tariff on activity $_j$; t_i the rate of tariff on activity $_i$, which is here assumed to be the only input; and a_{ij} is the share of i in the cost of producing j at world prices with no tariffs. Alternatively, in terms of value added we have:

$$P^1_j = \frac{V^1_j - V_j}{V^1_j}$$

where V^1_j is the value added per unit of output in activity j made possible by the tariff; and V_j is the value added per unit of output in activity j at world prices, with no tariffs.[14]

Exaggerated claims have been made for the concept of effective protection. Thus Corden has argued:

> Ordinary *nominal* tariffs apply to commodities, but resources move as between economic activities. Therefore, to discover the resource allocation effects of a tariff structure one must calculate the protective rate for each activity, that is, the effective protective rate. This is the main message of the new theory of tariff structures.[15]

Given these effects on the market for resources, the pattern of irrational industrialization which we have observed is supposedly explained in terms of the distorting effects of an irrational tariff system introduced by governments in these territories.[16]

It is argued that one major correction to these distortions—and, as a consequence, a likely solution to the problem of the patterns of industrial flows—would be to rationalize the tariff and exchange rate structures in order to eliminate the market distorting features of the present arrangements. This can be achieved, it is said, through the imposition of a uniform *ad valorem* tariff combined with some measured devaluation of the foreign exchange value of the currency. A uniform *ad valorem* tariff would neither penalize exports nor encourage imports. At the same time, a devaluation of the foreign exchange value of domestic currency would tend not only to stimulate exports—because their prices would be cheaper in terms of foreign currencies—but also to deter importation because the price of imports would rise in terms of domestic currency. In this way incentives would be offered to export-oriented industrialization and toward the establishment of industries to produce the capital goods inputs which are presently imported. In other words, there would be a minimization of the deviation from "correct" market norms and a maximization of the permissive conditions for private initiatives.

It is difficult to imagine a more naive formulation of the problems and issues of industrialization. Confining ourselves to an examination of the technical bases of these measurements that are supposed to determine the level of effective protection, we can readily observe a number of crucial weaknesses. In the first place, these measures are based on static partial-equilibrium analysis and have been built upon a very mechanical application of fixed input-output coefficients. They assume that the goods under consideration are homogeneous, with perfect elasticities in the supply of imports and the demand for exports. Further, it is usually assumed that the protected activities employ the same input ratios in both the home country and the rest of the world. Finally, all tradeable goods are assumed to remain traded, even after tariffs and other protective devices have been imposed. When these assumptions are partially suspended, it is not surprising that the resulting measures of the height of effective protection vary quite significantly. In view of all this, it follows that the social process of industrialization cannot be either explained or remedied on the basis of such a limited, partial, unhistorical, neoclassical analysis.

Indeed, our analysis of the whole historical process in these countries points to the fact that the tariff system is not an independent policy instrument freely used by these governments in pursuit of a particular developmental strategy. In fact, it is a dependent variable responding to many factors, not the least of which is the fact that the tariff structure has in reality been designed by the multinational firms to serve their own needs. True governmental independence in the implementation of tariff schedules is limited. Indeed, government policies in this sphere are distinguished less by their autonomy and independence than by the way in which they have historically been forced to compete with each other in offering incentives to the foreign multinational firms.

Consider the actual way in which these firms have often been established. It is common for some governments to conduct feasibility studies and then to prepare shopping lists of the most attractive projects. In other cases—although international pressure is reducing the likelihood of this—such lists may simply be drawn up without bothering with feasibility studies. Partly on governmental initiative (e.g., through the establishment of industrial corporations, publicity, etc.), but largely as a result of the efforts of the multinational firms to secure, preserve, and extend marketing outlets around the world, the governments and the multinational manufacturers come together in order to discuss the possibility and feasibility of the local production of the imported commodity. In the course of working out the details of their production plans the companies are in a position to virtually direct the governments as to the level of protection needed to make the proposed operations "feasible" for them. When faced with what is likely to be a take-it-or-leave-it situation, the government more often than not concedes to these requests. After all, as these governments see it their *primary* interest and objective is to promote the maximum inflow of foreign resources, foreign technology, and foreign skills in order to create their "apparent" industrial structure. In the last analysis, given the weakness of their bargaining positions—some other country can always make a competitive offer—they recognize that these flows depend on their acquiescence to these foreign demands.

The major weakness of the neoclassical interpretation stems from the poverty of its historical understanding. It assumes that the allocation of "capital" is simply determined by availability and will with equal ease respond to such local incentives. But this has not been the logic of multinational corporate expansion. What neoclassical theory has been forced to analyze and interpret as a "local" strategy of industrialization—because of its failure to grasp the full nature of the historical process—is largely a product of changes internal to the central mechanisms of industrial capitalism in the metropolitan countries. Neither the growth and spread of the multinational corporation, nor the way in which this has dynamically induced changes in patterns of investment, marketing, and the nature of technological transfers, can be comprehended simply as "local" phenomena. In this whole process the tariff system is more akin to what classical political economy had long recognized it to be—a political product. Thus, while it remains true that such protection is significant for the industrialization process in the typical small underdeveloped economy, the tariff system is itself a dependent variable determined by political and economic factors that are beyond its control as long as these economies continue to adhere to their present neocolonial form.

As we have already indicated and shall argue at greater length in Part 2, protection, or rather the planning of external trading relationships, is of crucial importance in the transition period. But such planning has to be conceived in a radically different manner than is the case with most existing tariff systems, which focus on influencing costs and prices through the market. As Preobrazhensky long ago pointed out with reference to the period of primitive socialist accumulation in the USSR:

> If there is sometimes a protectionist tariff policy in countries with a weakly developed industry, aimed at protecting a particular industry from the competition of a capitalistically more developed country, this has nothing in common, beyond external forms, with socialist protectionism. In the one case it is a matter of protecting one industry from another *belonging to the same economic system.* In the other we have the protection of one mode of production, in a state of infantile weakness, from another economic system mortally hostile to it which even in the period of its senile decrepitude will inevitably be stronger, economically and technically for a time, than the new economy.[17]

We have sought to extend the argument as presented by Preobrazhensky. He was concerned with two capitalist economies at different levels of industrialization, one of which was attempting to transform its mode of production to socialism.

Here we are concerned with center-periphery dependency relationships as they have evolved under neocolonialism. Here the tariff system performs an essentially different function. It no longer protects one industry from another but *becomes instead the condition for maximizing the drain of surplus from the periphery to the industrial center.* The local tariff systems are basically instruments of the expansion and development of the multinational firm. They reflect the creation of trans-national corporate economic systems and the way these relate to and protect themselves from each other. It is the corporate, not the national, character of the tariff system which is truly significant.

Conclusion

Although there are further aspects to this crypto-industrialization process, our analysis should be sufficient to demonstrate the extent to which dependency structures and underdevelopment are being reinforced despite the rapidly increasing gains in average per capita incomes. While these rising levels of per capita product mislead (if only because they avoid such issues as income distribution), we have dwelt more on the basic inadequacies of these dynamic processes for generating a self-sustained transformation of the material base of these societies. Material underdevelopment in the small underdeveloped economy—which we have interpreted as involving the dynamic divergence of resource use, ownership, and production, and the divergence between domestic demand and the needs of the population as a whole in the absence of a vibrant and indigenous technology which can provide an organic basis within the social system for linking these two processes—continues despite the per capita income increases.

As this is occurring, state efforts to create an indigenous capitalist class have not been particularly successful. The "nizers" who are created to "manage" the joint state-capitalist ventures are limited in their production, management, and technological exposure. As a result of their position within the multinational firm and the dependency relationships which the multinational corporations generate, there is no scope for creative innovation. Technological dependency reproduces itself through the systematic generation of a certain type of manpower: people capable of assembling durable consumer goods, but not of designing them; people who sell, but do not design their own marketing strategy; people who produce, but lack any creative relationship to technology. Meanwhile, the petty traders, the landlords, and the indigenous businessmen cannot accumulate capital in sufficiently large amounts to develop local technological and productive forces even if they are inclined to do so. The *objective* socialization of capital results in the loss of local capital to the center—through overpricing, over-invoicing, underpayment of profit taxes, excessive fiscal concessions, and so on. Even the savings of the workers and the better-off farmers are drained abroad, again because of the dominance of the multinational financial institutions over the savings-investment process in these countries.

With these developments it is not surprising that there has been a failure of an indigenous capitalist class to develop and to create its own local material base for self-reproduction. In addition to the social forces involved, the objective constraints of a small national market reduce the incentives and the capabilities of private capital to raise the level of production forces. Progressive state intervention of a capitalist kind, which is aimed at easing these constraints, is also unlikely to be successful. The basically undemocratic nature of these states deprives them of the political legitimacy and support necessary to command or solicit from the population the sacrifices necessary to make such a transformation technically feasible, *while at the same time reinforcing a social system which channels the benefits of transformation to private appropriators of the social surplus.*

This is why we have argued time and again that the historical options of these economies are limited either to a comprehensive socialist strategy for transforming the productive forces and liberating the political and social order, or to the continuation of the present neocolonial mode. In the latter case, economic change will continue to be a dependent by-product of developments in the capitalist center. And even if isolated exceptions due to favored political access to capitalist markets are possible (e.g., the force and presence of international capitalism in Taiwan as an offset to socialism in China), as a general rule these economies will be incapable of transforming themselves. Moreover, as the historical situation continues to change, certain objective factors (e.g., the technological gap, shifting international political alliances) reinforce the stringencies of this analysis.

While directing our attention to these matters—particularly our presentation of the industrialization strategy—has provided a useful preface to the analysis in Part 2, it has also served to illuminate several other important issues hinted at in the beginning of this chapter. Insofar as the income gains observed here have depended on a rapid volume of foreign capital inflows and outflows through the multinational corporation, it highlights an important danger confronting the small underdeveloped economy pursuing a socialist strategy of economic transformation. When faced, as it seeks to disengage from international capitalism, with the short-period problems of domestic resource bottlenecks, foreign exchange availability, and slowly rising income levels, the temptation is to tone down socialist policies and to seek various accommodations and partnerships with capitalism, since it is believed that these account for the other countries' "successes." In addition, the spectacle of the industrialized socialist countries contending for "similar" partnership arrangements with capitalism (trade treaties, management contracts, etc.), and making other political accommodations in order to ease *their* resource bottlenecks, will strengthen the temptation to tone down socialist policies, and thus weaken the will to persevere.

The rationalization of these developments in other socialist countries is often presented in the local context as the desire to socialize something more than poverty. The appeal of this position should not be underestimated. This is all the more so since it reinforces dependent psychological attitudes in regard to productive forces, the environment, and technology. While, as we have shown, much of the appeal rests on an objective misunderstanding of the nature of dependence and underdevelopment, developing an understanding along the lines of this study is important for raising one's consciousness of the material problem of underdevelopment in the small economy during the present neocolonial phase.

Notes

1. In a two-part article on the noncapitalist path, Tshume has also pointed out that in these societies:

   "The state exhibits a *relative* autonomy in relation to social classes because no single class is developed enough to dominate others. This relative autonomy makes the state power a more fragile thing than is common in societies with developed class formation: state power is more easily won by revolutionary democrats . . . and more easily wrested from them by imperialist (external) and pro-imperialist, pro-capitalist internal forces." (A. Tshume, *The African Communist;* italics in original.)

   While not ourselves agreeing that thereby power is more "easily won," the general drift of the argument is quite similar to that presented here. In a footnote on the same page, Tshume quotes R. Ulyanovsky ("Some Aspects of the Non-Capitalist Way for Asian and African Countries," *World Marxist Review* [September 1969]):

   "Because of the embryonic class relations in most of these countries, there is either no mechanism, or only a very minor one, for direct subordination between the petit-bourgeois intellectuals in power and class organisations, wherever such exists. The petit-bourgeois intellectuals holding the key posts in the state, the party, the army and the economic apparatus, are relatively free of the chief classes of society. That is why the state tends to take steps which variously meet or clash with the interests of the labouring social sections. This creates the illusion that the (state) power is above class."

It should be noted that these observations are made in the context of an analysis of the noncapitalist path where it is presumed there are strong tendencies toward petty-bourgeois, revolutionary democratic regimes.

2. This term is taken from the word "Africanization." It is used fairly frequently in Tanzania and has been introduced to the social sciences vocabulary by M. Von Freyholdt in her paper "The Workers and the Nizers."
3. See the paper by I. Shivji, "The Silent Class Struggle"; and J. Wells, "The Construction Industry in East Africa."
4. See C. Y. Thomas, "Meaningful Participation," pp. 358-59.
5. The author was fortunate in having the opportunity to examine contracts. Because of their confidentiality, a source cannot be given.
6. The role of protection is more extensively discussed in the next section.
7. For an excellent detailed study of underdevelopment in the context of high mineral export growth, see N. Girvan, *Foreign Capital and Economic Underdevelopment in Jamaica.*
8. For detailed evidence documenting the consequences of what J. Rweyemamu calls "perverse capitalist industrialization," see his forthcoming book, *Underdevelopment and Industrialization in Tanzania.* Some of this material has been released in Economic Research Bureau Papers (University of Dar-es-Salaam). For a similar and earlier documentation for some parts of the Caribbean area, see H. Brewster and C. Y. Thomas, *Dynamics of West Indian Economic Integration.* The evidence in these studies indicates the low domestic value-added ratios created by these industries.
9. See Girvan, *Foreign Capital and Economic Underdevelopment in Jamaica.*
10. C. V. Vaitsos, "Transfer of Resources and Preservation of Monopoly Rents." For further data see C. V. Vaitsos, "Bargaining and the Distribution of Return in the Purchase of Technology by Developing Countries"; and M. J. Yaffey, *Balance of Payments Problems.*
11. This subject is discussed further in Chapter 9.
12. For a representative sample of industry studies of the import effect of import-substitution policies, see J. M. Katz and E. Gallo, "The Industrialization of Argentina"; S. Macario, "Protectionism and Industrialization in Latin America"; N. H. Leff and A. D. Netto, "Import Substitution, Foreign Investment and International Disequilibrium in Brazil"; A. O. Hirschman, "The Political Economy of Import Substituting Industrialization in Latin America"; C. F. Diáz-

Alejandro, "On the Import Intensity of Import Substitution"; N. Islam, "Comparative Costs, Factor Proportions and Industrial Efficiency in Pakistan."

13. This has since been integrated into the Faculty of Agriculture, University of the West Indies.
14. See W. M. Corden, "The Structure of a Tariff System and the Effective Rate of Protection"; and B. Balassa, "Tariff Protection in Industrial Countries."
15. Corden, op. cit., p. 222.
16. Out of a large number of recent studies in this field, the Williams College Group specialized heavily in this area. As a representative sample of their work and those of associates in support of this thesis, consult H. J. Bruton, "The Import Substituting Strategy of Economic Development." This reviews the findings of the first twenty-four research memoranda in the AID-Williams College Contract. A second review is by John Sheahan, "Import Substitution and Economic Policy," and covers the work done under the Williams College-AID auspices for the period July 1969 through June 1972.
17. E. Preobrazhensky, *The New Economics*, p. 121 (emphasis in the original).

Part 2

Economic Strategy

4

On Converging Resource Use and Demand: The First "Iron Law" of Transformation

On Converging Resource Use and Demand

In this part of our study we shall discuss some major issues of economic strategy during the transition period. In our analysis of underdevelopment we argued that as a material objective phenomenon in small underdeveloped economies the dynamic of this process has centered on the productive relations which give rise to the divergence of the pattern of domestic resource use, domestic demand, and the needs of the broad mass of the community. It is in this pattern that the qualitative nature of structural dependence manifests itself. This indicator has been advanced in preference to such conventional measures as the rise in national per capita income, the rate of capital accumulation, the degree of unemployment, the degree of literacy, and so on.

From our point of view it follows that material development can be interpreted, in the most basic and fundamental way, as the initiation of economic processes which overcome this divergent pattern of needs, domestic production, and domestic consumption. And since these divergences are rooted in such basic structural relationships as foreign ownership and control of domestic resources, export specialization for metropolitan markets, the pervasiveness of foreign decision-making over domestic economic processes, etc., overcoming them requires nothing less than a revolutionary break with capitalism and imperialism. In the absence of such decisive disengagement, economic transformation will never be achieved—even though in isolated cases such as Kuwait, Taiwan, and Singapore, either special natural resources or favored political access to capitalist markets may allow high levels of income per capita and/or the development of a significant and prosperous export capacity in certain light manufactures.

It was indicated in Part 1 that a serious attempt at initiating economic processes that are aimed at reversing these cumulative divergences means securing on a political and social basis an entrenched worker/peasant alliance; this alone would make comprehensive planning of the type we have outlined possible.[1] We pointed out that such comprehensive planning means planning both production and consumption and therefore makes possible the elimination of the usual capitalist sequence of output and consumption changes being adjusted *ex post facto* via the market. It also institutionalizes mechanisms of planning and implementation so that there is in fact no *operational* distinction between planners and implementors—even though for analytical purposes we may wish to separate them. Furthermore, because of the very comprehensiveness of this planning approach to resource use and demand, the main limits on the economy's output capacity become the level of accumulation and the social costs which the community as a whole is prepared to sustain.

By enlarging the scope of conscious decision-making, the interdependencies through space and time and the interrelated dynamics of economic processes become amenable to rational management and control. The fully comprehensive nature of underdevelopment and measures for dealing with this become manifest in a way they cannot to an individual entrepreneur, particularly when, as is the present case, the entrepreneurial function is likely to be confined to a foreign businessman and/or his local client counterpart. From this perspective, an economic strategy becomes essentially a way of planning resource use and consumption in order to attain previously established material goals.

If the material manifestations of underdevelopment have

been expressed as the dynamic divergence in the pattern of domestic resource use, domestic demand, and needs, in the absence of an indigenous technology to provide the basis for an organic link between them, then the principal material goal must be to seek a dynamic convergence of these relationships. When put in this way, two basic problems of an economic strategy tailored to achieving this goal become clear. The first is to find out how to effect a convergence of the pattern and rate of domestic resource use and domestic demand as it has developed and is likely to develop (if we interpret the latter from universal human experience and relate it to the context of the particular society). The second issue centers on finding out how the community's demand can be structured so that it conforms more closely than at present to domestic resource availability and domestic use. This latter problem essentially means determining how the needs of the community can be made to converge with its demand patterns. Apart from extrapolating from experiences in both capitalist and socialist countries, there is no specific or dogmatic answer to this problem. The goods consumed in each society will reflect in some measure its values, culture, preferences, and so on. Accordingly, the precise composition of output cannot be posited from general formulations. All that can be done is to suggest that certain priorities seem to exist everywhere. These are indicated when—as in the case of housing—they have an impact on some aspect of the strategy for transformation and the principles of consumption and distribution of output.

The concept of the divergence of domestic resource use and domestic demand, which we have said expresses certain dimensions of the quintessential material dynamic of underdevelopment, cannot be interpreted statically. Indeed, the tendency has been for a cumulative tendency toward divergence, notwithstanding recent experiences of industrialization aimed at the domestic market. Two factors, both of which are intrinsic to the structure of international capitalism, support this basic long-term historical trend. The first has been demonstrated by the incapacity of these systems to develop an adequate and relevant indigenous technological and scientific capacity. As a consequence, in these economies there is no basis for forging an organic link between resource use and demand. Often, there is no domestic resource endowment in even the most rudimentary form. What exists, and is said to constitute an inventory of material resources, is a random search for specific metals by colonial offices or firms that have special search licenses. By the very nature of the ends sought and the ways in which the searches have been "organized," the full details are not known even by the governments of the host countries.

The second factor has been the long-run historical tendency for the global and domestic income elasticities of demand for those types of products which are not produced in the typical small underdeveloped economy to be higher than for those produced at home for home consumption and export-type commodities. The resulting income changes and the changes in demand which follow reinforce the divergence between domestic resource use and domestic demand. The growth of import-substituting industrialization has not changed this, since what has been described as industrialization is essentially a process in which multinational corporations, although they produce goods with high income elasticities of demand, do so by means of imported knocked-down equipment for local assembly. Because the bulk of the value added in the production process already lies in the imported knocked-down components, the result is that changes in domestic demand have had limited impact on domestic resource use. This pattern of high income elasticities of demand for goods which are not produced at home (i.e., industrial goods) has been a universal phenomenon, manifesting itself irrespective of the prevailing social system. As a result, it is inconceivable that these demand pressures can be contained, let alone reversed, at any realistic economic cost to a small economy since they satisfy human needs everywhere. The consequences of this for planning demand are therefore very important.

In view of these arguments, it follows that if the basic

strategy of transformation is the convergence of domestic resource use and domestic consumption, certain important policy issues will have to be settled. First, a long-run assessment has to be made of the nature and consequences of transformation for the now predominantly agricultural sectors of our small underdeveloped economies during the present neocolonial phase. This will be attempted in the next chapter. Second, strategies for producing industrial goods will have to be developed and systematically articulated. This becomes crucial in light of the long-run historical tendency that has decisively favored, and will continue to favor, the consumption of industrial goods while our modal-type economy is distinguished by the common belief that its capacity for industrialization is limited, both by its size and by the cost of industrialization in the present era. This element of our strategy is therefore pivotal to the whole transformation process, as we shall see in Chapter 5. Finally, some attempt has to be made to indicate the extent to which prevailing demand can, and does, accurately reflect needs, and the direction of major efforts required to fulfill needs which lead to direct increases in the welfare of the broad mass of the people, and which may not be readily and ordinarily forthcoming as average income levels rise. This issue is taken up throughout the next two chapters, and some further problems along these lines are dealt with in Chapter 8.

Economic Surplus: Size and Allocation

These basic policy issues relate directly to problems that center on the economic surplus of the community. There are two sets of strategic decisions involved. The first is the determination of the appropriate rate of accumulation of economic surplus; the second, the pattern of allocation of the mobilized surplus among the various branches of economic activity. In the socialist literature on underdevelopment, the emphasis has focussed heavily on the former set of decisions, mainly by drawing a distinction between savings (as this concept is used in neoclassical economic theory) and the social surplus as it is in fact generated from a community standpoint. Where the latter set of strategic decisions, which focus on allocation, have been mentioned, it has frequently been in terms of the larger generalities, such as the distribution between Department I and Department II. We shall ultimately focus on the second set of strategic decisions, but for the rest of this section we shall concentrate on the problems of the overall rate of accumulation.

Except in the numerous theoretical exercises in basic algebra by the neoclassical economists—which are supposed to constitute their ideas of economic model-building—the optimal rate of accumulation inevitably varies over time both among countries and within countries and depends on a number of crucial factors, none of which are easily quantified. Having said this, it is important to make it clear that our concept of economic surplus does not conform to the "traditional" view, which simply focuses on the amount of financial resources the community saves and thus makes "available" for investment. Viewing accumulation from this perspective is not consistent with a comprehensive program of socialist planning. In its simplest and most basic sense, such a comprehensive planning perspective requires that the social surplus available to any community be seen as that part of the community's output which, through time, does not constitute the society's essential consumption. The community's output is that which can be attained with full and rational use of available resources in the "given state of the arts." The social surplus is not a static conception which refers to a "fund" of savings to draw upon and which places limits on the extent to which, in the process, we can "sacrifice" consumption in some absolute sense. Dobb correctly pointed out this prevalent confusion:

> It has been a fairly common assumption in the past . . . that the essence of the problem is *financial* in the sense that what limits the possibility of such a transition is the availability of financial resources as a basis for large scale investment . . . According to this view (which I shall call the traditional view) the available and

> mobilisable "savings fund" of the community is the crucial bottleneck which sets a limit to the possible rate of economic development . . . to speak of development as being limited by the size of the basic savings "fund" in the sense we have just spoken of it (or alternatively by the institutional mechanisms for mobilizing such savings) only makes sense on the assumption that the margin between production and consumption can *only* be enlarged by lowering consumption and cannot be enlarged to any appreciable extent by enlarging total production. As soon as we drop this assumption and allow the possibility of an increase in total production, the limit upon development of which we have spoken loses its absolute character, and may even cease to have such meaning as a limiting factor at all.[2]

To cease to have meaning as a "limiting factor at all" can be interpreted, in the context of our analysis, to mean that it is indeterminate, outside of the historical context of the society we are concerned with. This means that the determination of the optimal level of accumulation requires a study of a complex set of factors which do not allow for any a priori estimation. Let us give a few examples. First of all, to determine the optimal level of accumulation it is necessary to know the resource limits on accumulation; that is, the availability of those labor resources, natural resources, and foreign exchange without which the given level of accumulation would mean that some investments are frustrated. We also have to know the social costs involved in dealing with the problems of easing these resource constraints; and have a very clear idea of the particular target rate of growth the community desires to achieve—which in turn reflects a host of economic, social, political, and even strategic considerations. Thus we may state categorically that to be socially efficient the planned levels and rate of accumulation have to reflect economic and technical factors (e.g., the levels of income, capital intensities in various sectors, availability of the appropriate resource mixes, etc.), and political and social factors (e.g., the required levels of consumption, the degree of control over the productive process which the worker/peasant alliance can command, etc.).

It follows that none of these basic factors, and the capacities they imply, are independent of the form and content of the way the surplus is used or the historical-social context of the particular society. That is why we have pointed out the impossibility of giving an a priori specification to the optimal rate of accumulation. All that we can tentatively say by way of generalization is that, given the dynamic relationship which exists between consumption levels, nutrition, health, and productivity in the typical underdeveloped economy, the optimal rate of accumulation is *very unlikely to be as high as the maximum rate which is technically possible.* This is simply because reducing the levels of real consumption below a certain point, in the typical underdeveloped economy, would be counterproductive in its effect on labor efficiency.

When considering the problems attached to the determination of the overall rate of accumulation in the context of underdevelopment, it is particularly important to bear in mind the distinction we drew earlier between savings, as used in the neoclassical literature, and the social surplus, as we are using it here. This distinction stems from the observation which Paul Baran made long ago that in the typical underdeveloped economy the economic and social system is so organized that there are certain substantial sources of surplus that are both actually and potentially available for productive investment but that only a comprehensive planning machinery, under appropriate political and social direction, can mobilize for productive use.[3] This surplus can be identified in a number of forms. There is, first of all, the present loss of social surplus which occurs in the form of excess overseas profit repatriation and which follows from the dominance of foreign enterprise over local economic activity. In the previous chapter we referred to the frequent malpractices of the multinational firms engaged in import substitution: the over-invoicing of imported raw material and machinery, the under-invoicing of exports, the importation of written-off machinery, etc. All of these constitute important sources of surplus drain. In addition, where the enterprise is of the traditional type (i.e., a primary exporting corporation selling its output to the parent company or other associated enterprises for further processing), and where trans-shipment and other facilities are controlled by the parent company, then the price set on the output of the local subsidiary is frequently an accounting device which bears less of a relationship to local production costs and profit levels than to the overall strategy of the company in minimizing its tax liability. Thus it is not surprising to find situations like this:

> From 1938 to 1959 the general U.S. price level rose by 138 percent. During these years the price of the bauxite produced in the United States doubled. Yet the price of bauxite imported from Surinam [Guyana] was almost the same in 1959 as it had been in 1938 [but this] did not prevent [the companies] from raising the price of aluminum, which went up by 78 percent between 1948 and 1959.[4]

The price level of bauxite did not in fact begin to rise until after tax concessions were granted to United States companies operating through Western hemisphere trade corporations.[5]

A second important source of surplus product derives from that part of the national product which the landlords, moneylenders, and traders appropriate in the rural economy and either hoard or spend on conspicuous consumption. Sometimes the major agencies of rural misappropriation of the surplus are the foreign enterprises which are engaged in the production and sale of primary staples overseas. Thus in the plantation economies these firms engage in all the forms of surplus drain which we have identified in their industrial counterparts.

A third important source of surplus loss is reflected in those resources which are used to support those aspects of the proliferating state bureaucracies which are primarily concerned with the spread of political patronage. This frequently also reaches the rural areas as state capitalism increasingly seeks to extend itself into agricultural production. It can be seen in the burden of charges being placed on the peasants for the support of cooperatives, marketing boards, official transportation of produce, etc.

Two final sources to which we can refer briefly are the

"excessive consumption" of the new elements of the bourgeoisie and the unemployment and underemployment of labor; these are major distinguishing characteristics of these societies. Sometimes this extensive underutilization of labor is accompanied by underutilization of land, particularly in plantation-type economies where a plantation's underutilized land "reserves" frequently accompany land "shortages" and rising land prices and rents.[6] In some cases there is also underutilization of foreign exchange resources. This is usually produced by maintaining rigid dependence on some one or other metropolitan standard (e.g., Franc Zone, Sterling Area), resulting in the multinational financial institutions dominating the local monetary situation.

What can we conclude from all this? As Baran has pointed out in his discussion of the identification and measurement of the various forms of economic surplus:

> These are essentially reducible to the fact that the category of the potential economic surplus itself transcends the horizon of the existing social order, relating as it does not merely to the easily observable performance of the given socioeconomic organization, but also to the less readily visualized image of a more rationally ordered society.[7]

It is in view of this that we have already indicated the incorrectness of trying to establish a priori an optimal rate of accumulation, abstracted from the historical, social, and political context. We would like to add two observations to this. First, the larger the proportion of potential surplus and unproductively used surplus product the state can mobilize, the less the immediate pressures on the rate at which real consumption can increase for the broad mass of the population, other things being equal. Second, the greater the degree of democratic participation and willingness on the part of the community to absorb the social costs of transformation, then the higher the optimal rate of accumulation for the society. Beyond this, there is nothing more we can generalize about, except to direct attention to the equally important issue of which policies should guide the allocation of surplus in order to achieve structural transformation. This task will occupy us for most of the remainder of this book, but before proceeding to this we shall elaborate briefly on the dynamic implications of convergence in the economic transformation of the economy, and discuss some issues of "measurement" which inevitably spring from the way we interpret the effects of economic backwardness and underdevelopment on the economic structure of the small economy.

Convergence in a Dynamic Context of Development

In the following chapters we shall focus on the strategy of convergence of resource use and the needs of the community in the context of the development of a vibrant and indigenous technology. As we shall observe, such a strategy contains its own material, economic, scientific, social, and political dynamic. We shall seek to establish the convergence of these relationships as a *necessary* condition for transforming the mode of production and raising the level of utilization of productive forces, so that poverty and underdevelopment will no longer remain crucial features of the economic system. As we shall present it, the strategy of convergence allows for the establishment of those material relationships we referred to earlier (resource use, production, technology, demand, needs). It is these relationships that give an economic system its internal autonomy and determine its capacity for sustaining growth and development. In the development of this strategy we shall concentrate on what can generally be described as the earlier phases of transformation (i.e., the phases of planning aimed at the development within the economy of a technology and productive base consonant with the satisfaction of the community's needs). As we shall argue in some detail, such a policy *does not imply crude notions of autarky*. It is true that during the initial phases of transformation the main achievements are the generation of a capacity to produce industrial goods—since there is a strongly progressive requirement to do so if the community's needs are to be satisfied. In the process of doing this, however, the community generates not only a capacity to spread the use of industrial techniques into all elements of the economic process and to produce industrial goods (which also favors the long-run global tendencies in material consumption), but it also creates a dynamic basis for engagement in the international economy through the export of industrial goods. Put in a dynamic context, the strategy of convergence is not simply constrained by the requirement of satisfying local needs in an autarkic sense, but allows for engagement in export activity where such *exports are an extension of domestic demand and domestic needs.* This is made possible by the extent to which output, the entire production system itself, technology, and the use of local resources, are all governed by the dynamic of convergence, so that exports, when they do develop, naturally follow as dynamic extensions of these considerations.

With technological growth and a system of resource use and production based on such an internal dynamic, the development of an export capacity in industrial goods is in effect a further dynamic development of the mode of production. But it is *a development which can only be achieved after dynamic convergence has already been attained.* This is a necessary condition if exports are not to represent the production and sale abroad of goods that are inconsistent with the prior satisfaction of local needs, which remain the basic and overriding condition of resource use.

One crucial consequence of this dynamic development is that in this situation the capacity to earn foreign exchange is no longer constrained by unequal exchange, or by the sluggish growth of the world market for primary products. Instead we now find that, by and large, foreign exchange earnings come to be determined by the output capacity of the export sector itself. This output capacity will in turn be constrained, as indeed will all other activities, by the level of accumulation the community is prepared to accept in support of the growth of this sector. Trade is then as it were a "super-engine" of growth. This follows because the *necessary and basic internal productive conditions will have been established to ensure that participation in a capitalist-dominated international economy does not result in a global division of labor which works against the local community.* Non-equivalence and inequality in exchange will therefore be removed as a result of *internal* changes in the relations of production and the development of productive forces along the lines to be indicated. In other words, inasmuch as trade reflects the structure of production, the production structure in turn will reveal modes of organization and production capable of withstanding the anarchy of the present international order.

Such developments are interpreted in this study as the necessary preconditions for yet a further stage in the transformation of the productive system—that is, the integration of the national economy into the world socialist economy on the basis of genuine independence and equality. In any other situation, wide disparities in size, together with the marked differences in the levels of productive efficiency of existing socialist states and the typical small underdeveloped economy, pose the dangers of inequalities in international economic relations within the socialist economic system. In other words, true independence is a function of internal organization and development and cannot be the unilateral concession of one nation state to another in the present world order.

As we shall also see, domestic (mainly natural) resources are expected to play a crucial role in the strategy of convergence. However, despite their importance in a dynamic context, this is not an *enduring* role, in the sense that it dominates the choice of economic activity *in perpetuity*. The internalization of technological growth, although initially dependent on adapting domestic resources to domestic needs, allows the productive system to become progressively "footloose" in terms of domestic resource constraints. This is a very crucial development. Thus, paradoxically, we find that even though the domestic resource constraint, or rather the availability of domestic resources, plays a crucial role in the initial stages of our strategy, later on this role is diminished as production becomes more or less "footloose" in terms of the availability of local resources. We may therefore say *that the domestic resource availabilities and constraints are replaced by the wider conception of man and the society's creative technological potential, which are now, as a result of planning and changes in production relations, becoming institutionalized in the mode of production and the very way of life.* In this situation the preconditions for achieving "plenty" are established and only then can the prospects for a transition beyond socialism be entertained.

This, then, is a very brief summary of the dynamic perspective against which our strategy has to be seen. However, despite the dynamic interconnections of these stages in the transformation process, the *first must remain the most vital and crucial. This is because dynamic convergence of resource use and needs is a precondition specific to the requirements of overcoming underdevelopment, small size, and the domination of neocolonial relationships in the international economy.* It is only after dynamic convergence has been achieved that the society will have reached a stage beyond the present neocolonial mode. But to achieve this requires a recognition that raising the level of the utilization of productive forces and social changes in the relations of production are both co-terminous at all stages in the development of socialism. To argue otherwise is a very dangerous form of idealism, little removed from the naive conceptions of poverty and smallness to which we have alluded frequently.

Divergence of Resource Use and Demand: Problems of Measurement

The complex idea of the relationships between resource use, demand, technology, and needs has both quantitative and qualitative dimensions. The qualitative dimensions are related to the dynamic interactions between people in the society and their relationships to the material environment. The quantitative dimensions relate to the products consumed and the products produced at home. Even though it would be unscientific to attempt to make a quantitative measure of underdevelopment, the measurement of this divergence between resource use and demand is important for planning and other uses connected with interpreting the course of material production. In an earlier work we referred to this measure as being appropriately described as the "import domestic expenditure coefficient."[8] We argued that the traditional indices, such as per capita income, per capita energy consumption, indices of the standards of living, etc., while of some use, were deficient and misleading in highlighting the material reflection of underdevelopment in the small underdeveloped economy during the present neocolonial phase.

Although our interpretation depends on the nature of the relationships between domestic production, imports, exports, and domestic expenditure, the traditional import indices used in the economic literature do not adequately display the crucial characteristics we are aiming at. Thus the import propensity (i.e., the ratio of total imports to gross national product) would be misleading if a great deal of importation was required as an export input and the exported commodity was not consumed at home in any significant way. Of course, this situation characterizes many of the primary exporting sectors: thus we find large volumes of imported inputs used in export production—machinery used in the production cycle, materials used in the extraction of the primary material (such as caustic soda in bauxite production), or inputs in agriculture directed to the export market (such as the use of fertilizers in the production of pyrethrum or sisal). In these situations the course of imports related to the behavior of GNP would clearly belie developments in the domestic economy. Similarly misleading is the import coefficient (the ratio of total imports to total expenditure or supplies). In this case the value of imports is found both in the numerator and the denominator. Given this, the movement of the ratio would not accurately reflect developments in the domestic economy since these would depend on the size of domestic output as compared to total output. Finally, the import content of domestic production for domestic use would be misleading since production would only be a part of home expenditure. In view of this we argued that:

> Our proposal is that these concepts should be supplemented by a new one called the "import domestic expenditure coefficient," which relates the value of imports for domestic use to domestic expenditure ... It will be seen at once that we are concerned about the fact that there may be a large gap between the structure of production and the structure of demand ... It is not surprising that the concept which we have introduced should not arise in the developed countries, for their production and demand coincide, more or less.[9]

The continuing neglect of this approach, despite the number of years since publication of our views, is not very surprising. While this approach remains valid and constitutes a measure of some considerable usefulness, on reflection it seems possible to modify it in a number of ways to make it of greater generality and usefulness. Expressing the earlier relationship in symbolic form, we have as the import domestic expenditure coefficient, λ:

$$\lambda = \frac{Mu}{E} = \frac{M}{O} - \frac{Mx}{X}$$

where Mu is imports for domestic use, E is domestic expenditures, M is total imports, X is exports, Mx is the import content of exports, and O is gross national product. It can be seen that conceptually it would be better to break total imports, M, into two major categories: those imports which cannot be produced at home and are therefore complementary to domestic output, to be called Π; and the remainder, those which are competitive with domestic output and thus reflect the influences of product differentiation on domestic expenditure. This dichotomization allows us to see more clearly the influences the economic structure has on determining those imports which reflect domestic unavailability of substitutes to the imported product, as against the other types of imports.

Similarly, it would be a definite improvement to specify

and identify the differences between those exports which do not compete with domestic expenditure, which we shall call X^1, from the rest of exports. These exports clearly represent the exportation of goods which are not consumed at home. Furthermore, like all exports they can have an import content, represented by ϕ. Thus if we call the reinterpretation of the measure of the divergence between domestic resource and domestic demand, d, then we have:

$$d = \frac{1}{2}\left(\frac{\Pi - \phi}{E} + \frac{X^1 - \phi}{O}\right)$$

with O and E retaining their original meaning.

When this relation is manipulated we can see that the values of d can range between zero and unity. When it is equal to unity, then

$$\Pi - \phi = E \quad \text{and} \quad X^1 - \phi = 0$$

That is, domestic expenditures are wholly directed toward goods the country cannot produce, and whatever is produced at home is wholly exported. In this case we can say the country completely specializes in producing what is not consumed at home. The divergence between domestic resource use and domestic demand is at its maximum.

At the other extreme, the value of d is zero, and:

$$\Pi - \phi = 0 \quad \text{and} \quad X^1 - \phi = 0$$

That is, imports of those goods not produced at home are equal to the import content of those exports which do not compete with domestic expenditure, and exports which do not compete with domestic expenditure are in effect the re-export of imported goods. In this case domestic demand and domestic resource are completely convergent.[10]

It must be stressed that these measures refer only to the quantitative expression in the productive system of relationships between domestic demand and domestic output. To fully comprehend the nature of economic underdevelopment in these economies, we also have to take into account what we have stressed all along—that is, the nature of the social relationships which govern production and consumption. Nevertheless, the further development of the earlier work of Brewster and myself advanced here has important implications for planning and for determining the course of the quantitative relationships through time.

It should be clear, if our formulae are examined carefully, why we have argued in the previous section that the convergence of domestic resource use and domestic demand does not represent crude and simple autarky. A country can have a high export ratio *and* a high convergence factor if exports are an extension of the domestic market and imports reflect merely differentiation in the sources of purchases and *not* unavailability of the product at home. This is generally the case with the dynamic industrialized economies. The formulae not only highlight the structure of material dependence in underdevelopment, but also the structure of production in economies like Japan and Britain on the one hand, and the Soviet Union and the United States on the other. In the former, insofar as a small but significant proportion of imports consists of products (usually raw materials) which are not available at home, then the measure of divergence is wider than for those countries with a more generously endowed raw material base. This is true even though in general the ratios of the former countries are much lower than those prevailing in the small underdeveloped economies. In the underdeveloped economies the imports of consumption goods, investment goods, and raw materials all reflect domestic unavailabilities. In effect, imports of these goods are almost equal to total imports (i.e., Mu is nearly equal to π) and at the same time exports are heavily specialized output.

Finally, the measures presented here should not be seen in isolation from the analysis of other economic determinants. Indeed, their operational significance relies a great deal on the data available, and the judgment exercised, in defining competitive and noncompetitive goods. It also depends on the care which is applied to particular sectors. In general we would expect the so-called modern dynamic sectors, which reflect the movement from traditional and subsistence economy, to yield significantly higher divergency ratios. Thus as the economy becomes more and more propelled by international capitalism, and less and less by its own domestic social formation, the ratios tend to rise and underdevelopment to deepen within the economic structures.

Conclusion

We have offered an interpretation of structural dependence, economic immaturity, and the way in which during the present era international capitalism dynamically internalizes itself in the production system of a small underdeveloped economy. It follows logically that one of the most fundamental laws governing the transformation process is the planned implementation of a structure of domestic output consistent with domestic demand patterns. It is in this sense that this is presented here as an "iron law" of transformation and therefore a fundamental objective of planning. We have argued that transformation cannot be achieved through the growth of traditional agricultural exports because the whole structure of the world market and technology militates against this. Thus, for example, the early export success of Japan, in using silk to finance its early years of industrialization, could not be replicated in the present international economy. Further, we have argued that the exceptions to this sluggish export performance (e.g., Taiwan, Hong Kong, Singapore, Puerto Rico, South Korea, and so on) have depended on preferred access to capitalist markets and a way of life most people would not freely choose if they understood it. More significantly, we have argued that this export success has not led to economic transformation of these economies in the sense we mean it. Faced with these dynamic features of their own economies, and with the international economy as it presently is, there is no way out except in terms of the path which we have indicated here.

We have also put this transformation process in a dynamic context in order to underline the interconnecting phases or sequences of the development to socialism and beyond. It follows from this, as we have stressed repeatedly, that it would be gross naiveté to interpret the strategy of dynamic convergence of resource use, production, demand, and needs as the aim of simple self-sufficiency, where the economy strives neither to import nor export. On the contrary, our modal-type of economy will always be characterized by extensive trading links. But under such planning *trade serves a different function, because the economy itself is reoriented to serve different purposes.* The character of imports and exports changes. Exports become an extension of the domestic market and in this way are brought into conformity with the requirements of achieving convergence of domestic resource use and domestic demand.

Notes

1. See Chapter 2.
2. M. Dobb, *Papers on Capitalism, Development and Planning*, pp. 72-73.
3. See P. A. Baran, *The Political Economy of Growth.*
4. P. Reno, "Aluminum Profits and Caribbean People," p. 84.
5. See N. Girvan, *Foreign Capital and Economic Underdevelopment in Jamaica.*
6. See G. Beckford, *Persistent Poverty.*
7. Baran, *The Political Economy of Growth*, p. 24.
8. H. R. Brewster and C. Y. Thomas, *The Dynamics of West Indian Economic Integration.*
9. Ibid., pp. 78-79.
10. The development of this section owes a great deal to a long conversation one evening with my colleague Marc Wuyts of the University of Dar-es-Salaam, Tanzania.

5

The Transformation of Agriculture

In this chapter we will broadly outline some of the major elements of the strategy involved in the transformation of the agricultural economy. We shall also present a very brief examination of one case study (Tanzania), where the socialist transformation of an underdeveloped and dependent agricultural system is being attempted. We shall do this in order to highlight in a more concrete manner some of the profound implications and difficulties of the strategy we have proposed.

Needs and Agricultural Output

Given our perspective on the nature of underdevelopment and the strategy and policies of a planned convergence of production, demand, and needs, we can best further our discussion at this stage by posing two initial questions: first, what are the structural implications of this strategy for agricultural policies in small underdeveloped economies; and second, what are the priorities which should govern production strategy? We pose these questions in this way not in order to set up a spurious dichotomization of the production system into industry and agriculture, but because the *present* importance of agriculture in these economies frequently creates difficulties and confusion in comprehending and planning its *future* role.

Because the masses of the population in these economies are poor and because agricultural production has for historical reasons usually been overspecialized in the production of commodities for overseas markets, the prevailing levels and patterns of demand for agricultural products, both in the home market and abroad, cannot be taken as the major determinants in planning the agricultural economy. This is so for several reasons, two of which are basic and incontestable. The first is that, at the prevailing low levels of income, domestic demand is a poor guide to the requirements and needs of the population at large. On close examination it can be seen that often the foods consumed by the population at large in these countries are traditionally cultivated by means of the most rudimentary techniques, are low in protein, and are only adequate to ensure bare subsistence. The second reason is that, as we have already noted, the sale of primary products overseas, which often dominates domestic resource use, has been characterized by low prices and income elasticities of demand, as well as frequent imbalances between the rate of growth of foreign demand and the rate of growth of domestic output. The result has been the well-observed historical tendency for their export values to fall relative to those of the industrial goods produced in the metropolitan countries, as well as a considerable instability in the value of export earnings.[1] This in turn has not only had expected harmful consequences on rural incomes, employment, and investments, but has also reinforced the dynamic tendencies toward divergence between agricultural resource use and domestic consumption of agricultural products.

In the light of this situation, the most basic strategic objective is to find a dynamic basis for planning agricultural output in such a way as to orient the economy away from its present export specialization in tropical staples. The obvious alternative dynamic for guiding product specialization is an orientation toward the long-run needs of the broad mass of the domestic population. Only planning on this basis can help reverse the tendencies toward dynamic divergence.

However, the problem one frequently encounters with this proposal, which we should face up to at the outset, is the widely held view that in the present circumstances there are no alternatives superior to the present product specialization in terms of efficiency of resource use. On this basis, it is argued that national efforts and resources should be geared toward improving the levels of efficiency in export agriculture and toward combating falling prices through internal and external marketing improvements. Only later, it is argued, should diversification be attempted, when higher incomes permit greater flexibility. To us the main problem with this view is that it is essentially short term. It is short term both in its limited perspective on the future and in its historical analysis of the past. It fails to appreciate that *it has been nearly a century now that these countries have been investing resources, to little avail, in precisely such an attempt at achieving a level of efficiency which can offset unfavorable market situations.* Even as traditional a neoclassical writer as Sir Arthur Lewis has pointed out that:

> For the last eighty years the tropical countries have put practically all their agricultural research and extension funds and efforts into trying to raise the productivity of export crops like cocoa, tea or rubber and virtually no effort into food productivity. From their point of view this effort was wholly misdirected.[2]

Surprisingly, there seems to have been no full appreciation of the extent to which, when the *needs* of the domestic population are interpreted, inferred, and extrapolated from historical experiences around the world, the preferred commodities do in fact display a considerable degree of dynamic demand potential. The agricultural commodities that have displayed the highest income elasticities of demand and the most widespread consistency in the way in which they are consumed as per capita incomes rise to intermediate levels are: dairy products, milk, eggs, cheese, butter, meat of all types, vegetables, and fruits. When related to needs, these foodstuffs are also the most essential on *nutritional grounds* to any serious effort to raise the quality of individual effort, extend the lifespan of individuals, and to reduce the incidence of disease during the given lifespan.

In addition, there are two further points about the historically exhibited demand potential of these commodities. First, although the empirical data show that the income elasticity of demand for foodstuffs is significant only up to intermediate income levels, and that it falls to unity or less as income levels of the magnitude of the United States are achieved, nevertheless, when measured during both the trend upward and downward, the demand for this class of agricultural commodities exhibits the strongest dynamic properties. As the statistician Engel long ago established in his household budget surveys, while the share of what are called "rough" products declines (e.g., bread, basic cereals, etc.), the share of the "noble" products rises (e.g., dairy products, fruit, beef, veal, sugar, etc.).

Second, experience has also shown that as the industrial labor force grows, and along with it urbanization, expanded educational opportunities, etc., these structural shifts result in a pattern of food consumption that also favors these "noble" commodities. Furthermore, these patterns in food consumption seem to be highly rational from the point of view of health and nutrition. A scientifically established list of "ideal" rational norms of food consumption proposed by the Soviet Academy of Sciences shows, among other things, the following as desirable patterns of per capita annual consumption: meat (73-91 kg.); fish (7-16 kg.); milk (292-585 kg.); sugar (27-33 kg.); eggs (175-370 units).[3]

These data show the influence of income on the pattern of food consumption in unplanned circumstances. In addition to the general rise in the levels of education, which fosters an awareness of health and nutritional needs, the persistence of the secular rises in income in countries like North America and Europe underlines the rationality of this trend. In the context of planning and transformation, the potential that should guide output is the gap between the needs of the broad mass of the population and their prevailing levels of output and consumption. When cast in these terms the dynamic potential inherent in a drive to satisfy local needs is shown to be considerable.

Thus, for example, we find that in Western Europe the per capita consumption of beef is at present about 3.5 to 4 lbs. per week, whereas in Tanzania it is the equivalent of one half of one ounce per week; in the Caribbean area it is about 4-5 ounces per week. The estimated consumption of eggs in Tanzania at present is only 12 per person per year, as against more than 250 per person per year in Europe. Per capita milk consumption in Europe is estimated to be a little less than one pint per day, whereas in most underdeveloped economies it is less than one pint per week. Not surprisingly, it has been recently pointed out that "the projections show that in 1980, 42 developing countries with a population of 1,400 million would, *even if market demand is fully met*, have average calorie intakes below requirements." Earlier in the same report it was stated that consumption of animal-origin protein is closely linked with income—about 20 grams per capita in the developed countries as against 3 to 4 grams per capita in the developing world.[4]

Given these horrendous gaps between the need for food in underdeveloped economies and their level of consumption and output, how can it be argued that demand is to be determined by prices as generated in a capitalist market system? This contradiction between needs and demand highlights the contradictions between the capitalist sequences of demand-supply adjustments through time, and the rational planning of resource use in the context of the community's needs. It is nowhere better exemplified than in the prevailing situation where, despite domestic protein shortages, some underdeveloped economies *export* considerable amount of protein. It has been pointed out that:

> In certain African countries and Brazil, for example, livestock and meat are exported from some zones while in others large segments of the population remain on very low protein diets because they cannot afford to buy more of the meat which is produced in the country. Such "perverse" movements are generally founded, however, on solid economics.[5]

This quotation, remarkable even for a staid United Nations publication, shows clearly the implied identification of "solid economics" with the capitalist market relations in these countries. In the dramatic context of bad health, malnutrition, and the destitution which accompanies these conditions, it also serves to highlight the rationality of comprehensive economic planning for the community's needs. Such planning radically alters the prevailing market-conditioned notions of what is required and what should therefore be produced.

Empirically, it would seem that despite the wide gaps between domestic output, domestic consumption, and domestic needs, a concentration of resources in products to satisfy domestic needs, even at *desired* levels of consumption, would not be sufficient to fully utilize the agricultural potential in some of the economies under consideration. In any event, even if this were not the case, a broad-based strategy of disengagement from international capitalism would require that a certain degree of self-sufficiency in food consumption and self-sustainment in agricultural growth be attained on both economic and political grounds. This becomes even more imperative when it is recalled that the socialist countries as a group, or for that matter individually, have been unable to achieve large and consistent surpluses in the production of mass-consumption foods.[6]

Failure to be self-sufficient in the output of mass-consumption foods is not only a severe constraint on the growth capacity of the economy (and, in particular, on industrial growth), but for the small underdeveloped economy can also lead to a very profound dependence on international capitalism. This is made all the more crucial by the unavailability of alternative sources of food supply. As a result, the second major dynamic around which the agricultural program should be planned is to supply the desired quantities of domestic mass-consumption foods, such as cereals, sugar, tea, and coffee. These are used *directly*, either processed or unprocessed, or *indirectly*, after conversion into other agricultural produce (e.g., into cereal feed for animals).

Since the basic transformation strategy that governs agricultural production is the need to plan the convergence of domestic resource use—through the stream of production—into domestic demand and domestic needs, there remains one further major area of agricultural production and planning which is crucial. This is the need to plan production in order to satisfy the needs for those agricultural commodities required as basic industrial inputs. The main commodities that fall into this category are the textile group.[7] It is important for us to realize that the production of agricultural raw materials, as we have described it, must be geared first toward the domestic need for manufactured products and then, as an extension of the home market, to the overseas demand for the manufactured product. When such production takes place in the underdeveloped economies, it is for the most part not based on the overseas demand for the basic raw material input itself.[8]

It does not require a tremendous amount of imagination to realize the considerable dynamic potential inherent in the need of a population, short of everything, to feed and clothe itself. The potential impact which this can have on domestic resource use in the context of comprehensive planning can be readily appreciated. Such a potential is considerably superior to the prospects for the specialized primary products sold in the international capitalist market. With this approach, the volume of food requirements during the transformation period will not constitute a restraining factor on the level of effort and the level of efficiency of resource use attainable. The basic requirement is still the comprehensive command of resources to permit the development of linkages in domestic resource use, domestic production, and technology in order to satisfy this stream of agricultural requirements.

Basic Production Norms and Transformation

Now, it is not only necessary at the minimum to achieve self-sufficiency in food production along the lines indicated and thus to gear resources and production to domestic needs; it is also necessary to the strategy of economic transformation that the economic program for producing these agricultural commodities should aim at satisfaction of certain basic norms for guiding efficiency during the transformation period. These are:

1. Output should be planned to grow at such a rate as to permit planning the price levels of basic foods in such a way that the composite weighted index of prices of these foods does not rise faster than the similar index of industrial goods. As experience has shown, it is preferable that the food index rise at a somewhat slower rate than the index of industrial goods in order to ensure that the net barter terms of trade remain in favor of industrial goods and against agriculture. Of course, this should be self-evident, given the goal of achieving a situation in which economic surplus will be transferred from agriculture to industry as output increases. This is an inescapable condition if the community is to be able to finance a rapid industrialization program within what is, initially, an extensively agricultural economy.

The extent of this surplus transfer from agriculture to industry—or, more correctly, from the existing productive base to the new branches of transformation activities—will be governed by two considerations. One will be the availability of other sources of surplus (e.g., foreign balances, unproductive consumption, underutilized resources, etc.). The more these alternate sources are available, the less pressure will be brought to bear on the rural communities. Second, this surplus transfer should take place without the development of the famous "scissors" phenomenon, to the point where it affects productivity on the land and influences the quantity of *marketed* agricultural produce negatively. As the Soviet Union's experience dramatically demonstrates, if the internal terms of trade between industry and agriculture deteriorate too rapidly, this can have very negative effects on the farmers' attitudes and on their willingness to supply food to the population at large.

2. In order to ensure that the economy is not forced *to use scarce foreign resources on a significant scale and in an erratic manner* to finance the import of basic foods, it is necessary to plan so that agricultural output *of the mass-consumption foods grows at a comfortable margin above consumption requirements.* Whereas it is possible in times of serious emergency to squeeze the level of consumption of certain proteins (e.g., butter, cheese, etc.) in order to conserve foreign exchange, it is rarely possible to reduce the level of consumption of basic mass-consumption foods to any appreciable extent.

The pressures on available foreign exchange resources required to finance economic transformation will in most circumstances be quite considerable. This stems directly from the well-known situation in which many of the inputs for economic expansion are not initially available and producible in these countries. This is usually the case when there is a lack of know-how, or no historically acquired production structure, etc. As a result, if the level of domestic capital accumulation is to be effective in expanding the productive capacity of the economy, foreign exchange will be required as a very important and strategic complementary resource. This places a great deal of pressure on the requirement that planning should be aimed at maximizing the *effective* import-substitution potentialities in every sector in order to save foreign exchange. Domestic foodstuffs constitute an important sector in this regard since, as we have seen, agricultural export specialization is frequently combined with a marked dependence on imported foodstuffs. Furthermore, the more efficient and the more productive this type of agriculture can be made in achieving this substitution of home-grown foods for imports, the less impact there will be on rural incomes of deteriorating net barter internal terms of trade. In other words, it becomes possible for the single factoral terms of trade not to turn against agriculture as well, as long as the rate of efficiency increase outstrips the rate of decline of the net barter terms of trade.

Before turning to the implications of this type of strategy for the structure of agriculture in a transformed economy, it is important to note that agriculture obviously requires certain inputs, the demand for which is largely a *function of the efficiency of agriculture itself.* These inputs include fertilizers, farm tools and implements, and pesticides, all of which reflect the importance of the systematic application of science and technology to agriculture. It follows that as transformation in agricultural production proceeds it generates pressures of its own on the scientific and industrialization program. These pressures are to be welcomed, however, because they will be consistent with the strategy of convergence, and this is so because we have advocated centering the planning of agriculture around: (a) the internal need for its produce to be consumed directly, either as processed or unprocessed foods (mainly meat, dairy products, vegetables, grain, etc.); (b) the domestic need for that part of its output which is used as an input into other agricultural activity (e.g., feed for the cattle industry); (c) the domestic need for new raw materials as inputs in domestic manufacturing activity; and (d) the overseas demand for those industrial outputs using substantially domestic agricultural inputs (e.g., clothing). The main generative influence on domestic agricultural production cannot continue to be the simple export of primary products if transformation is to be achieved. Yet it is precisely such thinking that dominates agricultural strategy in most underdeveloped economies—even, as we shall see later in this chapter, in one which is attempting a socialist transformation of agriculture.

If such a broad restructuring of the output composition of agriculture becomes the basic planning focus, then two further aspects of this reorientation require examination. The first is to note the structural requirements of an efficient and transformed agriculture operating within such an output structure. The second is to acquire an understanding of the extent to which present planning is more often than not inconsistent with, and sometimes unknowingly antithetical to this strategy. Before we turn to these two issues, we should note once again that our emphasis so far has been on planning and therefore it should not be inferred that we are suggesting either the neglect of existing resources used in the export of primary staples, or the immediate abandonment of coffee or cocoa estates. The transformation of resource use has to occur on a planned basis. And while it is intended that this should be as speedy as possible, there are constraints both in adapting existing resources to new priorities and in obtaining sufficient foreign exchange to maintain the momentum of the transformation program.

Structural Factors and the Transformation of Agriculture

Examining the first of these issues, it is important to recognize from the start the extent to which historical experience indicates that a structurally transformed and efficient agriculture in a socialist society must over the long run have the following basic characteristics:

1. It must utilize productive farming units and operate through marketing and managerial arrangements—organized either as state or socialist cooperative farming units or as some combination of both—which are larger than is generally available to peasants; in the process it must therefore require a rationalization of the ownership structure in the rural economy.
2. It must use agricultural techniques which reflect the fact that an efficient agriculture is indeed highly capital- and skill-intensive in its productive and distributive organization.
3. It must systematically use new and modernized inputs as the basis for technologically transforming the productivity of land and labor.
4. It must, over the long run, achieve the transfer of a large proportion of labor out of agriculture and into other activities, both in the rural and urban sectors.

The above imperatives all relate to technical, material, and organizational issues. In addition, it is also necessary that:

5. Political-social relations must be developed which succeed in: eliminating exploitation in the rural economy; preserving *voluntarism* as the basis of transforming the peasantry; and establishing decision-making structures which will help to ensure the maximum democratic participation by the producers in agricultural planning.

This last factor is a crucial element in preserving the stability of the worker/peasant alliance and in consolidating socialist relations in the countryside. Without it, the alienation of the peasant from his products and his work situation will continue. Let us briefly discuss the analytical bases on which these propositions rest.

The historical data have been sufficiently abundant and clear long enough for it to have been recognized that the early growth of the industrial capitalist economies was necessarily accompanied by the often brutal consolidation of land ownership in the hands of large farmers. This consolidation still continues at a rapid pace and is reflected in the emergence of the agrobusinessman who depends less and less on labor and more and more on capital and other inputs. Thus we find that in West Germany, the number of farms decreased by 36 percent between 1949 and 1970, and it has been projected that by 1980 the decrease will be on the order of 72 percent. In addition, the average size of family farming units is rising: in France and West Germany during the last ten years it has gone from about 62 acres to 112 acres.[9] The famous Mansholt Plan of the European Economic Community also envisions a considerable reduction in the number of peasants and rural laborers between 1961 and 1980.

Some further data on the industrialized capitalist countries are shown in Tables 2 and 3 below, which illustrate how this agricultural transformation has continued at a rapid rate right up to the present. In all the countries listed in these tables, landholdings are becoming fewer, larger in unit size, and labor displacement is occurring at a faster rate than population growth. While the method of farm consolidation in capitalist countries may have relied on incentives created through the market, the universal necessity to achieve this over the long run, as a condition of ensuring increased efficiency, is clearly evident in the fact that similar tendencies can be seen in the socialist countries: Table 4 shows this.

Generally, the data readily support historical experience: if science and technology are systematically applied to agriculture, then, irrespective of the social relations on the land, this either requires or leads to a transformation of agriculture into producing units that are both larger and capital intensive, and not labor intensive. Moreover, if this transformation is to be achieved as part of a national transformation of the entire production structure, then the growth of agriculture relative to other sectors falls, and the proportion of agriculture's contribution to total output diminishes. Of course, this relative fall in agriculture's share in total output does not mean that agriculture does not grow or is stagnant. Nor does it mean that agricultural growth is undesirable. What it does mean is that planning should foresee that the relative balance over the long run will shift decisively in favor of industry and against agriculture, and therefore that immediate steps should be taken to accord this factor an *independent weight in the planning process.*

This shift in turn reflects the spread of industrialization techniques. As agriculture becomes more industrialized and hence more efficient, this universal tendency to consolidate agricultural land in countries where agricultural transformation has either been effectively completed or is occurring at a rapid rate demonstrates the inability of the mode of small-scale petty production to survive on its own. However, the *manner* of the transformation necessarily depends on changes in the predominant mode of production. Under capitalism it leads to the capitalist farm and the rise of the modern agrobusinessman. Under socialism, in contrast, attempts have been made to construct state and cooperative farms linked to the predominant socialist mode. Accordingly, during the transition the political, economic, and social bases transforming the structure of the rural economy from precapitalist and capitalist farms, plantations, and other semi-feudal estates to new socialist forms become a matter of top priority.

Table 2
Changes in Agricultural Structure

Country	*Period*	*Percent change in number of holdings*	*Percent change in average size of holdings (area)*
Austria	1951-60	– 7	+10
Belgium	1950-59	–21	+21
Canada	1951-61	–23	+28
Denmark	1946-61	– 6	+ 4
Germany	1949-62	–19	+19
Ireland	1951-60	– 8	n.a
Luxembourg	1950-62	–26	+31
Netherlands	1950-59	–12	+11
Norway	1949-59	– 8	+ 6
Sweden	1951-61	–17	+12
Switzerland	1939-55	–14	+10
United Kingdom	1950-60	–11	n.a
United States	1950-59	–31	+41

Source: A. Simantov, "Economic Problems Affecting Agriculture in Europe and Policies Called For," p. 236.

This long-term transformation of agriculture is made technically possible largely because of the widespread use of industrial techniques in agriculture, which in turn require the use of more capital per unit of agricultural output. Surprisingly, two bits of evidence suggest that this demand for capital intensity is not only very great but may even far exceed the levels generally projected by professional economists.[10] Table 5 below, derived from the famous ACMS article,[11] presents data quoted there from an unpublished study by Bickel which ranks the capital intensities of various activities in the United States. A study of this table suggests just how high agriculture ranks on the capital intensity scale—indeed, the estimate of its capital intensity is higher than for activities

Table 3
Changes in Active Population in Agriculture

Country	*Period*	*Annual percent reduction*
Germany	1950-60	4.2
Canada	1950-60	4.1
Sweden	1950-60	4.1
Belgium	1950-62	4.0
Austria	1951-61	3.5
Luxembourg	1947-62	2.9
United States	1950-61	2.8
Iceland	1950-60	2.8
Norway	1950-61	2.6
Denmark	1950-61	2.6
Netherlands	1947-60	2.4
Ireland	1950-60	2.2
United Kingdom	1950-60	1.7

Source: A. Simantov, "Economic Problems Affecting Agriculture in Europe and Policies Called For," p. 237.

which are generally assumed to be capital-intensive par excellence (e.g., iron and steel, machinery, shipbuilding, and so on). For all the listed activities, agriculture ranks fifth in capital intensity in the United States.

The second source of data is derived from a study by Zarembka of production functions in the United States and Northern Europe. The study concluded: "Thus the United States, with a higher ratio of capital to labor than West Germany, appears to have its comparative advantage in farming, which (according to the production function estimates) is more capital-intensive than manufacturing."[12] The evidence presented here, although it can be challenged on a technical level because of obvious difficulties of identification, measurement, techniques, etc., should not be ignored. It certainly conveys an impression which runs counter to prevailing presumptions and should be fully investigated for this reason alone. Too frequently in the radical literature, the cost in terms of resources, if not complexity, is too readily dismissed as excessively exaggerated. The assumption that improvements automatically follow a change of social and production relations, with no reference to such matters as surplus requirements, technology, and science, is a very dangerous one indeed.

It is worth noting that both the studies quoted here might very well understate the possible levels of capital intensity in agriculture for a society in transition because the level of human skills and training have not been included. Whatever conceptual difficulties might be posed by this resource and its measurement, observation suggests that a lack of skilled personnel, probably even more than capital, has been and will continue to be a major constraint in economies like Cuba, and more so Tanzania, which are seeking to transform the

Table 4
Socialist Countries: Agricultural Structure
(in percent)

	National Income				Labor Force			
Country	Industry		Agriculture		Industry		Agriculture	
	1950	1969	1950	1969	1950	1969	1950	1969
Bulgaria	36.8	59.4	42.1	24.4	11.4	37.9	79.5	37.6
Hungary	48.6	43.6	24.9	20.5	23.3	41.2	50.6	29.1
G.D.R.	47.0	60.7	28.4	11.6	43.7	50.0	27.3	13.3
Poland	37.1	53.4	40.1	19.2	26.2	35.1	54.0	37.4
Rumania	43.4	56.6	27.3	24.4	14.2	29.2	74.3	51.2
U.S.S.R.	57.5	54.6	28.8	19.7	27.5	36.4	47.6	28.7
C.S.S.R.	62.5	60.7	16.2	13.3	36.3	46.4	38.6	18.8

Source: H. J. Wienhold, "On Socialist Transformation of Agriculture"; data taken from *Statistical Yearbook* (Moscow: CMEA, 1970).

Table 5
Capital Intensities: U.S. Activities

No.	*Primary production*	
01,02,03	Agriculture	19.51
04	Fishing	3.24
10	Coal mining	4.87
12	Metal mining	13.34
13	Petroleum and natural gas	40.57
14,19	Nonmetallic minerals	10.37
	Manufacturing	
205	Grain mill production	5.36
20,22	Processed food	5.11
23	Textiles	2.76
232,243	Apparel	0.99
241,242,29	Leather products	1.01
25,26	Lumber and wood products	3.58
27	Paper	7.31
28	Printing and publishing	3.45
30	Rubber	3.73
31	Chemicals	8.32
321,329	Petroleum products	38.18
322,329	Coal	35.85
33	Nonmetallic mineral production	5.95
341,35	Iron and steel	8.60
342	Nonferrous metals	11.45
36,37	Machinery	4.86
381	Ship-building	4.76
382	Transport equipment	5.01
	Utilities and services	
511	Electric power	46.13
61	Trade	5.93
71	Transport	15.71

Source: K. J. Arrow, et al., "Capital-Labor Substitution and Economic Efficiency," p. 240.

rural sector rapidly. Agriculture, insofar as it relies on skilled personnel to transmit new inputs, will be drawing heavily on scarce resources.

The last, and weakest, analytical peg on which these propositions rest, is mentioned so that the reader can see the author's bias: we believe, based on a fair amount of reading of agricultural studies (reinforced by personal experiences in several countries), that *within the existing framework* farmers are by and large rational and efficient in their use of resources. To transform agriculture, therefore, requires new and modernized inputs which alter both the resource mix available to the farmer and the framework of social relations on the land. Those who argue that an extension of activity within the present resource framework can result in a dramatic expansion of agricultural production are in fact implying that the farmer is irrational and that is why the present resource and output mixes are inconsistent with transformation. The evidence for this seems slight. What can be readily conceded is that rearrangements of resources can lead to significant increases in output. But without new inputs around which these can be planned, and around which new arrangements can be organized, transformation cannot take place under socialism. At best, agriculture will remain primarily a means of subsidizing people to remain on the land in order to ease the social and political pressures which follow on rapid population growth, rural/urban migration, and slowly rising agricultural incomes.

While the progressive establishment of the above-stated technico-economic relations is crucial to the success of the transformation strategy in increasing agricultural output, it should be borne in mind that the historical factors working against a genuine and rapid transformation of the relations of production in the countryside are in reality considerable. But in spite of this reality, not only must this rapid transformation of social relations occur, but it must also be achieved in a basically voluntary manner if true socialist relations are to prevail. We shall take up this question again in Chapter 9, but here it is important for us to note that the *voluntary, co-*

operative, and participatory aspects of rural transformation have always been important cornerstones of socialist theory. Practice has so far been different, since specific historical configurations have resulted in a more or less forced transformation of the agricultural sectors of most socialist states. Yet this element of socialist thought must be stressed if we are to effectively combat the prevalence of this practice. As Engels declared long ago:

> When we are in possession of state power we shall not even think of forcibly expropriating the small peasants (regardless of whether with or without compensation), as we shall have to do in the case of the big landowners. Our task relative to the small peasants consists, in the first place, in effecting a transition of his private enterprise and private possession to cooperative ones, not forcibly but by dint of example and the proffer of social assistance for this purpose.[13]

This theme was again to be echoed and elaborated by Lenin in his famous Cooperative Plan.[14] Yet, as we have pointed out, these theoretical positions have been belied by the experiences of a brutal transition period. The overall effect of this can be seen in the stubborn persistence of agricultural problems in many of the socialist countries which has already contributed a great deal to the prevailing deformations of some of the socialist countries. The data in Table 6 show the present varied positions of the socialist countries in their "juridical" relations to the land.

We might well ask what the problems which underlie this gap between socialist theory and socialist practice are. Briefly, it would seem that they *objectively* derive from the contradictory position of the peasantry, as well as from the specific historical conditions facing each country. While, on the one hand, peasant relations to the land have been subservient to the dominant mode of production (capitalist or precapitalist), and as a result the peasants have been exposed to social and economic exploitation in the countryside; on the other hand, the peasants own some resources privately and frequently employ labor on a small scale, usually in the form of family labor. While the peasants are therefore anxious to end rural exploitation and to support struggles along these lines, the end to exploitation is frequently seen as occurring by way of greater security of private tenure and real income, both of which the peasant believes can only follow from an expansion of holding size and from the preservation and extension of unrestricted rights to the use and disposal of land.

Table 6
Socialist Sector and Size of Farms in the Agriculture of Socialist Countries

Country	Percent share in agricultural area used 1960			Average size of socialist farms 1969 (in hectares)	
	Total socialist sector	Including State sector	Including Coop. sector	State farms	Coop. farms
U.S.S.R.	100	47	53	21,400	6,000
Albania	88	3	85	—	—
Bulgaria	99	7	92	4,042	4,136
China	100	2	98	—	—
Czechoslovakia	89	26	63	4,195	627
German Dem. Republic	94	8	86	824	801
Yugoslavia	15	10	5	—	—
Korea	100	7	93	—	—
Cuba	70	70	—	—	—
Mongolia	100	2	98	—	—
Poland	14	13	1	440	210
Rumania	94	30	64	5,883	1,954
Hungary	97	20	77	5,230	1,811
Vietnam (DRV)	76	1	75	—	—

Source: H. J. Wienhold, *On Socialist Transformation of Agriculture*, Appendix, Table 1.

Strong social forces inclining toward increasing rural differentiation and to the rise of the "kulaks" are inherent in the position of the peasants. In the ex-colonial territories with which we are basically concerned, this tendency toward rural differentiation has often been supported by the colonial power in the form of various "progressive farmer" policies, which have continued to find strong state support in the post-independence period. The result has been to produce a highly variegated rural structure in many of the underdeveloped areas, with various combinations of small peasants, middle peasants, estates, plantations, cooperative farms, state-aided farms, landless laborers, communal farms, etc. The balance of the particular structure, combined with the specific historical situation, largely determine the potential nature of rural transformation. Thus, for example, in Cuba, where the previous rural economy was distinguished by the domination of foreign plantations, their nationalization has paved the way for a much more rapid establishment of socialist forms of land ownership and use than could be achieved in a country with a predominantly peasant farming structure. This accounts for Cuba's progress in the establishment of public ownership of the land as shown in Table 6.

Returning to our main thesis, if socialist relations are to characterize the countryside then it is imperative for the worker/peasant alliance to abolish systematically all exploitative relations on the land and to pursue policies aimed at maximum cooperation—right from the start of the transition period. It may even be that the success or failure of the worker/peasant alliance in pursuing these policies will itself determine whether or not socialism can proceed further! This seems to be the case for a number of important reasons. In the first place, if methods of brutal consolidation and coercion (which characterized the early history of capitalism and socialism in the USSR) were to be tried, they would simply expose the country in question to hostile international propaganda and might very well establish the pretext for imperialist intervention. Second, as Dobb and Nove have shown in their studies of the Soviet Union, not only does agricultural production have to increase, but, more to the point, it is the *marketed* surplus we should really be concerned with.[15] It is only by increasing this output that the nonagricultural sections of the community—particularly the working class—can be fed. Furthermore, the marketable surplus must rise if foreign exchange is to be earned or saved.

Such increases in output are based on a substantial rise in the productivity of the peasants and on the willingness with which they labor. The experiences of the Soviet Union have shown that if democracy is not preserved in the rural areas the peasants will be driven to retaliation and to the sabotage of the transition efforts. Given the nature of the political base of the alliance, this raises enormous difficulties which cannot be resolved if the state attempts to preserve its power by using force in the countryside.

While the success of socialism lies in avoiding these negative features—hostile propaganda, intervention, a fall in the marketed surplus, etc.—it also depends on the ability of the new state, through changes in productive relations on the land, to systematically apply innovations. Improvements in technology and shifts in output patterns away from traditional lines, as indicated earlier, can best be accomplished with a highly motivated peasantry. Similarly, improved management of the rural economy and a shift to comprehensive planning involving the rural community at every level are also heavily dependent on the level of commitment and the degree of motivation of the population. It follows that we can hardly overstate the importance of the correct development of political and social relations in the countryside.

In conclusion, it is interesting to note the stress on cooperation in the recent efforts to establish socialist relations in the countryside in such different situations as those of China and Tanzania. But, as we shall see in the next section, in Tanzania the elements of size and overdependence on international capitalism pose a perpetual danger in constraining the success of these efforts.

The Limitations of Agricultural Policy in Transition: The Case of Tanzania

There is an increasing awareness of, and literature on, Tanzania's experiments with rural socialism, the *Ujamaa* village program.[16] In this section we shall briefly examine some aspects of Tanzanian agricultural policy in order to highlight certain implications of the strategy discussed above, and to discuss more concretely the extent to which policies, even in a radical context, can in practice be contradictory to those outlined above. In particular we shall seek to demonstrate: (1) the extent of the divergence of present policies from those suggested in this text in terms of product choice, (2) the relatively indifferent production achievements of the strategy pursued in Tanzania, and, as a consequence, (3) the extent to which there is a real danger that current efforts, particularly where they are persistently inconsistent with some aspects of the strategy outlined here, may constitute a serious misuse of resources and hinder the prospects for the successful transformation of the economy.

The published data on Tanzania show that a large proportion of public-sector resources has been allocated to agriculture. In the 1964-1969 plan, just over 27 percent of central government capital expenditure was earmarked for *directly productive* agricultural activities. In the 1969-1974 plan, the proportion was just over 29 percent. Apart from the first two years of the second plan (1969-1970, 1970-1971), when *directly productive activities* accounted for one-quarter of government capital expenditure, the proportion declines to 18 percent, 14 percent, and 13 percent respectively for the remaining plan years. For the entire plan period, manufacturing averaged 44 percent of *directly productive expenditure.* However, over 60 percent of government capital expenditure was allocated to economic infrastructure. Since the largest items in this class are roads, electricity, rural water, agricultural improvement/drainage, and livestock, agriculture has actually claimed a major share of public-sector resources. Furthermore, a great deal of skilled manpower has also been directed into the agricultural/rural program. In more recent times this has been considerably strengthened by the newly announced policies of rapid decentralization of the state structure in order to bring greater democracy and efficiency to rural planning and development.[17]

The present plan target for total agricultural output (1969-1974) is an increase of approximately 5 percent per annum for marketed livestock products, 7.3 percent per annum for marketed crop products (mainly exports), and 3 percent per annum for subsistence agriculture. An approximate estimate of the growth of the labor force over the plan period is 1.5 percent per annum. To achieve these targets, which require overall agricultural expansion at a rate of about 7 percent per annum, output per head must show striking increases, somewhere in the region of 5-6 percent per annum. Allowing for the fact that acreage expansion could account for about half the output growth, yields would have to increase at about 3 percent per annum. But unless political mobilization in the countryside is considerable, these are comparatively difficult targets to achieve if agricultural reorganization and output increases are attempted in a basically voluntarist manner, with no complementary support in the form of a radical change in input-output mixes.

Despite the socialist thrust of the government, a great deal of the agricultural effort, and the major planned output increases, have been focused on the expansion and extension of primary export production, and here it contrasts with the strategy of transformation outlined in this book. Judging from comments in public documents and reports or seminar discussions of agricultural development and planning, this policy seems to have been based on the idea of achieving further specialization and efficiency in order to combat declining prices, maintain earnings of foreign exchange, and eventually develop a capacity for diversification.

Data relevant to the planned performance of the primary

export sector are shown in Table 7. It can be seen that the planned target-increases in output of the main primary crops, with the exception of sisal, all averaged above 6 percent per annum. The data for 1971, however, indicate that *substantial discrepancies* developed between the output targets hoped for in the plan and actual production. In addition, these crops—all oriented for sales abroad—have been exposed to all the unsatisfactory market situations we have discussed. As can be seen from the data in Table 8, both the value of output and the export prices obtained for the major crops have been very disappointing. Only coffee and cashew nuts had in 1971 reached unit prices above those of 1960. But even so, the unit price of coffee in 1971 (11.3 percent above 1960 prices) was about 10 percent less than the 1971 price. And given the shortfalls in production in that year, the value of sales was less than that for any of the previous five years! It is not surprising that agriculture's contribution to gross domestic product has unintentionally been falling. The data in Table 9 reveal the extent to which this has been the case.

It would not be unduly harsh to conclude that achievements in agriculture have overall been very disappointing. This is even true when measured against the marked scarcity of the resources that have been devoted to this sector. The reason for this development is simply a failure to accept the fact that, whatever may be the need for foreign exchange, and whatever are the short-run pressures on employment and income, *primary export production in this historical era does not contain enough dynamic demand potential to transform agriculture.* The income and price elasticities of the products Tanzania exports are low. In addition, substitutes always exist to stifle any threat of significantly upward rising prices. Moreover, insofar as primary export production is uncoordinated among the Third World countries, their individual pursuit of national advantage will always lead to frustrating price movements in the world commodity markets. It is difficult to understand how these disappointing results were not anticipated by the planners. One would have expected a much more basic program for agriculture in an economy in transition to socialism.

Table 7
Planned Output/Actual Output of Agricultural Crops in Tanzania
('000 tons)

	Second Plan target rates of growth per annum	*Second Plan target 1971*	*Actual output 1971*	*Discrepancy (–) less than target for year 1971*
Cotton (lint)*	+ 9%	123	66.0	-67
Coffee (clean)	+ 6%	72.0	45.8	-26.2
Sisal	- 2%	186.0	181.1	- 4.9
Cashew nuts*	+10%	180.0	126.3	-53.7
Tea	+ 9%	13.3	10.5	- 2.8
Tobacco*	+ 6%	21.6	11.9	- 9.1
Sugar	+ 7%	136.0	95.8	-40.2

Source: Economic Survey 1971-72, United Republic of Tanzania.

* Based on crop year.

Table 8
Value of Output of Selected Crops (Marketed Quantities and Exports) in Tanzania
(million shillings)

	Average	*Coffee*	*Cotton*	*Sisal*	*Cashew nuts*	*Tobacco*	*Tea*	*Total*
1966-1967	Exports	269	300	218	96	25	44	952
	Export price index (1960 = 100)	97.2	91.8	73.7	117.8	—	99.5	—
1968	Exports	265	283	159	107	40	45	899
	Export price index (1960 = 100)	93.8	100.7	57.2	111.9	—	93.6	—
1969	Exports	257	235	160	119	35	48	854
	Export price index (1960 = 100)	90.3	92.4	63.3	126.9	—	88.7	—
1970	Exports	312	247	179	115	45	42	940
	Export price index (1960 = 100)	121.1	91.1	96.1	130.4	—	84.9	—
1971	Exports	221	217	136	127	41	48	790
	Export price index (1960 = 100)	111.3	98.3	56.8	108.5	—	82.7	—

Source: Economic Survey 1971-72, United Republic of Tanzania.

Table 9
Percentage Contribution of Agriculture to GDP at Current and Constant Price

	Monetary sector (current prices)	*Subsistence sector* (current prices)*	*Monetary sector (1966 prices)*	*Subsistence sector* (1966 prices)*
1966	45.3	23.8	45.3	23.8
1967	42.0	23.2	43.3	23.6
1968	41.3	22.8	42.7	23.1
1969	40.7	21.6	42.0	21.6
1970	41.1	21.0	41.0	20.8
1971	38.2	19.9	38.7	19.7

Source: Economic Survey, 1971-72, United Republic of Tanzania.

* Subsistence sector includes agriculture, hunting, forestry, and fishing.

In addition to this reliance on primary exports, there has been no consistent success in, or indeed program for, the exploitation of domestic demand for high-protein foods, even at the prevailingly low levels of protein intake. In 1971 total food imports were estimated at 176 million Tanzanian shillings—just over 10 percent of the value of domestic exports in that year! The import demand for milk and milk products in 1971 was approximately 50 million shillings. Imports of these have grown at a compound rate of 11.5 percent in value terms and 7.3 percent in quantity terms during the past ten years.[18]

In addition, the general strategy of agricultural planning appears to have been based on the policy of maximization of existing resource use, mainly through the eventual rural organization of production in *Ujamaa* villages combined with cooperative marketing and distribution. While one cannot deny the need of *Ujamaa* development to provide a social and institutional framework for building socialism, success requires that the organization and output of producing units be consistent with the long-run and dynamic profiles outlined in this book. This must be the case if the *Ujamaa* village is to become the institutional framework for transforming the national, and in particular the agricultural, economy. The *Ujamaa* village must be the framework through which indigenous science and technology are both developed and applied to economic activity, agricultural as well as nonagricultural. It must be the institution where the organic link between resource ownership, use, and demand is forged. Failure to do this will merely mean the substitution of one institutional form for another, and the persistence of economic underdevelopment in new guises.

In particular, to be able to transform agriculture *Ujamaa* villages will have to be the framework that makes possible the systematic infusion of new inputs into agriculture. This, as we have seen, is necessary to ensure a continuous self-sustaining reorganization of the rural economy such that higher levels of output per unit of land and labor are attained, and a vast proportion of the people are peacefully and equitably transferred from agricultural into nonagricultural activities located in both the rural areas and the urban centers. At the moment, the *Ujamaa* emphasis is on reorganizing what appears to the planners to be abundant—cheap resources (i.e., land and labor). But such a policy is self-limiting and must be seen and *planned* as such. The relative abundance which seems to exist now will disappear and it will do so all the more quickly as the growth of the *Ujamaa* villages is more rapid! As plans are now, the *maximum* possible rate of growth of these villages, other social and political factors being equal, is assumed to be the *optimal* rate of growth. The result is that the very premises of extensive activity in the rural area are rapidly being eroded by that activity itself.

A pertinent observation on this issue was made in 1970 and bears repeating:

> As I read the Tanzanian Plan for Agricultural Development it seems to me that the strategy for development is based on the concept of improvement rather than modernization: I do not mean that the Plan does not have a strategy of technological change—there are certain suggestions for changing techniques of production. What I do mean is that there is no clear-cut strategy that emphasizes the elements of modernization, applied research, increased inputs of chemical fertilizers, pesticides and the like, expansion of an extension service and credit system to be linked to technological innovations. Indeed, improved seed appears to have been mentioned *once* (in connection with cotton), and fertilizers *twice*: once in connection with FAO trials and once in connection with an expanded credit program primarily for flue-cured tobacco. There appears to be limited emphasis on pesticides and the like. The Plan stresses the avoidance of mechanization, but I would like to stress that there can be modernization without mechanization. The symbols of modernization can be seeds and fertilizers, not tractors.[19]

In general, the contradictions manifested in Tanzanian planning have stemmed from a number of factors, including poor planning and a lack of vision about the requirements for transformation during the early phases. In addition, however, there seems to be strong evidence that the *present* importance of agriculture to national survival has its own overwhelming effect on the planners' attitude toward the role of agriculture and is in part responsible for their inability to see the interaction between social relations and the form and content of production. This effect is magnified when an economic and social system is more dependent and when production relations are less geared to the community's needs. In the typical small underdeveloped economy, dependence has been high and, as we have seen, the divergence of the productive system from the community's needs quite marked. In view of this, it is difficult to comprehend how one can simultaneously stress the socialist reorganization of the rural countryside, and production and output almost exclusively along classical colonial lines. Not surprisingly, this contradiction has been manifested in the loss of public resources in support of agricultural crops which have been unequally exchanged in the world's commodity markets, and in the frustration over the agricultural benefits of the enormous *Ujamaa* effort. In other words, the worst of both possible worlds.

A further factor has been the effect created by the pressures for doing something now in order to meet existing demands, rather than to transform the system itself. Often this effect becomes transmitted into attitudes which tend to either overlook the requirements for transformation or to dismiss them as being impractical or visionary: they are assigned no independent weight in short-term activities, and there are thus neither forward nor backward links between intention and practice. There is in a real sense little planning. Finally, the tendency among urban-based planners (foreign and local) and some elements of the petty bourgeoisie to romanticize the virtues of poverty and/or to overestimate the qualities of rural life as it stands has been of inestimable significance. These are not sufficiently seen and understood as malformations of human existence—the very factors which call forth socialism in theory and practice in the first place.

This brief review has sought to show how far traditional policies in fact have a hold on the Tanzanian economy, even as public professions of socialism become louder and surer.

The problem lies in the attempt to develop revolutionary political theory and practice without a concomitant expansion of the ideology for conquest of the material environment. It is this which explains why Tanzania finds it strategically "necessary" to follow an agricultural production policy aimed at improving the primary export sector's performance. In this sense it differs little from that which preceded the experiments with socialism. Furthermore, where efforts are directed at improved domestic production of livestock and dairy production, performance has been extremely low, even though the stated targets are, at their maximum, the prevailing rates of growth of consumption of those products and not the needs of the population! The resource flows to traditional agriculture continue to dominate, performance continues to be disappointing, and underdevelopment becomes more and more manifest. In this situation, clarification of the issues can help show that the postponement of what must be done does not make what is to be done any less urgent. And if what is to be done is *not* done, then socialism remains a chimera. Indeed, an evaluation of the drive toward socialism, as much of our argument shows, must be based heavily on the way people are organized to control their environment and on their success in doing so. When put this way, failure to transform a society is not explained as a by-product of poor education, low income, insufficient capital, small markets, and so on, but as a failure of socialism to develop. The development of socialism cannot be measured independently of a simultaneous evaluation of the relations of production *and* the level of development of productive forces.

Notes

1. There is a vast literature on this subject. As a sampling of the range of positions taken on the data see, A. Emmanuel, *Unequal Exchange;* C. P. Kindleberger, *The Terms of Trade: A European Case Study;* R. E. Baldwin, "Secular Movements in the Terms of Trade"; and J. Bhagwati, "A Sceptical Note on the Adverse Secular Trend in the Terms of Trade of the Underdeveloped Countries."
2. Sir W. A. Lewis, *Aspects of Tropical Trade, 1883-1965*, p. 25.
3. Data quoted in E. Mandel, *Marxist Economic Theory*, p. 611, and taken from P. Mstislavsky in *Partilinaya Zlizn*, no. 12 (1959).
4. J. Abbott, "The Efficient Use of World Protein Supplies," pp. 2-4 (our emphasis).
5. Ibid., p. 4. As pointed out in this article, the only exceptions to this marked animal-protein deficiency in the underdeveloped economies are the Río Plata countries of Latin America.
6. We shall cover some of the factors related to this later in this chapter and again in Chapter 9.
7. The basic importance of textiles will be brought out in the analysis of industrialization in the next chapter.
8. In the final section where we discuss the case of Tanzania, we are able to highlight the significance of this difference in emphasis.
9. Data quoted by H. Wienhold in "On Socialist Transformation of Agriculture." The data presented here were obtained from the *Green Report*, West German Bundestag, 6th Election Period Printed Matter VI/372 (Bonn, 1970), p. 22 (in German).
10. For a discussion of this point see J. Flanders, "Agriculture Versus Industry in Development Policy." The evidence cited here is quoted in this article; however, it should be noted that the issues as presented in this study are not indicative of any "conflict" as such.
11. K. J. Arrow, et al., "Capital-Labor Substitutions and Economic Efficiency."
12. P. Zarembka, "Manufacturing and Agricultural Production Functions and International Trade: United States and Northern Europe," p. 965.
13. F. Engels, "The Peasant Question in France and Germany," in *Selected Works*, vol. III, p. 470.
14. V. I. Lenin, "On Cooperation," in *Alliance of the Working Class and the Peasantry.*

15. See A. Nove, *An Economic History of the USSR*, and M. Dobb, *Soviet Economic Development Since 1917*.
16. See L. Cliffe and J. Saul, eds., *Socialism in Tanzania*, and Tanzanian Economic Society, *Towards Socialist Planning*.
17. For more details consult *Annual Plan, 1971-1972* (Government Printer, United Republic of Tanzania).
18. See T. Zalla, *Dairy Development in Tanzania*, which is based on a *Report to the Ministry of Agriculture, Food and Cooperatives* (Tanzania, 1972).
19. M. Yudelman, "Agricultural Development in Tanzania" (our emphasis).

6

Industrialization and Transformation

In this chapter we shall attempt to specify the basic patterns of industrial allocation required to overcome underdevelopment in a small economy during the present neocolonial phase.

The Transformation Role of Industry

Structural transformation, disengagement from capitalism, socialist development—all these imply industrialization in the basic sense of the progressive spread of industrial techniques of organization and resource use into all branches of economic activity, as part of the struggle to make the material environment serve the community's needs. This relationship between industrialization and the degree of development of the productive forces is readily perceived when one looks at the global distribution of industry and the marked concentration of industrial production among those countries which have solved the problem of mass poverty and have achieved self-sustaining increases in the level of material production. Indeed, this is so generally accepted a feature of the international economy that high incomes and wealth are often taken as synonyms for industrialization.

In view of this, it is not surprising that the poor underdeveloped Third World countries contribute only approximately 6.5 percent of the world's manufacturing production. More strikingly perhaps, this comparative underindustrialization is combined with a disproportionate production of the major raw materials used in manufacturing production. While these countries contribute approximately 4 percent of the world's manufactured steel output, for example, they are the source of approximately 23 percent of the world's iron ore. Similarly, while extracting approximately 59 percent of the world's bauxite, they only account for 3 percent of the world's primary aluminum. This is equally true for the production and manufacturing of phosphates, rubber, copper, lead, petroleum, zinc, and so on.[1]

There is a fair amount of empirical data relating to the industrial structure and growth of a number of countries. A number of recent studies have sought to establish "industrial patterns" on the basis of cross-sectional analyses of these industrial statistics. These "patterns" have been presented in the hopes that they would serve the underdeveloped and underindustrialized economies seeking a "scientific" method or pattern, as guides with which to plan their industrial establishments.[2] It is surely naive to imagine that this information can simply be "copied" and will provide a strategy of industrialization. If this were so, the ahistorical basis of such an approach would quickly become evident, since it is clear that such "patterns" ignore objective differences in the circumstances that faced the already industrialized countries during their early stages of industrialization, and the underdeveloped countries attempting to industrialize during the present neocolonial phase.

Two of these objective differences have turned out to be crucial. One is the very fact that there are a number of countries which are already industrialized; the other is the vast increases in the initial costs of acquiring industrial equipment, which have been rising since the early phases of European industrialization. Indeed, as we saw in Chapter 3, these two factors are extremely significant in the prevailing processes of multinational corporate expansion in the underdeveloped countries.

Bearing these very important cautions firmly in mind, it nevertheless seems reasonable to make a number of general inferences based on empirical data from both capitalist and socialist economies. These demonstrate with sufficient reliability that industrialization involves:

1. A significant rise in the share of manufacturing in total output and in its absorption of resources.
2. A growth in interindustrial transactions in the manufacturing sector, as it becomes more differentiated.
3. A qualitative shift in the output of manufactured goods in favor of those which require complex technology and capital-intensive techniques.
4. A substantial upward displacement in the relative output per worker in industry as against primary and tertiary activities, so that the sectoral shift in favor of industry raises the national average product per worker and increases the labor-absorptive capacity of the economy.
5. A self-sustained rise in labor productivity occasioned by (a) consistent technical progress, (b) the continuous enlargement of the market, thereby bringing economies of scale through time, and (c) the progressive use of higher levels of capital per worker.
6. A spread of industrialized techniques to the rest of the economy.
7. A qualitative shift in attitudes and relationships to material phenomena, subject to the overriding forms of class and other relationships.

As this process occurs, expenditure on manufacturing output shows a high income elasticity of demand:

> Under any social and political system, there can be little question that until high levels of income are reached the demand for the products of the industrial sector as a whole expands more rapidly than real income. This seems to be true of both *laissez-faire* and centrally planned economies, even though the composition of demand for industrial products may be different in these two

cases; it seems to be true regardless of the distribution of income.[3]

If, as communities develop, the incomes available for satisfying their needs rise rapidly and their demand structure is transformed in such a way that it leads to an increasing demand for industrial goods, then for this demand to be satisfied the underdeveloped economy will have to achieve the spread of industry and industrial techniques into all facets of material production. As far as industrialization is concerned, therefore, a consistent strategy will have to conform to the demands of planned agriculture as we have analyzed it above, and thus ensure balance and proportion in the growth and composition of output, and will also have to lead to the generation of the bulk of material output from industry per se.

Although this overriding constraint is widely recognized, its basic implications for planning are in practice often disregarded or fudged under the guise of real, imagined, or contrived pressures. Naturally, such a constraint has the basic implication that—whatever might be the social rate of return of the particular projects which together constitute the "plan" (the usual method of justifying investment priorities in these countries) and which have been selected by the use of the usual techniques of project analysis and selection (with the usual time horizons)—the balance of resource flows which follows must decisively favor industry. And, as we shall analyze later, *this will be industry of a particular kind.* If this does not occur, then the problems of structural transformation are not being confronted and the plan has no analytical basis in the system of underdevelopment.

One hears many supposedly well-meaning rationalizations of why development plans in small underdeveloped economies cannot conform to the requirements of this approach. Apart from the arcadian view of agriculture implicit in certain approaches and the usual rationalizations in support of the policy of further specialization (i.e., further entrenchment in the international capitalist system) in order to obtain income, know-how, etc., with which to diversify later (both of these were considered earlier), the real issue has been the lack of a commanding vision with which to permeate the planning process. Beset by a multitude of foreign experts, advisors, and the bourgeois literature on "pragmatic" planning which, as we noted in Chapter 1, is all that is available and "addressed" to their circumstances, there has been a subtle resignation by many policymakers, even in small underdeveloped economies like Tanzania where socialist policies have been opted for, to what has been perceived as the inevitably enduring nature of poverty and underdevelopment. Half-understood notions of size and survival clearly limit the policymakers' ability to perceive that the people are capable of transforming the environment. That this misperception has maintained such a firm hold during a period of history distinguished by the fact that in the space of less than five decades socialism has achieved the structural transformation of economies in which one-third of the world's people live, demonstrates the dominance of the imperialist perspective about both the economies and the capacities of the people within them, as well as the devastating psychological influence of underdevelopment over a person's perception of his or her own capacity and freedom to create.

Of course, we are not implying that the industrial imperatives which can be discerned in modern history are mechanical and irresistible natural laws. They are resistible in theory, but only at a cost we believe no society really wants to bear. Indeed, we believe that rather than having occurred *in vacuo* and in response to natural laws, industrialization is a social process necessary to enable society to master the material environment in the service of its own needs. In this sense the pressures to industrialize cannot be resisted rationally. Furthermore, the industrial imperatives are not mechanical either, in the sense that the dominant flow of resources to build up an industrial structure should follow an equal and unchanging pattern. There are periods when resource flows to agriculture, or to other activities, may have to take precedence. But unless structural transformation is achieved, these must be construed as temporary expedients created by unforeseeable situations (e.g., the proverbial "acts of God") and their effects on the rural economy, or as emergency measures to alleviate social and political strains in the rural economy at certain points in time. Indeed, the latter consideration might well be the only justifiable rationale behind the patterns of resource flow that have emerged in Tanzania, but the issue has never been articulated this way. As a result, the consequences of present policies have not been fully appreciated.

The priority of resource flows to industry neither implies nor presupposes any "conflict" between industry and agriculture, as is frequently stated in the neoclassical literature. Such a way of stating the issue would be, from our analytical standpoint, most artificial. The basic strategy is one of the planned convergence of domestic resource use, domestic demand, and the needs of the community. All that we have argued so far is that it is the industrial component of the community's needs that has the greatest dynamic properties for a policy of planned production geared to satisfying the needs of the community. It is this basic strategy which reveals the priorities of resource flows, priorities which constitute the essence of transformation.

Similarly, our strategy does not presuppose that there is a genuine conflict between capital, or any other productive factor intensity, in determining the pattern of investment priorities. As we shall see, *investment priorities and the choice of technique are in our model determined almost completely by the strategy of transformation and by the product choices to which this gives rise.* If there is scope for de facto substitution of resource combinations beyond this, and if the alternatives are real in the sense that their social costs/social benefits cannot be evaluated on the basis of deductive reasoning from the underdevelopment/planned transformation model, then the choice will clearly have to be exercised through an evaluation of the alternatives, with reference to the known resource availabilities and social constraints in the community. Our own belief, however, is that choice of technique as it has been presented in the neoclassical literature (i.e., the choice between the intensive use of broad factors such as capital or labor in production) is fairly limited in practice. What might be more important as a factor contributing to substitutability, given the resource basis of our strategy, is the choice of raw material input required in making a particular industrial output. We shall say more about this later.

Before leaving this section, it is appropriate to note that there seems to us to be a considerable amount of genuine confusion in neoclassical arguments concerning the choice of techniques. One confusion is worth highlighting here, since we are concerned with assessing the transformative role of industry. It derives from the confused way in which the same arguments about the choice of techniques are expected to apply to the entire economy and/or to specific industrial processes. In the previous paragraph, we discussed the usefulness of the choice of technique in terms of the latter situation *after* product choices have been formulated on a different and higher level of analysis. The confusion in the neoclassical literature often derives from the "unsuspected" transposition of such arguments as those concerning the ratios of use of "two factors of production"—labor and capital—in a particular activity to maximize some objective function (such as income, employment, or savings, etc.), into generalizations from these conclusions to the whole economy. Thus the insuperable conceptual difficulties which already exist in their attempts to measure capital are compounded by the utterly unrealistic nature of the assumptions which are needed to make this transposition hold. Bagchi, writing on the choice of technique, was forced to point out that "the neoclassical approach demands such assumptions about the world to which it is to be applied as to make us despair that it can ever say anything really useful about the world we actually live in."[5]

Contradiction and Confusion: Project Evaluation as Industrial Planning

In the previous section we saw that the necessity for comprehensive industrialization follows directly from the overriding requirements of a dynamic convergence of resource use—through the production stream, and embracing indigenous technology—to the needs of the community. Such an approach makes the usual way of presenting the problem (i.e., as agriculture versus industry or capital versus labor) logically absurd as a guide to industrial priorities. Given the recommendations of the neoclassical literature, one commonly finds that planning consists of little more than the mechanical application of the so-called objective techniques of microeconomics to a number of individual projects in order to test their feasibility. Depending on the results, these projects are then aggregated to determine the optimal investment plan. Since these projects all require financing, the cutoff point is determined by the amount of investment funds at the disposal of the state. This procedure is even more arbitrary because a significant proportion of the funds "available" to the state derive from foreign sources, including multilateral aid agencies, and are frequently found to be closely geared to particular projects, which are in turn dependent on the provision of local counterpart funds. The net effect, therefore, is that the projects which have been prepared locally merely constitute a shopping list for aid, and the choosing of the projects—i.e., *the actual detailed composition of the plan itself*—is largely influenced by aid donors. When, as is the more frequent practice, the shopping list is passed around to private investors through local industrial development corporations, similar influences operate via the overseas private companies. How can such an exercise constitute planning for structural transformation? How can it be argued that such a process is rooted in an analysis of underdevelopment and the aims of socialist transformation? Yet we find that this approach has been elevated into what is virtually a religion of contemporary planning among Third

World countries. And, not surprisingly, we find that "aid"-granting governments and multilateral aid agencies insist on these procedures.

If these weaknesses in the basic approach are not already a devastating refutation of the idea that present practices constitute planning, there are three major weaknesses *inherent in the techniques* of project evaluation which ensure that there is no *logical* reason that they will do what they are expected to do—frame an investment program—whatever other uses they may have as aids to decision-making. Before considering these limitations it is important to recall very briefly what these techniques are all about. Basically, they involve listing, evaluating, and making a comparison of the social costs and social benefits of an investment project. Social benefits are measured as additions to the flow of output arising from the investment. Put this way, certain basic problems of project evaluation are immediately clear. When, for example, the output of the particular project is not to be sold in a well-organized capitalist market, the valuation of benefits cannot be determined by simple recourse to market prices. Approximations have to be devised and the methods of devising these raise considerable difficulties. Furthermore, even if the output of the project *is* to be sold in well-organized markets, the project takes time to complete and production takes place through time, so that it is future prices we are concerned with. But accurate projections of future prices are almost impossible to make, even under "ideal" market conditions, let alone under the conditions of uncertain economic progress which characterize capitalism in underdeveloped economies.

Similar problems of estimating social costs (i.e., the future value of the resources used up in production) also exist. If productive resources are not marketed in a well-organized capitalist market so that the resources are priced in the act of exchange, then, in the absence of comprehensive planning which can provide an alternative basis of valuation, market prices will be a poor guide to the real costs of resource use in the capitalist context. The problem, therefore, is one of devising an approximate measure of prices. And even if resources are sold in a well-organized capitalist market, the problem of determining future costs under conditions of uncertainty remains.

To compare social costs and social benefits, however they may be estimated, it is necessary to find a "social discount rate" in order to discount to present values all future streams of payments and receipts. The question therefore arises as to *who* determines this social discount rate. The determination is very important, since actual calculations readily show that the results of project evaluation will vary significantly depending on the particular rate. This computational and conceptual difficulty is of further significance because it reflects our earlier arguments about the choice of techniques—i.e., the nature of the choice as between capital and labor intensity. Again, we find in practice that the particular choice varies significantly with variations in the discount rate.

In addition to all these problems, certain further major conceptual difficulties of measurement remain. These derive from such varied real-life situations as the non-homogeneity of resources, and the difficulties attached to valuing labor in the context of considerable unemployment. The fact that resources are heterogeneous makes it difficult to find a single measure of the opportunity cost of such frequently applied resource categories as foreign exchange, land, skills, etc., while the existence of widespread unemployment highlights the importance of the *social perspective* which is used in determining an "efficient" valuation of resources. Thus, in the context of significant unemployment the neoclassical economist would argue that given the requirements of optimal resource use, the real, true, or social cost of labor is its opportunity cost. In a situation of extensive unemployment, the institutional workings of society are such that the opportunity cost of labor is obviously likely to be *less* than the wage rate which is *actually* being paid by employers in the labor market. But as far as the state is concerned, the real cost of labor is the wage rate which it *normally* pays its workers *less* the value of the unemployment relief it offers.

When we turn to the community as a whole, if we find that the prevailing wage rate significantly constrains the levels of nutrition achievable, and if differences in income and wealth within the community affect the commitment to work, etc., then the cost of labor has to be measured as the wage actually paid against the impact of these other factors to determine the levels of output per head. In these situations, *what* is the "correct" social valuation of wages? The answer would largely depend on who makes the choice.

These technical difficulties would pose themselves, in one form or another, whatever social arrangements govern the society, since they relate to difficulties of estimation and valuation that go beyond the confines of one society. Since they reduce the reliability of the actual results, the major problem we face is how to use these techniques as the basis of determining an industrial investment program. It is here that the logical limitations of these techniques in relation to this task are important.

The first of these limitations is what the neoclassical welfare theory, on which much of project analysis is based, itself recognizes as the constraints of second-best theory. These demonstrate that it is impossible to derive an optimal pricing of inputs and outputs in a partial equilibrium situation—that is, moving to a Pareto optimum in one sector may or may not improve the community's welfare. Once this is conceded, Pareto optimality, which is the implicit aim of the selection techniques, cannot ever be achieved. Moreover, since in any concrete situation the amount of deviation of planned pricing from Pareto top-level welfare optimal pricing cannot be either estimated or evaluated, it must remain true that the impact of the particular project on the welfare of the community cannot really be determined.[6]

The second limitation of these techniques is that economic development, no matter how limitedly construed, requires the employment of some form of general equilibrium analysis. Microeconomic techniques, by definition, cannot do this, so all direct costs and benefits cannot be measured accurately, both for the reason stated previously and also because existing techniques have no way of satisfactorily evaluating the qualitative externalities of a project. Insofar as externalities and complementarities are key elements in helping to frame decisions in this context, reliance on these techniques would be disastrous, all the more so since industrialization is considered here as leading to huge structural changes in output, values, etc. In this situation the marginalist limitation of these techniques becomes self-evident.

There remains the most crucial of these limitations. This follows from the implicit assumption in the literature that these techniques are neutral and objective, operating *in vacuo* (i.e., independent of the social system). In other words, they can be applied equally well to any economic system if the maximization criteria are specified. In fact, they are neither neutral nor objective. Rather than being independent of the social system, they imply that the "system" for which the projects are planned *can generate its own development*, a proposition which directly contradicts the realities of the economies under consideration, even though it conforms to the realities of the already transformed economies.

Given the arguments stated above, it follows that the contradictions between project evaluation and industrial planning derive from the fact that the former is in practice used as a substitute for the latter. To the extent that this practice prevails, we find that current usage reflects one further dimension of the multifaceted way in which dependent decision-making internalizes itself within these economic systems; what is taken to be neutral, objective, and scientific is essentially a set of principles which yields decisions consistent with the maintenance of the status quo.

Soviet "Heavy-Industry" and Neoclassical "Import-Substitution" Strategies

Leaving these issues aside temporarily, we find two fundamental approaches in the literature to the problem of determining the correct sequence of investments in an industrialization program. The first, the so-called Soviet model, is based on the strategy of concentrating investments in heavy industry—particularly by focusing these investment flows on the production of the machines and plants needed to produce other machines and plants. The literature on this approach is considerable and covers the controversies among Soviet economists during the early stages of that country's industrialization, the historical-economic analyses of Russian experiences with industrialization, and the theoretical propositions derived from Marxian analysis, particularly the Marxian schema of classifying output into two major departments.[7] Dobb sums up the general position fairly well:

> So-called investment priority for heavy industry has come to be regarded, in discussing policies of development, as a leading characteristic of Soviet industrialization. This and the coupling of rapid industrialization with collectivization of agriculture are generally treated as composing the hallmark of the specifically Soviet mode of development.[8]

He also points out the significance of this in the context of underdevelopment:

> In underdeveloped countries faced with the problem of either launching or sustaining the momentum of an industrial revolution, its economic *rationale* has been more frequently appreciated; and in the last ten or fifteen years discussion has shifted to the general applicability of this method to underdeveloped countries and whether or not it can be regarded as a general condition for achieving a high rate of growth.[9]

Other socialist writers have taken this model to be an axiomatic principle of development. Dobb quotes Baran:

> Large investment in producers' goods industries is tantamount to high rates of growth sustained during the entire planning period, and correspondingly a program directed toward economic development via consumers' goods industries implies automatically not only smaller initial investment but also much lower rates of ensuing growth.[10]

The origin of the formal demonstration of this relationship goes back to G. A. Feldman of Gosplan, who developed the

Marxian two-departmental schema so as to include in Department I only the net additions to capital and in Department II, the consumers goods sector, all consumer goods including raw materials and replacement provisions for the existing capital stock. As a result it was possible to demonstrate that the rate of growth becomes crucially dependent on the productive capacity of the capital goods sector, as defined. In other words, for Marx's "expanded reproduction" to occur, the absolute amount of accumulation in Department I must be higher than in Department II.

Judging from the rate at which the Soviet economy was transformed industrially, there is little doubt about the efficiency of these sequences. The major problems which relate to this strategy are those of ensuring the avoidance of the "forced" collectivization of agriculture that characterized the Soviet Union. *But such a model is of use only where the requirements of heavy industry, and the range of heavy industry required, permit their feasible development all around.* In other words, while the starting point of the strategy is correct (i.e., the limits on industrialization are set by the surpluses generated and devoted to industry and *not* by the markets for industrial goods), in small dependent economic systems the volume of feasible output becomes crucial to the social costs of industrialization. Indeed, it is for this very basic reason that we have distinguished the *small* underdeveloped economy.

The reaction of socialist writers to the recognition of the considerations we have pointed out here has been to swing the pendulum to the other side, and to presume, without any further analysis or evidence, that *socialist industrialization is not feasible where the Soviet heavy-industry model cannot be applied.* It is this which has left the theoretical field wide open to the "pragmatic" neoclassical import-substitution programs. The importance of this problem can be seen from the fact that despite the existence of countries like Sweden, Bulgaria, North Korea, Belgium, etc., Huberman and Sweezy could blithely assert in discussing Cuba:

> But above all it became increasingly clear that Cuba's demand for industrial products was not, and under no conceivable circumstances could become, large enough to justify the establishment of a wide variety of modern, technologically efficient industries. By committing herself to a program of industrial diversification, Cuba would in effect be condemning herself to industrial backwardness.[11]

Statements such as these not only betray the uncritical acceptance of the market notion of demand as a constraint on output, without reference to the needs of the community as distinct from purchases, but also represent common and unsupported prejudices about the real "variety" of modern industry and the impact of size in determining the social costs of establishing it. That this position is not an isolated slip but represents a certain prevalent type of unsuspected "prejudice" can be seen from the following references in a very successful textbook by another radical writer, R. Sutcliffe:

> This challenge in underdeveloped countries is blindingly clear; but with very few exceptions it is hard to see immediate prospects of the sort of dynamic social and institutional responses upon which an industrialization program must be built. It is partly that existing social and political structures do not often appear to be well-equipped to meet the challenge. In addition, *the size of many, though not all, underdeveloped countries is utterly inadequate to support an integrated modern industrial economy. Small economies are perfectly viable as long as they remain in the position of dependent "colonial" economies largely supplying primary products to the industrialized world.* It is only when an industrialization program is envisaged that their economic size is seen to be inadequate.[12]

What more striking recognition of the enduring and insurmountable nature of the problems of the small underdeveloped economy during the neocolonial phase can be stated? Can there be a more blind acceptance of the constraints of size?

As we can clearly see, although it has not been systematically articulated as a radical position, there are only two prospects which such a dim view permits. One is the economic integration of nation states in order to overcome size, and the other is the adaptation of technology to the requirements of particular economies. We shall examine the economic integration strategy in Part 3, but whatever the merits of this particular approach, the only realistic conclusion is that at present there is little likelihood of meaningful political/economic integration among a significant enough number of states to permit a serious combined effort at structural transformation. It follows that other strategies, apart from waiting for the achievement of economic integration, will have to be devised if these economies are to play a role in the liberation of mankind. Further, although there is some merit to the view about the need for technological adaptability, as we shall indicate, *the development of an adaptive technology of this sort presupposes certain dynamic bases of development.*

The second type of model found in the literature is the one which presently prevails among the Third World countries. This emphasizes the initial need for incentives to ensure domestic import substitution in light manufacturing, mainly in the assembly of consumer goods, with the expectation that in time this will induce a continuous, regular, backward expansion into intermediate and heavy industries.

In Part 1 we have examined the weaknesses of this type of crypto-industrialization process and established why linkages cannot be successfully forged on this basis. The problems, as we saw them, were not merely *technical.* We are prepared to concede that technically the links backward can be made, and in economies where the size of the market for intermediate and heavy goods industries justifies it on a private calculus (e.g., Mexico and Brazil) attempts have already been made by capitalist enterprises to forge these links. The main obstacles to such a process in small economies, where the private calculus may not justify it, are political and institutional, in the sense that comprehensive planning is not possible under prevailing social conditions, and that an indigenous capitalist class cannot both develop itself and at the same time take sufficient command of the state to force the population to undertake this industrialization, while it remains the private appropriator of the surplus product.

Indeed, if this were not the case such a smooth development from consumer goods industries backwards to heavy industries among all Third World economies would undermine the very rationale of the multinational firms' participation in these economies. As we have already argued, their imperatives spring from the internal dynamics of change in the capitalist center and their aim, as far as the local peripheral economies are concerned, is to exploit the local market with the *minimum amount of technological transfer and the maximum amount of dependence on imported inputs.*

Although this model is beyond doubt the favorite capitalist one, *it is important to note that it does not accord with the historical experiences of such small capitalist countries as Britain and Belgium (which industrialized early), and Australia, New Zealand, and South Africa (which are presently industrializing quite rapidly).*[13] Given the unrelatedness of this model to the actual experiences of the capitalist states, the question is why this has become the neoclassical approach to industry and underdevelopment. It often seems as if this model has been advocated because the neoclassical economists have eschewed historical analysis and started from certain a priori economic relationships, with the result that industrialization plans are, as we saw above, little more than a collection of shopping lists of feasible industries—derived from the application of such neoclassical criteria as the minimization of scarce factor use, the maximization of the wage cost/total cost ratios, and so on.

On close examination it can be seen that, apart from the conceptual and other weaknesses discussed in the previous section, a number of further weaknesses are evident in the existing studies which support these hypotheses. Combined with the presumption of eternal backwardness and the deliberate focus on "pragmatic" policies to be adapted to conditions in these countries, these largely explain the terms of their recommendations. Let us take a couple of examples. The ratios of factor combinations, etc., are often derived as averages of the data from individual firms. The result has been that the data inevitably tend to mask many important variations in existing practice. Further, the very definitions of industry have been arbitrary and reflect market divisions in the capitalist systems—we can find such practices as the casual separation of the tanning and footwear industries from livestock production, or of clothing from growing textiles. It is therefore no surprise to find that the results are often quite misleading, although they may not generally be appreciated as such. In the Brewster-Thomas study this type of analysis was summed up as follows:

> The methods, advanced as they were by some of the empirical and theoretical work of Professors Florence, Kahn, and Chenery in the late 1940's and early 1950's, may now be more properly elevated to a theory of investment priorities. The logic of this theory is simply that the scarce factor inputs should in aggregate be minimized per unit of output. In some of the more subtle formulations both input and output have to be measured in social, as distinct from private, values. Thus, less-developed countries should minimize, for example, the inputs of capital, fuel, and skills and should promote industries with relatively high wage-cost elements, low degrees of localization, small size of operation, low capital-output ratios, low fuel-cost ratios, and so on. Only the net result of the various criteria can finally establish the priority, though the adding-up problem has not been left as lucid and amenable to implementation as might be desired.
>
> It must be admitted that this procedure has a strong rationale, that is, the incontrovertible fact that the relative scarcity of the factor inputs in less-developed countries differs from that of industrial countries. However, the result of these methods has been the recommendation, and in some instances the implementation, of a pattern of industrialization which is striking in at least two respects. Firstly, it is the reverse (though not for this reason incorrect) process of the industrial pattern pursued by those nations succeeding Britain's lead, even the more recent ones such as South Africa, Australia, New Zealand. Secondly, the outcome is a structure of industry which has extremely exiguous internal links, low employment and income potential relative to the magnitude

of the development problem, and little or no rational continuity with the future course of industrialization. Examples of procedures of this kind may be found in the work of Dr. Bohr, Professor Lewis, and the Stanford Research Institute. In this connection it is interesting to note the selection of the industries which were found most suitable in the first two classes, to newly developing areas. [Class 1: Boots, shoes, soap and candles, cooperage, leather goods, bedding and mattresses, jewellery, clothing, paint, hosiery, rubber goods, brooms and brushes, glass, electrical machinery and tanning. Class 2: Cardboard boxes, furniture, sheet-metal work, cutting and small hand-tools, fabricated plastics, steel wire, stoves, ovens, agricultural machinery and implements, textiles, dyeing and finishing, and earthenware]. When we consider the question of industrialization in this way some uncertainty arises about the economic soundness of spreading the available resources over a patchy, loosely linked collection of small-scale fabricating industries which, in the aggregate and by the usual criteria may well have a lower priority than the so-called unsuitable industries.[14]

The Convergence Strategy: Basic Materials and Basic Goods

This combination of "prejudice" and "pragmatism" has succeeded in masking the real potential for economic transformation of the small underdeveloped economics, condemning them to a history without a future—to neocolonialism and dependence. Our basic strategy for transforming these economies is to plan the convergence of domestic resource use, domestic demand, and needs in such a way as to create the basis of an indigenous technology. To do this, we must first establish what constitutes the major resource content of demand and what scope there is for regulating this demand to a country's resource configuration.

An examination of the input/output matrices of industrialized countries shows that, despite the multiplicity of final products, the material content of these products is skewed in favor of a very narrow range of basic materials. Two of these—iron and steel, and textiles—form the backbone of modern industrial consumption. If paper, plastics, rubber, glass, leather, cement, wood, fuel, aluminum, and industrial chemicals (primarily the alkalis, chlorine, and sulphuric acid) are added, then we can account for the overwhelming bulk of the basic materials used in industry. Most of the value added in industry is derived from these industries, and as a result they constitute the empirically verifiable range of strategic linkages and should form the cornerstone of an industrialization program.[15]

Given the preoccupations of economists, it is perhaps not altogether surprising that the widespread ramifications of this simple observation and the analysis of its implications for economic transformation have not been pursued either in socialist or neoclassical literature. Yet, given the developments in technology and the composition of industrial demand in transformed economies, it is clear that if these goods are not produced locally the organic linkages between domestic demand and domestic output will forever lie abroad in the countries from which these imports are derived. The growth of domestic demand will then simply result in transferring the bulk of the value added abroad. An effective industrialization strategy must therefore seek the vertical integration of the demand structure with domestic resource use. This means that the investment priorities which must override all other priorities are *the choice of product* from this strategic sector of products, and the *intensive* use of domestic resources within this sector of possibilities. Some data on the value added in selected industrial products are shown in Table 10.

It is especially important for us to be clear about the analytical properties of this proposition. Accordingly, the remainder of this chapter will be devoted to a discussion of the production economics of this pattern of industrialization, particularly as it relates to economies of scale, since the issue of size, judging from the quotations above, is often brought up to preclude rational discussion of any form of heavy industrialization in the small underdeveloped economy.[16]

Before turning to this let us make some further observations about the basic materials sector as delineated here. We must first of all be aware that the vector of industries, which has been described here on the basis of empirical examinations of input-output data for the industrialized economies, meets two further important dynamic criteria in addition to the high proportion of the value added which they absorb. These in turn go a long way toward justifying their importance in transformation. First, as we have pointed out, there is a lot of empirical data to support the proposition that in general, and over the long run, the income elasticity of demand for industrial goods is very high. Because of the uniformity and broad basis of this trend, it is taken as indicative of real needs. However, although the composition of these goods when finally consumed may vary somewhat, their basic materials content remains broadly stable. Thus it is not surprising that the industries with the highest growth elasticities are to be found in precisely this category, as Table 11 demonstrates. The data are derived from the empirical studies of the patterns of industrial growth, cited earlier, conducted by Chenery and by the United Nations. The growth elasticities measure the rate of change of per capita of value added (V_i) in a given sector in relation to the change of per capita income (Y), i.e.:

$$\left(\frac{dV_i}{V_i} \div \frac{dY}{Y} \right)$$

The second criterion which these industries satisfy is that they have high technical linkages with other activities, both backward and forward. Thus their planned production can ensure dynamically increasing intersectoral linkages and differentiation within the internal economy. There are of course a number of precautions to be taken in the measurement of input/output relationships of this sort. In particular, a great deal of the measured relationships in the capitalist countries may reflect the structure of industry (e.g., the amount of vertical integration, the degree of monopoly, etc.) which prevails. Despite this, we believe the general impression to be fairly reliable. Stated simply, that impression is that over a range of industrially developed countries the techno-material linkages emanating from this set of industries are the greatest. In Table 12 we present data showing the size of interindustry linkages for certain basic materials sectors, in Italian, Japanese, and United States industry. Here we clearly observe the strength of interindustrial transactions.[17]

It is interesting that our idea of basic materials comes close to Sraffa's concept of basic goods. When the basic materials of industry are combined with our focus on agricultural production to satisfy the needs of the broad mass of the population, it can be seen that the convergence strategy requires a *focus on the production of the goods which enter into the means of producing all other goods*, whether indirectly (e.g., via basic foodstuffs consumed by labor) or directly (e.g., the use of iron ore in the making of steel commodities).

Table 10
Estimated Value-Added in Selected Industries

Industries	*Materials cost as percent of product*
Clothing	83.7
Paper	62.7
Paint	62.4
Rubber tires & tubes	61.0
Aluminum (primary)	59.7
Rubber (synthetic)	58.6
Footwear	56.6
Woolen manufactures	55.8
Cotton goods	52.6
Rayon fabrics	51.3
Industrial chemicals	50.9
Glass containers	45.4

Sources: H. R. Brewster and C. Y. Thomas, *The Dynamics of West Indian Economic Integration*, p. 142; quoted from AID, *Manual of Industrial Development* (June 1958).

In the absence of joint products, Sraffa defined a basic good as follows: "The criteria is whether a commodity enters (no matter whether directly or indirectly) into the production of *all* commodities. Those that do we shall call *basic*, and those that do not, *nonbasic* products."[18] Relaxing the simplifying assumptions stated here, he later generalized the formulation of this concept as follows:

> In a system of K productive process and K commodities (no matter whether produced singly or jointly) we say that a commodity, or more generally a group of n linked commodities (where n must be smaller than K and may be equal to 1), are *non-basic* if of the K rows (formed by the 2n quantities in which they appear in the process) not more than n rows are independent, the others being linear combinations of these. All commodities which do not satisfy this condition are *basic.*[19]

Table 11

Commodity	*Growth elasticities*	
	Chenery	*United Nations*
Machinery	2.80	1.98
Metals	2.14	1.99
Paper	2.69	2.04
Petroleum	2.22	1.55
Rubber	2.00	1.58
Chemicals	1.66	1.66
Textiles	1.44	1.21
Wood products	1.77	1.53
Leather goods	1.64	0.89
Clothing	1.69	1.36
Nonmetallic minerals	1.62	1.16
Total manufacturing*	1.62	1.37

Sources: United Nations, *A Study of Industrial Growth*, and H. Chenery, "Patterns of Industrial Growth," p. 638.

* Categories 20-39 of the Standard Industrial Classification.

Table 12
Inter-Industry Linkages (Italy, Japan, U.S.A.)

Item	*Backward linkage*	*Forward linkage*
Iron and steel	66	78
Nonferrous metals	61	81
Paper and products	57	78
Petroleum products	65	68
Chemicals	60	69
Textiles	67	57
Rubber products	51	48
Lumber and wood	61	38
Leather and products	66	37

Source: H. Chenery and T. Watanabe, "International Comparisons of the Structure of Production."

As Sraffa himself has pointed out, the derivation of those commodities which are basic depends to a large extent on an intuitive grasp of economic processes. The growth of computers and the increases in the amount of highly disaggregated input-output data have tended to improve our knowledge of the technical processes of the economic system and will progressively make it less and less necessary to rely on intuition. Nevertheless, in the context of underdevelopment the position still broadly remains one in which Sraffa's conclusion holds:

> The formal definition just given is not nearly so satisfactory from the economic standpoint as the intuitive criterion of "entering or not entering," the means of production of all commodities, which it supersedes. It has, however, the advantage of greater generality.[20]

What the above demonstrates is the close similarity between constructing an economic system which integrates domestic resource use—production—technology—demand—needs, and the ability to produce the means to produce commodities. Unless this is achieved, the economic system cannot function with an internally directed autonomy. As we saw in the previous chapter, this does not necessarily imply limited external trading relationships.

In conclusion it should be borne in mind that there are no necessary and automatic connections between producing the basic materials for industry and the form and type of the final products. On the contrary, we have merely sought to establish those basic materials which are dominant in satisfying industrial needs. As we have pointed out, historically these have been confined to a vector of possibilities, with high growth occurring within a stable range. These *basic materials*, as inputs, will have to be linked to the *basic goods*, as outputs. But the latter are determined by the particular society's needs so that the whole process of production is one planned in the context of the transformation requirements for basic goods—to which all other considerations must be subservient.

Resource Use and Resource Flexibility

If, as we have argued, a strategy of comprehensive planning for structural transformation requires the domestic production of those basic materials which are required as primary inputs for the manufacture of the basic goods of the community, then, in order to make this strategy fully effective, it is necessary to ensure that these basic materials are substantially derived from domestic resources. It is only in this way that the major industrial thrust will ensure the dynamic interaction of domestic resource use and domestic needs. This therefore constitutes the *necessary*, if not the sufficient, condition for the growth of an indigenously oriented technology—that is, a technology rooted in the use of domestic resources and servicing domestic needs. It also follows logically from this that a comprehensive and rational planning of industrialization must be preceded by two necessary conditions: an up-to-date and reliable inventory of the country's natural resources and the establishment of facilities for rapid and effective technological training.

Elementary as these principles would seem, it is still true that almost all of the Third World countries have passed their years of "industrialization" without either the systematic compilation of such an inventory, or any major attempt at the establishment of the necessary technological facilities.[21] As we have pointed out, it is often the case that the natural resource endowments of these countries are not known and so have to be estimated from studies initiated during the former colonial administrations. Given the nature and functioning of the colonial economic system, the search for natural resources has reflected the needs and priorities of the metropolitan power.

Similarly, the experience has been that, almost without exception, the provision of major and large-scale training facilities has simply been reduced to the policy of "taking over" institutes, colleges, etc., established during the colonial administration. Frequently, this policy of "taking over" has not been accompanied by significant shifts in either the numbers of persons trained or the nature and content of the training. Thus it is not surprising frequently to find situations such as in Africa, where one of the world's best endowed regions for hydropower (at the present level of knowledge) utilizes less than 0.6 percent of the known hydropower facilities.[22] Or again, there is Guyana, where not a single kilowatt of power has been derived from the world's longest vertical drop waterfall, Kaiteur Falls. Examples such as these can be provided *ad nauseam.*

Since it is only an actual inventory which can establish the natural resource situation of a given country, we cannot make any rigid a priori estimates of a country's transformative potential. The scope for structural transformation will be heavily dependent on the resource configuration which is discovered in each and every society. *Although this point cannot be overstressed, there are at least six important technological considerations which serve to lessen the sheer burden of this constraint on the development of the basic materials sector.* We shall indicate these technological considerations in this section in order to demonstrate the range of possible flexibility, despite the existence of this overriding constraint.

The first of these technological considerations is that the various technical processes for producing basic materials often allow for the possibility of the physical substitution of one resource input for another in order to produce the same product, but with a different material composition. Thus we find that plastics can sometimes substitute for leather, aluminum for steel, cotton for synthetics, wood for glass, etc. It follows that if demand is planned *both* to satisfy the community's needs and to converge wherever possible with domestic resource availability, then demand planning can take place in such a way as to take account of deficient resource endowments where they exist, as well as to exploit abundant resources where they exist. It is for this reason that, in the context of planning and rational resource use, basic material substitutability can in many instances turn out to be much more crucial than the present preoccupation with labor/capital substitutability would suggest. Yet, as we have seen, the economic literature has devoted little or no attention to this situation.

The second technological consideration which gives rise to flexibility in the face of this constraint is that the raw material inputs of some basic materials are to a certain extent variable in composition. The variability of input mix gives rise to further flexibility for this range of industrial activities. Thus charcoal can replace coking coal in iron metallurgy, or power can be fueled with nuclear energy, oil, coal, or hydroelectricity. It may also be that an abundant unused resource (e.g., molasses or bagasse—by-products of sugar production) may be used for making a much-needed basic output, such as making plastics or providing energy. Again, the importance of this consideration becomes manifest in the context of planning and rational resource use.

The third area of flexibility is that often technological developments abroad can be exploited in such a way as to make up for deficient resources at home. Thus, given the importance the underdeveloped countries attach to iron and steel production, the recent changes in the technology of making prereduced ore increase the range of technological options because they open up the possibility for iron and steel manufacture to take place in countries where iron ore supplies may be deficient, since prereduced ore may now be imported fairly cheaply. Of course, not all the technological considerations are equally advantageous. Thus the benefits of iron and steel manufacture will be somewhat reduced if the industry has a significant import content. However, the force of our proposition is that if the alternative is no steel manufacture, then reliance on imported inputs for a local steel industry is to be preferred—even though a project evaluation may show that the product cannot be produced at "competitive prices." Here, the preference is indicated at the level of basic analysis of the dependence/transformation model.

A fourth area of technological flexibility derives from the recent dramatic improvements in bulk transportation methods. Where a country is forced to import a crucial resource input because it is physically unavailable, this lessens the cost of transportation. It is not surprising that these improvements have followed on the needs of Europe, Japan, and America to find cheap ways of moving natural resources—such as natural gas, oil, and iron ore—across long distances. Again, reliance on this consideration is really making the best of an unsatisfactory situation, the absence of the raw materials at home.

The fifth technological consideration is that some of the basic materials (e.g., wood, leather, paper, etc.) are renewable resources. Thus with national planning both the quantity and quality of these resources can be improved in terms of their natural, virgin availability even as they are being used up. Thus, to take one example, the improvements in forest resources made possible through the planting of the eucalyptus in tropical areas (as has been demonstrated in trials in Africa and more widespread cultivation in Australia and Latin America) have opened up wide possibilities for some of the underdeveloped economies in their search for fibrous material.

Finally, technological changes have hitherto been strongly biased in favor of getting more output per unit of raw material input, as well as in bringing into regular use more and more of what were previously regarded as marginal inputs. In general, it seems that this development has reflected both the pressures within the industrialized countries to reduce their dependence on raw material sources outside of their national economies, as well as the search for reducing unit production costs. Some of this, indirectly and unintentionally perhaps, can with careful planning be made to spill over to improve the resource potentialities in some of the underdeveloped economies. But selective importation and adaptation of foreign technology presupposes the existence of a significant national technological capability.

The above considerations clearly highlight the scope of resource flexibility even as they acknowledge the importance of the resource constraint in economic transformation. Further, they serve to make certain other issues abundantly clear. First, while it is true that the only basis for establishing a long-run production structure which is consistent with the needs of the community is through the growth of a domestic technology, adaptive to the twin conditions of local resources and local needs, for such indigenous technological growth to take place domestic resource use and domestic needs have to be the dominant foci for the planned production. While we may therefore say that these establish the *necessary* conditions for technological growth, to be *sufficient* planned production will have to be integrated into the planned development and spread of scientific training facilities.

Second, it is clear from our analysis that from the point of view of comprehensive planning the notion of resource endowment cannot be very meaningfully analyzed under the broad categories of land, labor, capital, etc., as is the prevailing practice. Specific resource configurations will have to be brought into the analysis if we are not to miss the complexities of industrial processes. Indeed, as we have argued, raw material input substitutability is likely to be more crucial than broad substitutabilities of labor for capital, and so on.

Finally, our analysis also makes it very clear that *the resource configuration of a country cannot be considered independent of the demand structure and the needs of the broad mass of the population.* It is the latter consideration which gives significance to production. As a result, the existence of flexibility in the goods needed, as well as their material input requirements, means that the range of choice made possible because of the planning of demand is essential to the industrialization program. It is only in this sense that the constraint of size can be overcome. But, as we can see, such flexibility presupposes a certain approach to the organization of economic and social activity.

Economies of Scale: Assumptions and Realities

Insofar as the types of economies we are considering are partly distinguished by constraints of size, the question of economies of scale inevitably becomes most crucial to any planned strategy of transformation, particularly as all of these basic industries seem at present to be characterized by the need for large volumes of output to be economical. From this it is often presumed (and, as we have pointed out, not questioned further) that the social costs of industrialization will inevitably be prohibitive. This follows from a rather hazy and casual application of the so-called dictates of the concept of economies of scale, and has resulted in much of the confusion we find when considering the literature on the role of industrialization in small underdeveloped economies. We shall examine some issues related to this concept in this section.

Although in the economics literature the concept of economies of scale has been derived from the inverse relation that is said to exist between unit monetary cost of production and the level of output of an enterprise, there is in truth much ambiguity deriving from mixed-up interpretations of what may be different levels of cost curves and movements along a given set of cost curves. The consequence of this, noted by the neoclassical writers themselves, has been a fair degree of skepticism about such notions as "optimum output levels." Nevertheless, it would be fair to conclude that presently the view predominates that economies of scale are, in one way or another, crucial in determining the nature and levels of manufacturing production.[23]

In strict production terms, economies of scale may be derived from the empirically observed inverse relationship between levels of physical output and the physical input ratio. Major factors influencing this relationship are the length of the various output runs and the possibilities of deriving unit cost savings on physical inputs because of the phenomenon of cubic dimensions. Because of indivisibilities in many production processes, the amount of physical input used tends to rise at a slower rate than output. In engineering circles this is frequently referred to as the "0.6 rule"—the rule which says that physical input unit costs rise at a rate approximately equal to the rate of increase of output raised to the power of 0.6. This rule expresses the mathematical relationship between the volume of a spherical or cylindrical object and its surface area. Although expressed as "capital cost" economies (i.e., economies in the cost of capital construction), these economies indirectly affect the unit cost of production. The nature of these effects will of course depend on the relationship of fixed to variable costs and the amount of depreciation costs. Expressed this way, economies of scale are therefore largely returns to scale devoid of the monetary influences such as the prices of the inputs used in the production process.

In the complex real world of production, however, these economies are normally expressed in terms of monetary units. This permits a very wide variety of other factors to impinge on these purely technical/physical considerations and thereby to affect further the nature of the relationship between unit costs of output and production levels. These influences can be seen in a number of situations. For instance, we often find that when available raw materials are cheap and abundant, industries may be established which do not meet the technological optimum for reaping full economies of scale. In this event cheap available supplies compensate for higher production costs when production levels are below the optimum. Second, we often find that the location of production and the impact of this on transport costs make it worthwhile to establish industries even when the plant size is far below the optimum. This is particularly marked when the input requirements of the product, and/or the product itself, are heavy, bulky, and therefore costly to distribute. Thus, for example, the large number of cement industries of widely varying sizes found around the world is partly a reflection of these considerations and attempts to minimize transport costs. Third, we know that the variation which exists in the prices of inputs in a particular process, usually labor and capital, are very marked among countries. In view of this, the true meaning of measures of unit costs of production becomes difficult to interpret.

In addition to all of these qualifications and complications, it is of further importance that we note that many of the studies of economies of scale have been conducted in the industrialized capitalist economies. In addition to the distorting effects noted above, we thus have to take into account such other real difficulties as: (1) determining the correct conversion rate of the local currency into foreign exchange (in order to move from domestic prices to an international standard of comparison to facilitate cross-country comparisons); (2) the degree of monopoly and the extent of monopoly pricing (in order to distinguish the relationship between unit costs and unit selling prices); and (3) external economies (in order to isolate factors external to the enterprise which affect costs of production and selling prices).

Given all these complex factors, it is frequently the case that *the relationship between physical input and output factors belies the relationship of money costs of production, output levels, and the prices at which the output becomes available.* Thus we find that in many underdeveloped economies the anarchy of the present productive system confuses the real significance of economies of scale. High unit costs of production in many lines of manufacturing, brought about by the capitalistically induced proliferation of plants, have been, by this very fact, compensated by the high levels of local protection afforded to these plants. How else can we explain the fact that in 1967 the total number of cars and trucks produced in the Latin American Free Trade Area was just over 650,000 units and the number of producing plants as many as 67? In Venezuela alone, 13 firms produce annually about 62,000 vehicles, whereas in Chile 19 firms produce annually about 16,400 vehicles.[24] In this confusing situation not only are the output capacities of individual plants very small, but the level of utilization of this capacity is also a small proportion of its potential. And, despite all this, the levels of private profitability of these operations are very high indeed! Thus we can see how complex and unclear is the effect of economies of scale on production costs, selling prices, and social and private rates of return.

From the point of view of the national interests of the underdeveloped economies and their relationship to their main suppliers in the industrialized countries, another important consideration is that there is in practice a marked difference between unit costs of production in the industrialized economies and unit prices of imports. This difference reflects two distortions which are basic to the operation of capitalist enterprises in the metropolitan countries. One is that, in the pursuit of profit, these firms systematically exploit the existence of different slopes in their average revenue curves in the home and overseas market. In practice, this often leads to systematic dumping abroad, particularly in the Third World countries where resistance to this practice is likely to be low. Although it has been argued that dumping can be beneficial to the receiving countries in certain restrictive situations—because they receive the product at a cheaper price—it can hardly be argued that this is so when the purchase of the dumped product leads to the *systematic* distortion of the developmental benefits of producing the dumped commodity at home. Evidence suggests that this is a much more widespread practice than is commonly supposed.[25] In such a situation no socialist government embarking upon comprehensive planning in order to effect the transformation of the country's economic structure can afford to allow its production decisions to be determined simply by the relation of its own production costs and the price of the imported equivalent.

The second distortion is an extension of our earlier argument and concerns the reverse use of monopoly power. Prices are raised for sales to the underdeveloped countries, in the same pursuit of monopoly gains, if the average revenue curve facing the firm makes this profitable. In view of this, it surely follows that the imported price equivalent of domestic production, "uncleansed" of all these considerations, will not, and indeed cannot, play a crucial role in the framing of an efficient industrialization program. Yet we must bear in mind the very fashionable trend in this direction represented by the success and increasing use of the Little/Mirrlees model of shadow pricing, where internationally traded prices (frontier prices) are imputed as the correct basis for valuing domestic inputs and outputs in a project. From our perspective, such a procedure merely *internalizes* within the *methods* of investment planning the distorting characteristics of the international economy. Rather than leading to "efficiency," as it is claimed, such procedures, insofar as they are not based on internal requirements and resources, can only serve to deepen the country's involvement in the international capitalist system.[26]

One corollary of this conclusion, which can be taken together with our earlier observations of the confusions which center on the interpretation and measurement of economies of scale, suggests that prices can only be rational—and therefore useful in guiding production decisions—insofar as they reflect domestic constraints and domestic demand priorities, etc. Efficiency considerations are not, and indeed cannot be, attained in the blind search for the "optimum" scale of operations. Rather, what is clear is that social costs must be measured, not in relation to idealized "optimum" levels, but to realistic and practical "critical minimum levels" if we are to operate effectively within the context of size constraints. The "critical minimum" can then be described as that range of the cost function over which the rate of inversion (i.e., rates of cost changes) is such that cost savings are greatest, and the social costs of industrialization are rapidly reduced, at the point where the level of production reaches a "critical minimum."

Despite the unreliability and the contradictory nature of some of the theoretical arguments in this field, two uncontestable points emerge for assessing our basic materials strategy. The first is that the inverse relation between unit costs and levels of output is not a regular relation—that is, the rate of inversion varies along the cost curve. The second point is that for all of the basic industries the empirical evidence suggests that they operate on a roughly drawn L-shaped cost function. Thus in the production of finished steel, a hypothetical increase in production from 50,000 tons to 250,000 tons reduces the unit cost of production by 36 percent, whereas a further increase to 750,000 tons would only lead to a unit cost gain of 25 percent. In integrated pulp and paper production an increase from 50 to 200 tons a day reduces unit operating costs by 50 percent, whereas a further increase to 350 tons a day reduces unit operating costs only by a further 20 percent.[27] With such a slope to the cost function, in technical terms the critical range becomes that part of the cost function in which sensitivity to output changes is greatest—i.e., the maximum point at which the rate of change of average cost with increases in scale is greatest.

When this approach is adopted, the preliminary planning requirement for determining production is whether the desired (or planned) domestic demand for any of the basic industries, now or in the near future, approaches the "critical minimum" as defined above. At this point, further gains in social cost savings obtained by waiting for output requirements to grow and approach the optimum *are outweighed by the structural imperatives of transforming the economic system.* The customary reliance on optimal output considerations to determine decisions is very misleading in its implications for industrialization in a small underdeveloped economy. How can it be otherwise? All of these concepts of optima are derived from the preoccupations of firms operating in industrialized capitalist economies which are in a position to service the entire globe! They are not a reflection of the underdeveloped countries' own priorities. It is true that practical problems remain as to the implementability of our proposal, but these center on the sequence of industrial establishments in relation to surplus accumulation and foreign exchange availability. Sectoral choices and the pressures of immediacy have already been determined by analysis from the underdevelopment/planned transformation model.

Complementary Industrial Activities

Machine Tools: Even though the basic materials sector constitutes the cornerstone of the industrialization program and the dominant focus in the struggle to transform the economy, this sector cannot be planned in isolation from other industrial activities that are necessarily complementary to it. These other activities will have to be integrated into a comprehensive program which derives from the same basic imperatives of integrating domestic resource use and domestic needs on the basis of a vibrant indigenous technology. From this perspective, it has to be realized that the capital goods sector must be planned so that it is dynamically interconnected and capable of the *rapid development and transmission of technological changes.* With this objective in mind, it follows that one of the most important areas of the capital goods sector which has to be planned and integrated into the basic materials sector is that of the *machinery and machine tools industries.*

There are a number of features of this sector which have historically given it a crucial role in the development of technology and which, as a consequence, have made it an indispensable element in serious policies of industrial transformation. Fortunately, from the viewpoint of the small underdeveloped economy, certain characteristics of this sector tend to make its firm establishment not too difficult when comprehensive planning takes place and the initiative for technological development and application no longer lies with the multinational firm or a dependent capitalist client class. In the first place, the machine tools and machine-building sectors are not significantly capital-intensive. From a list of 139 industries in the United States (covering sections 20-39 of the Standard Industrial Classification) machine tools, machinery, and metal work industries have had capital intensity ratios of 1.96 and 1.71. Only ten industries have had lower ratios, even though the overall variation was quite considerable, ranging from 61 to 1.05.[28]

This evidence of the use of labor-intensive processes in this sector in the "capital-abundant" United States means that the capital costs of establishment are not nearly as crucial as in other "heavy" industries. One reason why the capital-intensity ratio has tended to be low is that this sector is not really amenable to standardized mass production methods. In actuality it mostly satisfies a demand for made-to-order output, using specific machines for specific purposes. However, if these industries are required to produce on the basis of precise specifications for nearly unique products, the machine tools sector has to be a highly skill-intensive sector. Thus we frequently find that although the industry employs relatively high proportions of labor to capital, it nevertheless tends to draw disproportionately on available highly skilled manpower.

A recent study by Pratten that examines machine tool production in a much smaller economy than the United States, the United Kingdom, highlights some of the present characteristics of this sector in highly industrialized capitalist economies.[29] In his survey Pratten found more than 200 firms producing machine tools in the United Kingdom. Together they employ about 80,000 persons, or one-half of one percent of the labor force. Furthermore, he points out that "it is not a capital-intensive industry."[30] The scale of production, as he describes it, is quite small, with "the annual output of machine tools [being] measured in terms of tens, hundreds, and occasionally thousands."[31] This naturally reduces the scope for flow production techniques, although it is noted in the study that some firms use them for assembly and some machining operations. It was also found that *all* firms produced their machine parts in batches, and that most of them assembled tools on the batch principle.

Although the evidence supports our view that this industry is less standardized than other heavy goods industries, and that it operates more or less on the made-to-order principle, *paradoxically this does not necessarily imply a bewildering variety of outputs.* In fact, many of the technical processes involved in their use—such as control mechanisms, servo-mechanisms, power transmission, etc.—are based on similar engineering principles. Thus Pratten found that there were seven basic groups of products produced by this sector, including the usual lathes, drilling and boring machines, and grinding machines. These seven groups were subdivided into forty-four classes of tools, with a range of models.[32] A great deal of the variation in models referred to differences in size, performance, etc., and were introduced in response to the highly variegated requests from customers. Not surprisingly, Pratten found that "economies attributable to larger factories appear to be small in relation to other factors affecting performance."[33] Thus it was shown that firms producing one-quarter of one percent of the industry's output for the United Kingdom market were not disadvantaged on account of size. This was true even if they produced only a limited range of standard tools, in which case only one or two percent of the industry's total output was necessary for a firm to be competitive.[34]

A parallel aspect of this variety of outputs is that it ensures that innovations, if and when they do occur in the production of a particular machine, can be rapidly and easily spread throughout a wide range of capital goods industries. Even in capitalist economies, with their private patents and monopolistic restrictions on the use of technical knowledge, this pattern has prevailed. Thus Rosenberg has observed

> the introduction of a relatively small number of broadly similar productive processes to a large number of industries. Throughout these sectors there are common processes, initially in the refining and smelting of metal ores, subsequently in foundry work whereby the refined metals are cast into preliminary shapes, and then in various machinery processes through which the component metal parts are converted into final form preparatory to their assembly as a finished product.[35]

Given this sort of dynamic interconnectedness, the premium this sector necessarily places on flexibility, adaptability, and creative responses to specific orders makes it a truly dynamic component of technological change.

In his study of the Chinese machine industry, Chu-Yuan Chang observed a very high correlation between performance in the machine-building sector and labor productivity in industry.[36] This suggests that even in newly established machine tools sectors, productivity gains can be quickly realized. Ultimately, this springs from the nature of the creative interaction this sector provides between what a country has and what it needs. As the Chinese, Russian, and Japanese examples show, all contemporary economies start with a stock of already acquired machines. In the first stages of planning, therefore, the approach is basically one of adaptation and selection in order to strengthen the existing basis of the machines sector. It soon becomes possible for internal technological advances and adaptations to take place, but the initial phases should not be regarded as simply involving imitation and a crude emphasis on wholesale copying. As Strassmann has correctly pointed out, "One can borrow most effectively if one also has the capacity to be original."[37]

In other words, this sector tends by its very nature to encapsulate technological change within itself. Failure to develop local machinery and machine tools must mean dependence on overseas machines, the stultification of indigenous technological capacities, and a pattern of production where the machines in domestic use are a by-product of forces elsewhere, seeking to converge some other societies' resources to their requirements.

Given the arguments presented here, it is not surprising to find, as we saw in the data presented in Table 11 above, that both Chenery's and the United Nations' studies have shown that historically this sector has had phenomenally high growth elasticities. This same historical experience indicates that in order to be able to make full use of the potential of this sector, a great deal of attention has to be paid to the question of manpower requirements. The establishment of adequate training facilities to ensure the right amount of research expertise becomes a *sine qua non* of integrated and comprehensive planning for *every country.* That this training can take place at a very rapid rate is clearly seen in the experiences of China, Russia, and much of Eastern Europe. Indeed, in some of the larger underdeveloped areas such as Brazil and India, the numbers of trained persons have shown quite considerable increases. Leff, in his study of the Brazilian capital goods industry, found a three-fold increase of the skilled labor force, from 24,700 to 75,000 between 1958 and 1963.[38]

This need to provide a capital goods sector and trained personnel takes on a "national" character, as is seen in the experiences of Eastern Europe:

> East European countries have in effect dodged for a long time any serious cooperation in the field of metallurgy and machine construction: their policymakers have for many years stressed the idea that domestic production of electricity, steel, and machine tools is *absolutely necessary to each country*, no matter what its natural endowment may be. Even now the division of labor among these countries in metallurgy and machine tools remains limited.[39]

Rather than interpret this as "dodging" the issue, as its author suggests, this essentially highlights that such an approach is *the rational objective to be pursued by every country seeking to transform its economic base.* It is only by so doing that it can create a material basis for equality in international cooperation. What this quote further serves to emphasize is that even in periods of highest political and military cooperation, the necessity of a national development of a machine-building capacity remains. How, therefore, can any underdeveloped economy afford to ignore this and do otherwise?

Overheads: Power and Transportation. The second important area of complementary industrial development lies in the provision of *infrastructural and overhead facilities, particularly power and transportation.* Electricity has always played a vital role in socialist theories and practice of industrialization. During the early phases of Russian development it was seen as the "key" to industrial progress, and it was Lenin who made famous the slogan "Communism is the power of the Soviets plus electricity." The basic strategy implied in this emphasis on power is that if electricity is made available to all productive units in large and easily procured amounts, this can transform production functions. Its homogeneity, divisibility, and flexibility will allow its rapid and widespread use in both rural and industrial centers. Thus Spulber briefly traces Krzhizhanovskii's impact on the GOELRO plan:

> The plan of electrification of Russia, written in December 1920 . . . [saw] marvellous prospects . . . from the massive use of electricity. Bazarov . . . [said it would] relegate to the museums of the future socialist society . . . the barrack-type factory and their fitting social complement the skyscraper buildings . . . the most glaring manifestations of the cultural barbarity produced by the crude technology of the age of classical capitalism. A young technician, I. Ivanov, stressed in a famous article highly praised by Krzhizhanovskii that electricity would serve as the basis for communist technology in the same way that steam power had served as the foundation of early capitalist technology.[40]

Given the spread of these views, it is not surprising that energy output per capita is frequently taken as an important index of the level of industrialization. All industrial processes require power, and the spread and use of power facilities are therefore important to the growth of industry. Despite this, historical evidence suggests that electricity, and indeed all other overhead facilities (transportation, etc.), do not *cause* economic growth as such, but are indispensable *complements* to successful growth.

Although it is not widely known and appreciated, electricity costs are not crucial in most industrial processes:

> Apart from aluminum and iron pigs, cement and electrolytic chlorine, there are hardly any other products in which energy could possibly be the pivotal cost element. In most industries, including pulp and paper, glass, chemicals, textiles, rolled steel, and iron and steel forgings, energy input tends to be less than 8 percent of output. In the greater number of industries it is less than 6 percent. Even in the case of blast furnace products and cement, the energy input does not exceed 25 percent of the value of the product.[41]

What is required during the transformation process, therefore, is not a dependence on electrification as a panacea, but the assurance that electricity, and indeed transportation and all other overhead facilities, are comprehensively planned in order to maintain adequate supplies to cope with the industrial, agricultural, and social requirements of development.

Small-Scale Industry. The third major area of complementary industrial activity is the development of small-scale industry. Small-scale industries have much to commend them, provided they are expected to play an essentially ancillary role and are not expected to be *the* basis of the industrial thrust. Small-scale industries are flexible in many regards. In some cases, existing small-scale industries have developed from household and other service-oriented operations and have been able to survive the historical tendencies toward the concentration of industrial processes. This pattern of development and survival is particularly typical of small industry in the underdeveloped economy where some amount of industrialization has taken place. In other circumstances, existing small-scale factories survive in highly industrialized economies mainly because their operations are based on doing work on a subcontracting basis for the larger industrial enterprises.

When discussing the possible usefulness of small-scale industries, it has frequently been presumed that they are labor-intensive and therefore should be encouraged if only because they will help to provide employment and the opportunity for the display of entrepreneurial talent on as wide a basis as possible. To those advisors anxious to develop a domestic capitalist class and widely decentralized business ownership, this has been a very attractive policy. But in practice the data from studies of small-scale industries suggest that rather than being labor-intensive, "in general, the most capital-intensive type of manufacturing establishment is the small factory using modern machinery, and employing up to fifty workers."[42]

Small-scale industries cannot therefore be rationalized in terms of labor intensity or their ability to provide entrepreneurial talent because of the decentralization of business ownership which it makes possible. The justification must lie elsewhere, in their demonstrated social and economic efficiencies. Their social efficiency stems from their flexibility in terms of location, which means they can be a very important instrument for narrowing rural/urban industrial differentiation. Their economic efficiency stems from the pressures they can maintain in a planned economy to enforce the requirements of adapting technology to small size.

A look at the categorization of small-scale industries provided by Staley and Morse and the factors which determine their viability gives some idea of their potential range.[43] Small-scale industries often have the advantage of *favorable locational factors*, such as in: (1) the dairy products industry, where there there is the need to process inputs available over widely scattered areas; (2) clay blocks and tiles, where there is the need to produce for local markets a product with otherwise high transportation costs; and (3) service industries—plumbing, electrical repairs, machinery repairs, etc.—where the service has to be provided on the spot. There are also what can be called *market influences* which favor certain small-scale industries—such as leather goods and straw work—where the product is highly differentiated, often to meet specific orders, and where economies of scale are not significant or the industries concentrate on serving very small levels of specialized demand. Finally, there are certain processes which these industries are advantageously placed to perform—e.g., *distinct manufacturing operations on the more or less made-to-order principle*, such as some of the machine-building industries discussed previously, precision and highly skilled hand-work processes like those sections of the leather goods industry mentioned earlier, or simply operations confined to such straightforward processes as assembly, mixing, designing, or other light finishing operations. Given this sort of range, the complementary usefulness of small-scale industry is amply testified to.

Agricultural Industries. The last major areas of complementary activities which we shall draw attention to are those which relate to the agricultural sector. In the previous chapter we have already indicated that the agricultural sector transmits its own influences onto the industrialization program. This stems from the need to provide this sector with inputs crucial to its transformation—such as pesticides, fertilizers, building equipment, irrigation facilities, machine equipment, etc. All these are closely linked to the basic goods sectors—fertilizers to chemicals, machinery to iron and steel, and so on. Insofar as these influences operate, then planning basic materials to produce basic goods involves planning for agricultural uses. On the other hand, there is the need for the further manufacturing and processing of agricultural products—textiles, food preserving, canning, etc. In both these instances it is clear that there is a dynamic interaction between the basic materials sector and all other sectors of the economy. Indeed, this is true almost by definition, since this sector is basic to the provision of all basic goods. The principal factor which has to be borne in mind is the oft-repeated one: the interaction of agriculture and industry must be based on the principles of the intensive use of domestic resources to serve domestic needs, since only this can provide a true basis for domestic technological development.

Conclusion

We have already indicated that it would be incorrect to deduce from our strategy naive notions of economic transformation; we are not by any means suggesting that a socialist government pursuing a strategy of industrial convergence should not trade. The point advanced here is that since trade is a manifestation of, and a factor reinforcing, structural disequilibrium in the small underdeveloped economy during the present neocolonial phase, a solution to this problem has to be found at a structural level. From the point of view of the subject matter of this chapter, this principally means that industrialization, insofar as it creates a convergence of domestic resource use and domestic demand (needs), also simultaneously creates a dynamic domestic capacity to convert domestic savings into investment goods and thereby allows for the potential development of an export capacity in industrial goods. Such an export capacity is indispensable if the economy is to be able to make the pressures of domestic requirements (in the context of limited size) and productivity levels operating at home a lesser constraining factor on its earnings of foreign exchange, as compared to the position of existing primary agricultural exports.

Unless this structural shift occurs, the rate of domestic accumulation will remain an insufficient indicator of the rate of possible expansion of domestic capacity. This follows logically from the obvious fact that if an industrial capacity does not exist at home, then efforts at domestic economic expansion are contingent on the country's ability to obtain those goods which, because there is no domestic industrial capacity, cannot always immediately be produced at home. This means that in such a situation foreign exchange is a crucial resource input, since unless foreign exchange is available in the necessary amounts to be a full complement to domestic savings, these savings can be "frustrated," in the sense of not effectively transformed into material output. The only way to resolve this basic structural problem must be through an intensification of the search for local resources and technology. These are explicit features of the industrial planning strategy we have advanced, since that strategy in effect seeks, among other things, to narrow the range of goods which are not produceable at home.

From this we can infer the new emphasis on trading policies that must accompany other economic policies in the small underdeveloped economies during the transition. Basically, the ultimate and most vital tests of the efficiency of trade policies must be derived from an evaluation of their dynamic contributions toward increasing intersectoral transactions within the domestic economy. This can occur either by stimulating the use of domestic resources (by exporting manufactured products) or by trade arrangements with Third World countries (particularly neighboring ones) and other socialist countries. These trade arrangements must not seek simply to liberalize trade; their major emphasis must be to juxtapose and combine resource use and consumption patterns in the planned production of those basic materials and other products, in which domestic resources or demand requirements are deficient in the countries concerned.

Insofar as the industrialization drive is subsumed under the strategy of dynamic convergence, then several other important implications follow. First, industrialization itself tends to contribute flexibility to the economic system. This occurs not only because industry is more flexible and adaptable, but because the spread of industrial techniques and the industrial approach to dealing with material phenomena and natural processes generates flexibility in the use of resource inputs and adaptation to changing needs and requirements. Second, as we have argued, the organic link between domestic resource use, domestic demand, and needs has to be rooted in an indigenous technology. But how can this occur if the technologically intensive outputs are imported? The strategy of industrialization presented here seeks to overcome this by internalizing within the economic system, *by producing these items and not simply using them*, the dynamic bases for technological change that have historically been encapsulated in the basic materials and machine-building sectors. It is only this approach that can provide the material basis for a broadly conceived drive to transform the material basis of the society, in the widest possible sense.

Finally, our approach, by focusing on the present historical context (i.e., the neocolonial aspects of international relations), allows us to take fully into account certain features of the international economy and the urgency this gives to efforts aimed at internalizing the basis for productive transformation. Some of these we have mentioned explicitly in the earlier parts of this study—such as the widening technological gap and the present high level of costs of initial capital investments in the industry, as compared with the earlier periods of West European industrialization. Among the other important factors not mentioned so far are, first, pressures of population growth due to health improvements, and to rapid rural/urban migration. During the long history of Britain's industrialization, it was not until the middle of the nineteenth century that the rural labor supply fell. In the case of the Soviet Union, it was not until the mid-1950s that this occurred. But already in many of the underdeveloped economies the pressures of rural depopulation, combined with high population growth rates, require a strategy to cope with these neocolonial survivals. For this reason, we have emphasized the rural/urban balance and the noncontradictory roles of agriculture and industry.

Second, economies attempting to industrialize now have to do so in competition with each other and in a world where many countries are already industrialized. As a consequence, the global economy tends to be characterized by extremely assertive commercial and political struggles for markets, even though the threat of a nuclear holocaust has tended to minimize the role of direct conquest as a source of markets. In the earlier industrialization of Europe, the fact of conquest was crucial to the expansion and development of markets:

> In the decisive formative period of the capitalist mode of production, extending from the sixteenth to the end of the eighteenth century, the creation of the world market was of crucial importance . . . But all through this period of the birth of capitalism the two forms of surplus value appeared at each step. On the one hand, it was the outcome of the surplus labor of the wage workers hired by the capitalists; on the other, it was the outcome of values stolen, plundered, seized by tricks, pressure or violence from the overseas peoples with whom the Western world had made contact. From the conquest and pillage of Mexico and Peru by the Spaniards, to the sacking of Indonesia by the Portuguese and the Dutch and the ferocious exploitation of India by the British, the history of the sixteenth to the eighteenth centuries is an unbroken chain of deeds of brigandage which were so many *acts of international concentration of values and capital in Western Europe.*[44]

Today the imperialist ferocity is directed toward commercial and political manipulations, and entry into the world market as an industrial seller cannot be, if ever it was, the result of an easy evolutionary process. It is the recognition of the international character of the present capitalist order that makes it impossible to envisage any real alternative to the approaches toward industrialization we indicated here. Thus we cannot agree with Dobb, when discussing the Feldman model of investment priority in heavy industry, that:

> This is not to deny that there may be situations to which the Feldman proposition will not apply. In a completely free-trade world, with high demand-elasticities, it would make little difference to development whether a country could make structural steel and machinery itself, or produce other commodities (even primary commodities) with a sufficient market abroad, since by exploiting the latter it could procure the means to import the steel and machinery on which development depended.[45]

Even in these highly favored situations we maintain that a country's first priority is still the adaptation of its own resources to its own needs, and only thereafter can it embody technological growth as a matter of course within the social and economic system. Unless it can do this, unless it is *capable* of using its own basic materials for producing its basic requirements, then in a dynamic context it remains underdeveloped.

Notes

1. For further details see P. Jalée, *The Third World in World Economy*, Chapter IV.
2. See H. B. Chenery, "Patterns of Industrial Growth"; H. B. Chenery and L. Taylor, "Development Patterns Among Countries and Over Time"; S. Kuznets, *Modern Economic Growth: Rate Structure and Spread;* United Nations, *Patterns of Industrial Growth, 1938-1958;* and W. Hoffman, *The Industrial Economies.*
3. R. B. Sutcliffe, *Industry and Underdevelopment*, p. 245. This quotation is taken from a recent standard text and is presented here in order to show how generally acknowledged is the point we are making. Given the universality of this phenomenon, it would seem appropriate to deduce that the increasing preferences displayed for industrial goods do reflect real needs of the community—even after allowing for the role of "sales" promotion in the industrialized capitalist economies.
4. See D. Seers, "The Role of Industry in Development: Some Fallacies"; I. Livingstone, "Industry Versus Agriculture in Economic Development"; J. Flanders, "Agriculture Versus Industry in Development Policy."
5. A. G. Bagchi, "The Choice of Optimum Technique," p. 676.
6. For a review of the literature on welfare economics and a huge bibliography see E. J. Mishan, "A Survey of Welfare Economics, 1939-59." For a radical perspective see M. Dobb, *Welfare Economics and the Economics of Socialism.*
7. See E. Mandel, *Marxist Economic Theory*, pp. 627-30; M. Dobb, *Papers on Capitalism, Development and Planning;* E. Preobrazhensky, *The New Economics;* and N. Spulber, *Soviet Strategy for Economic Growth.*

8. M. Dobb, ibid., pp. 107-8.
9. Ibid.
10. Quoted in ibid., p. 284, from P. Baran, *The Political Economy of Growth.*
11. L. Huberman and P. M. Sweezy, *Socialism in Cuba,* p. 74. The last sentence of the quotation was quoted above in Chapter 1.
12. Sutcliffe, *Industry and Underdevelopment,* p. 334 (our emphasis).
13. As it has been pointed out, Canadian-type industrialization may merely be a higher order of dependence. See K. Levitt, *Silent Surrender,* and "Canada, the World's Richest Underdeveloped Country."
14. H. R. Brewster and C. Y. Thomas, *The Dynamics of West Indian Economic Integration,* pp. 141-43.
15. For an extended analysis of this element of the industrialization strategy in the context of economic integration and specific proposals for the Caribbean, see ibid.
16. While some of the earlier quotations focused on market limitations, we might point out that other writers have focused on other difficulties of size, such as individual entrepreneurs being able to accumulate enough funds. Thus Hobsbawm, in *Industry and Empire: An Economic History of Britain Since 1750,* has pointed out that in contrast to the British Industrial Revolution, where the techniques in use required small capital outlays and were therefore "within the capacities of a multiplicity of small entrepreneurs and skilled artisans, no twentieth-century country setting about industrialization has, or can have, anything like these advantages" (p. 25).
17. In the following chapter we shall discuss these linkages and the way they relate to planning as outlined in this study.
18. P. Sraffa, *Production of Commodities by Means of Commodities,* p. 8.
19. Ibid., pp. 51-52.
20. Ibid., p. 51.
21. In the penultimate section of this chapter we shall discuss the crucial role of the machine tools sector in this regard.
22. For further information see G. Dekker, "Climate and Water Resources."
23. See J. S. Bain, *Barriers to New Competition: Their Character and Consequences in Manufacturing Industry,* and J. Jewkes, "Are Economies of Scale Unlimited?"
24. See J. Baranson, "Automotive Industries in Developing Countries," and "Integrated Automobiles for Latin America."
25. See H. W. De Jong, "The Significance of Dumping in International Trade."

26. See I. Little and J. Mirrlees, *Manual of Industrial Project Analysis in Developing Countries.* We discuss shadow pricing in Chapter 7. It can be added here that the export pricing procedures of the industrialized socialist countries will also have to be evaluated empirically as their levels of trade with the Third World increase.
27. There are a number of studies which bring out these relationships. See Brewster and Thomas, *Dynamics of West Indian Economic Integration,* which presents a great deal of the information, as well as four United Nations studies: *A Study of the Iron and Steel Industry in Latin America, Pulp and Paper Prospects in Latin America, Pulp and Paper Prospects in Asia and the Far East, Pulp and Paper Prospects in Africa and the Near East.*
28. W. P. Travis, *The Theory of Trade and Protection,* Appendix II.
29. C. F. Pratten, "Economies of Scale for Machine Tool Production."
30. Ibid., p. 148.
31. Ibid., p. 150.
32. Ibid., p. 148. He points out that the Machine Tool Trade Association of Britain lists four hundred separate headings in its classification code.
33. Ibid. The other factors include flexibility, better supervision of quality, etc., in the smaller concerns.
34. Ibid., p. 165.
35. N. Rosenberg, "Technological Change in the Machine Tool Industry, 1840-1910," p. 422.
36. Chu-Yuan Chang, "Growth and Structural Change in the Chinese Machine-Building Industry, 1952-1966." The correlation between labor productivity and machine-building output was high indeed (R = 0.99).
37. W. P. Strassman, *Technological Change and Economic Development,* p. 226.
38. N. H. Leff, *The Brazilian Capital Goods Industry.*
39. Spulber, *Soviet Strategy for Economic Growth,* p. 76 (our emphasis).
40. Ibid., p. 142, n. 32.
41. Brewster and Thomas, *Dynamics of West Indian Economic Integration,* p. 145.
42. P. N. Dhar and H. Lydall, *The Role of Small Enterprises in Indian Development,* p. 19.
43. E. Staley and R. Morse, *Modern Small Industry for Developing Countries.*
44. Mandel, *Marxist Economic Theory,* p. 443.
45. Dobb, *Papers on Capitalism, Development and Planning,* p. 112.

7

Structural Interdependence, Pricing and Foreign Exchange

In this chapter we shall deal with three special topics which are important to our analysis of underdevelopment and the strategy of economic transformation. These are: (1) the relation of our concept of dynamic convergence of domestic needs—domestic demand—domestic resources and resource use—indigenous technology to the notion of structural interdependence as it has developed in the neoclassical economic literature; (2) the problem of determining the rationality of the price structure during the transition period; and (3) the crucial importance of foreign exchange to the small underdeveloped economy during the transition period. In the last two cases we shall also be touching on questions associated with the sequencing of production in terms of preferred industries.

Structural Interdependence: Planned or Market

As it has developed in economic literature, the idea of structural interdependence is straightforward.[1] Based on the "Leontief-type" input-output matrix, linkages can be measured backward or forward. Backward linkages are given as the proportion of intermediate consumption of the ith industry to its total output, so that:

$$\frac{\sum_{i=1}^{n} X_{ij}}{X_j}$$

where x_{ij} are inputs from the ith sector to the jth sector, n is the number of sectors, and X_j is the total output of sector j.

The forward linkages are given as the ratio of intermediate demand for the output of the given sector to the total supplies of that sector, so that:

$$\frac{\sum_{i=1}^{n} X_{ij}}{X_i + X_{is} + X_{mi}}$$

where X_{is} and X_{mi} are the changes of inventories in the ith sector and the imports of the ith sector output respectively. The limitation of using average measures and relying on direct input requirements, ignoring the indirect and secondary repercussions, was modified by Rasmussen. He defined backward linkage as the power of dispersion; so that:

$$U_j = \frac{\frac{1}{n} Z_j}{\frac{1}{n^2} \sum_{j=1}^{n} Z_j} \qquad \text{where } Z_j = \sum_{i=1}^{n} Z_{ij}$$

Z_{ij} being an element in the ith row and the jth column of the inverse matrix. U_j measures the extent of dispersion following on an increased final demand for the product of industry j. By analogy the forward linkage is:

$$U_i = \frac{\frac{1}{n} Z_i}{\frac{1}{n^2} \sum_{i=1}^{n} Z_i} \qquad \text{where } Z_i = \sum_{j=1}^{n} Z_{ij}$$

Comparing these measures with the propositions advanced in this study, it will be seen that in our analysis the interdependence sought within the national economy is the dynamic interaction of natural resource availability, its use, indigenous technology, production, demand, and needs. These basic relationships express the *primum mobile* of planned transformation. As such, they are both wider in their ramifications and more basic to planning than those which one can expect to find in a private market economy, where interdependence is greatly influenced by the structure of competition, the degree of concentration of industrial ownership, the vertical and horizontal integration of production, the extent of the market, and the particular ways in which monopoly power is used.

Given the way these features of the economic system impinge on linkages, it follows that the engine of expansion in this market economy context centers on the scope and manner in which input/output linkages lead to *inducements by way of increased profitable opportunities*, which are in turn expected to generate increased private initiatives in one sector leading to a logical sequencing of output in other sectors (backward or forward), because the scope for further initiatives has increased. In our proposition it is clear that the inducement element is not very significant. In the context of comprehensive planning the priority of exploring these linkages through planning must be accepted as axiomatic from the outset. Therefore they must be systematically, not randomly, developed. The rate of expansion of output and the consequent linkages are thus governed by social resource availability and not private profit calculations.

In other words, what we are seeking to maximize in the first stages of transformation is the relationship between changes in needs and changes in per capita demand for goods and services, on the one hand, and changes in per capita demand for goods and services and the rate of change in the value added locally (to which production to satisfy the demand gives rise), on the other. Both relationships will have to be weighted by the extent to which the value added is created by the intensive use of domestic and not foreign natural resources. In view of this, the second element of the two ratios can be expressed as follows:

$$r \cdot \left(\frac{dv}{v} / \frac{dy}{y} \right)$$

where r is equal to the ratio of domestic basic material resources used in production, v is the value added in industry, and y is the per capita product. It is obvious that in practice this value will vary with: (1) the ratio of home expenditure to total expenditure, (2) the levels of capacity use, (3) the degree of efficiency, and (4) the pattern of resource utilization—in addition to other less important factors. The important point is that we should not look for a "key" sector, or a specific industry, to set a chain of linked investments in motion, but should attempt to elaborate analytically the foundations of the investment program. We might add that *after* the economy is transformed and industrial exports no longer constitute a bottleneck, the second stages of transformation will require that changes in demand include overseas purchases of local output.

Many of the industrial activities discussed above require economic processes which, on the basis of empirical data, seem to be intensive in their use of machines and equipment as compared to labor. But it has already been noted that this might well be true of other major activities, such as primary agricultural exports, which are prevalent in many of these underdeveloped economies, as well as of domestic foodstuff production in those countries with "successful" agriculture. This shift to new techniques of production is therefore one of the requirements of transformation that cannot be bypassed and the issue cannot be tackled, except marginally, through such favored neoclassical approaches as factor price adjustment. As we have argued at some length, the choice of technique is largely determined by the choice of product and the program of investment. The scope for factor substitution does not realistically appear to be wide. There are therefore only two further points which are worth making on this score. One is that industry and agriculture as we have discussed them so far do not exploit the full range of the investment program. An important area of "needs" still has to be met, and in the next chapter we will see what bearing this will have on the employment question, since in a planned economy the full use of the labor force is taken as a given.

The other point, one which we made earlier, is that preoccupation with labor/output ratios may mask one important absolute measure. One advantage of small economies in which there is an employment problem, is that the size of the country often means that in absolute terms its labor force is also small. Consider what this implies in a country where, for example, a number of industrial complexes are to be established producing basic materials, with its own (albeit limited) machine sector. In this situation the absolute size of employment in these sectors becomes large *relative* to the total labor force. This means that it is possible to expose quite rapidly a large percentage of the labor force to highly technical and modern industrial processes.

Thus we see that except insofar as there are technical relationships of an input-output nature to be observed in all production processes, there is little real similarity between our notion of dynamic convergence and the ideas of structural interdependence *à la* Hirschman, which merely combine the technical input-output relations in all production processes with incentives and inducements to invest. In our approach these empirically determined relationships are merely one element in a comprehensive strategy of transformation.

Prices as Politics: Shadow Price and Rational Price

We cannot in this section pretend to a comprehensive and detailed treatment of the problem of pricing during the transition. This is a very important issue, one which relates not only to such fundamental theoretical problems as the relationship of prices to value, but to others of a much more practical nature, such as the role of markets, calculating the effectiveness of investments, and the relationship of domestic prices to international prices—which, in an open dependent economy, is obviously of particular significance. What we shall try to do in this section is to raise some general issues in direct and indirect support of the following major propositions that seem to govern the transition period:

1. Planning must lead to the elimination of spontaneous price formation.

2. Prices must be seen as an instrument of economic policy and not as an end in themselves.

3. Given the structural changes which occur during the transition, the measurements of "objective valuations" which presently dominate the East European literature and which are based on programming techniques are unsuitable.

4. As an extension of the above, in the absence of a basic materials sector there can be no basis for a truly "rational" pricing except insofar as it is an expression of political priorities.

Since the October Revolution, controversy over the theory and practice of price formation during the transition period has always played a vital role in both neoclassical and Marxian theories of political economy. Indeed, it was the Austrian economist Von Mises who opened up the modern phase of the debate in 1920 when, in his famous attack on socialism, he argued that as an economic system it was bound to be an irrational one, since it had no means of establishing a rational basis for pricing resources. His argument was based on the premise that prices can only be established during an act of exchange, and that such exchanges necessarily presuppose the existence of a market for resources. It is only the relative prices of the means of production which prevail in the market that can be the true indicators of relative scarcities. As a consequence, only decisions based on these prices can guarantee rationality in resource use.

Later economists in the same tradition, such as Von Hayek and Robbins, had to modify this argument since the neoclassical theory of general equilibrium had in fact conceded that prices could be determined outside of a market. This could be done by a system of equations, provided the necessary information on technology, consumer preference, and the amount of resources were available. If, as it was generally conceded, under central and comprehensive planning the required information would be available, it followed that in theory a planned economy could be a rational one. Their objections then shifted to the *practical* difficulties. They argued that such a system of equations would not only be too complex to be solved but that even if an actual solution could be discovered the lag in the process of solving these equations, transmitting the solutions to decision-makers for a decision, and implementing the decisions arrived at would compound each other, making it impossible in practice to rely on these as a basis for allocation of resources.

Lange was the first major socialist economist to respond to these arguments. Since the theoretical possibility of a rational pricing system could easily be demonstrated conclusively, he concentrated on providing what was in effect a practical response to the practical issue. His solution was based on publicly owned enterprises, which were decentralized in their decision-making processes and competing with each other for resources on the basis of rules laid down by a central planning authority. In effect, these rules were the rules of perfect competition. Lange argued that this procedure would allow for a practical trial-and-error approach to the problem of determining a rational pricing structure.

A number of weaknesses to this approach have repeatedly been pointed out in the literature. Lange sought to reproduce a market, but in so doing he failed to recognize that there can be no *true* independence of decision-making as regards resource acquisition and use if in fact all the means of production are publicly owned! The proposed solution therefore embraced the worst of both possible worlds, since it not only gave up the advantages of centralized decision-making as regards resource use in the period of transition (and thus retained some of the anarchy of the market), but it also sought to have price formation determined by supply-demand adjustments through time, thereby arriving at prices as an *ex post* solution.

Later Dobb was to take up this point quite forcibly by contrasting market coordination of resource use as an *ex post* occurrence, and the waste it necessarily implied, with the advantages of *ex ante* planning of the size and allocation of the social surplus. Such planning ruled out the underutilization of resources which occurred during the fluctuations of economic activity characteristic of capitalism, while at the same time permitting a rational and comprehensive approach to the question of resource allocation. Thus, planning was to be preferred because it made far more efficient accumulation possible and permitted a more comprehensive approach to the basic issues of transforming the economic structure. Dobb was of course downgrading the significance of optimizing the use of given resources, and consequently the importance of marginalism in the approach to economic development during the transition period.

At this point we can make one very important observation: in *practice* the problem of rational pricing in the Soviet Union was resolved not through the creation of institutions which replicated the market, as Lange first suggested, but through comprehensive planning and an administrative approach to price formation which tended to reflect the political priorities, social costs, and resources available at that time. It is obvious that these, by their very nature, could not have been static and fixed. Indeed, as we know, economic development has taken place at a rapid rate, so that it would be logical to expect that the practice of price formation would, through time, be subject to further changes. Today, these developments are reflected in the shift in theoretical interest, which now focuses on problems of optimization and marginalism. This can be seen in the work of such Soviet economists as Nemchinov, Kantorovich, and Novozhilov.[3]

In view of this relationship of practice and theory, we would like to advance the proposition that the present theoretical preoccupations of Soviet economists are largely the direct products of the transformation that the economic system of the Soviet Union (as indeed that of Eastern Europe) has undergone since the establishment of socialism. *It is only because such a transformation has taken place that the problems of rational pricing can be conceivably and realistically approached in terms of marginalization and the optimization of given resource use.*

As the socialist economies have become industrialized and transformed, and as their output has become highly differentiated, thereby requiring a complex range of decisions, they have found that problems of optimization and rationality of given resource use multiply, while the problems of major structural adjustments recede. These require both new theoretical and practical bases for a rational pricing system.

These processes have been favored by two factors. The first has been the rapid development of computer technology and the second has been the tendency toward greater decentralization and independence among enterprises—the latter in part a product of the growing complexity of economic activities, as well as a reflection of pressures for greater democracy and participation in national life. Together they have reinforced each other by providing the operational basis for the stress and importance attached to programming techniques and the search for solutions of optimal plan fulfillment.

In these approaches, optimal prices are derived as the solution of the "dual" in programming—i.e., the price ratios which lead to minimization of resource use as one objective, and the maximization of output as the other. As such they have been described as the "objectively determined valuations" which represent the "significance of the different resources to plan fulfillment." The construction of optimal prices and an optimal overall plan are therefore seen as two sides of the same minimax problem, while the solution of these prices for a large number of processes presupposes computer-type operations.

It is important to note that these programming techniques are essentially aimed at short-period problems. As Kantorovich has observed, "The planning and allocation problems envisaged here relate to comparatively short periods of time (a year, a quarter, a month)."[4] Because of this, these techniques cannot be relied on to provide "rational" prices in situations where investments take a long time to gestate *and* where, because of the structural impact of these investments, external costs and benefits are large relative to direct costs and benefits. Given this, it would be extremely foolish to treat the *present* preoccupations of Soviet and East European economists as indicative of the pricing requirements of an underdeveloped economy during the transition period. Furthermore, these economies will not only be faced with haphazard and unrealistic price relations inherited from the previous order, but with the *absence of a basic materials sector, making it impossible to put a "rational" domestic resource valuation on domestic output.*

We are not concerned with presenting these theoretical developments in the industrialized socialist economies for their own sake. But an examination of certain features of both the theory and practice of pricing indicates the nature of the interaction between the two and is thus of great relevance to our understanding of the problems of pricing during the transition period. Accordingly, we shall make a few brief observations at this stage.

The first is that planning in all these countries has been generally successful in eliminating spontaneous price formation during the transition period. This has been accomplished despite the fact that planning has been accompanied by a system of broadly market-determined pricing for consumer goods and small commodity producers, mainly in the rural economy. This shows that the *fundamental* issues of rational pricing center on the *appropriate valuation of the means of production.* Second, their experiences have shown that prices do not necessarily coincide with values during the transition. Indeed, when, in the earlier periods of their development, material balances were used as the system for testing the consistency of production plans, prices were in effect being virtually disregarded *in favor of the priority of rapid structural adjustment and increases in the physical output of cer-*

tain basic goods. Third, their experiences have shown that prices as such do not, and indeed are often not expected to, *determine the allocation of resources.* They have merely been tools and instruments in attempts to arrive at efficient resource use. All the major economic decisions in these societies—such as the consumption/investment ratio, the major types of industry to be set up, and planned proportional development—have been made, in practice, largely on the basis of social and political criteria and not on that of "objective valuations" or the labor theory of value.

Finally, the recent stress on programming techniques can be seen in their actual use and the attempts to develop a network of modal computer centers in each of the socialist countries. For the 1966-1970 plan in Hungary, 43 plan variants were calculated; in the USSR, 20 cost variants were considered in the 1970 interbranch balances and 15 variants in the physical units.[5]

These features of socialist pricing practice should not be interpreted to mean that in the early stages of transformation these countries have used inefficient pricing methods *because the present programming techniques were not then in widespread use. The efficiency of a technique is relative.* There were inefficiencies of resource use, but basically all the major inefficiencies were integral to the problems generated by efforts at economic transformation. *They could not, during the transition period, have been solved by the methods and techniques of achieving efficiency in the post-transformation period.*

When we carry our discussion to the present context of underdevelopment, there should be no great difficulty in evaluating these observations as they relate to pricing in the underdeveloped economies. In these countries, the actual problems encountered have not focused on combining a rational pricing system with comprehensive planning (i.e., the two sides of the same coin of optimal plan fulfillment and objective valuations). This has been so simply because comprehensive planning does not exist in these countries. Instead, the focus has been on determining rational prices, or shadow prices, for the current valuation of state-aided investment projects, which are only a part of total investment outlay. As we previously pointed out, these investment projects have often been simply aggregated after their "efficiency" has been established on the basis of project selection of this sort. These aggregate investments constitute the plan. In view of this, the impact of the valuation procedures which they use is not confined to the projects they are directly applied to, but to the overall planning strategy of the state as well.

Of course, in the socialist economies shadow prices are also used as a guide to the valuation of investment projects. As in the underdeveloped countries, these shadow prices have often remained shadows, in that they are not usually the prices actually paid—although some economists, notably Kantorovich, have argued that they should be the prices in actual use to bring about a situation where the enterprise and its norms of functioning are a microcosm of the optimal national plan. If these enterprises can in fact become true microcosms, the optimal plan is the summation of individual enterprise plans. But even at a theoretical level, such optimality can only be achieved this way if the economic system is already transformed and the efficiency of given resource use is taken to be the dominant form of expanding material output. Clearly, such a situation is completely unrelated to the prevailing context of underdevelopment.

In the previous chapter we discussed problems of project evaluation and pointed out the logical impossibility of devising an efficient plan on the basis of the simple aggregation of a number of projects which have been derived in this way. In the present context, we are therefore not considering those issues that concern the use of cost-benefit studies *after* they have been completed; instead we are seeking to focus on the technical and computational basis of valuing outputs and inputs in the *preparation* of projects, on the assumption that market prices as they exist are irrational because the market itself is defective.[6] One approach to solving this problem that has gained considerable acceptance, and that we mentioned in the previous chapter, is the Little/Mirrlees procedure for shadow pricing.[7] Confronting the difficulties of deriving "objective valuations" in situations where existing markets are inefficient and defective, Little and Mirrlees suggested valuing all inputs and outputs at their frontier prices—i.e., at the prices at which the goods can be traded in the world market. Where the goods in use are not traded, appropriate techniques are indicated for valuing these nontrading inputs. The essential principle of this form of valuation is that every decision to utilize a national resource is, in rational terms, a choice between buying the resource abroad or making it at home; the objective is clearly maximization of output on the basis of given resources. In other words, we have here the basic comparative cost principle of international specialization. Such a procedure observes the Pareto optimal rule—that the marginal social cost of each good must be equal to the world price of that good in order to take into account the fact that a country has the opportunity of transforming its resources through international trade. This is clearly a restatement of the fact that a country has the option to use resources to produce for home use, to produce for export, or to produce imports, and that the exercise of this option on this principle maximizes global income at the level of given global resource use.

If such a principle did generally guide the pricing of inputs and outputs in project selection in the typical underdeveloped economy, then it would certainly mean that *investments in these economies must, to be efficient, satisfy the test of transformation through trade.* Given the prevailing level of restrictions on trade, such a procedure is in effect implying an even more total integration of the country into the world economy than at present. But, as things stand, it is precisely the present degree and pattern of integration of these economies in the international system that provides the dynamic base for generating and sustaining their underdevelopment characteristics. Inevitably, therefore, we would expect to find that few if any of the industrial and agricultural priorities listed above can be proven "efficient" on the basis of these static principles of comparative cost. The patterns of resource flow which are likely to emerge are those which strengthen the present divorce between domestic resource use and domestic demand (needs).

This problem of domestic resource transformation through international trade emerged in the early stages of transformation of the industrialized socialist economies. The solution they arrived at, and correctly so, was to disregard existing world prices. The interest these countries presently display in world prices and the domestic transformation of their resources through trade has followed *after* they have developed a domestic capacity to participate in the world economy without themselves being systematically subjected to exploitation through unequal exchange. It would therefore be highly unrealistic to expect that an underdeveloped economy in transition can be guided by the *present practices of the industrialized socialist states, or indeed any practice derived from the existing global distribution of income and production.*

An observation similar to this was made by Preobrazhensky in his discussion of the period of primitive socialist accumulation:

> We have selling prices which are much higher than those that obtain abroad [but] in the entire period of this accumulation they will be much higher than foreign prices—and that is the essence of the matter. We accumulate only on the basis of struggle against the world law of value, although the dimensions of nonequivalence gradually decline, which is the aim of our policy, to be attained precisely through accumulation.[8]

From all this it follows that there are, and indeed can be, no short-cut approaches to the derivation of a rational pricing structure during the period of economic transformation. Prices will have to reflect political priorities, social constraints, available resources, and the basic choices that are made among the alternative priorities. A rational pricing system has to be construed, therefore, as an instrument of social progress and not as an objective in itself. As such, operationally, its rationality cannot be divorced from the nature of the particular society and the sorts of problems which confront it.

Foreign Exchange and Industrial Sequencing

The difficulties attached to the use of such instruments of allocation as the world price of traded and nontraded products, the domestic market, and "objective valuations" derived from the programming of the optimal plan in determining the sequencing and patterning of investments during the transition period are still further complicated when the role of foreign exchange is correctly assessed. In the case of industrial investments, it is obvious that one of the major constraints affecting the allocation and sequencing of these investments is the availability of investment funds. While these funds are derived from the surplus product (i.e., that part of current output not needed for consumption), theoretically these can become available as surpluses generated in the industrial sector being ploughed back into industry, as surpluses generated in agriculture being transferred from agriculture to industry, or through foreign exchange earned from the export sector (mainly through the sale of traditional commodities) being directed to industry. Frequently in the socialist literature, the major concentration is on the two former categories—i.e., the size of the surplus generated locally—because the economic models in use are not as "open" as the ones we are considering here.

One of the most characteristic features of the underdeveloped economy is the extent to which most of the machinery, plant, equipment, materials, and know-how in *present use*—and therefore the means of maintaining *the current levels of expansion* of the economy—are imported from abroad. Now, we also know that this importation does not simply reflect the influences of product differentiation—i.e., it is not simply a preference for foreign over domestic supplies of these products, as would be the case for similar purchases in the developed industrial economies. Instead, it indicates the basic incapacity of the economy to transform its domestic resources into required capital goods. This limited substitutability between domestic output and imports reveals that there is a category of goods which is crucial to maintaining the prevailing levels of industrial expansion but which is at the same time more or less not producible at home. Such a situation would represent, in the early stages of the transition, an *inherited level of foreign exchange that must be earned if the economy is to follow its optimum expansion path for the prevailing resource structure in use.* The greater this constraint (i.e., the lower the elasticity of domestic output of these commodities), the more crucial will be the role of foreign exchange in determining the prevailing levels and rate of growth of domestic output.

It can readily be deduced that in addition to these inherited foreign exchange requirements which condition the rate of expansion of the present domestic resource structure, the strategy of new investments we have proposed also creates additional requirements for foreign exchange—because the newer processes, equipment, skills, etc., which are required may *initially* have to be imported. Furthermore, if, despite efforts to the contrary, domestic output of foodstuffs falls below the needed requirements of the population, then additional foreign exchange will be required to finance food imports during the early stages of transition. These foreign exchange requirements, while they express the basic limitations of the existing economic structures, are not of course unalterably fixed. Indeed, our entire strategy depends on the premise that domestic resources will be developed in order to increase the substitutability between domestic output and the types of imports which characterize the untransformed economy. But in practice these developments inevitably will *take some time.* The result is that initially, and paradoxically, *our strategy entails the expansion of the "not-producible-at-home" category of goods.* It follows that earnings and use of foreign exchange become intimately intertwined in the process of transition. At the level of planning, these will be clearly revealed by the gaps in the material balances matrix—the gap between input requirements and the output of the home market.

In such situations foreign exchange is not to be interpreted as simply foreign savings brought in to supplement the domestic surplus, but is in fact required as an *indispensable complement* to local savings. It is the *necessary condition for filling the gap between domestic inputs and domestic output requirements.* In this situation an exclusive preoccupation with the size of the domestic surplus available during the transition period would be incorrect, since if the necessary foreign exchange required to purchase inputs which cannot be produced at home is not available, the domestic factors cannot be transformed into the physical and technical requirements of our strategy. It is in this sense, therefore, that we pointed out earlier that the size of the surplus available is an insufficient indicator of the rate at which transformation can take place. It has to be weighted by the foreign exchange content of the indicated investments and the sequencing of foreign exchange earnings.

In this context effective import substitution requires that the values of the inputs *necessary* in order to enable the new industries to operate efficiently (i.e., the capital equipment for initial construction *and* other foreign inputs required for the operation of the project) have to be less than the value of imports which would have entered into the country during the lifetime of the project. If they are less, the sequencing of the given industrial investments *is in no way constrained by the foreign exchange test, the general case for the industry, as a domestic activity, having already been established in our earlier arguments.* If the foreign exchange required is more than the effective saving of the project, then foreign exchange costs play a crucial role in sequencing the flow of projects.

There is, in addition to this, a summation problem, because if all industries satisfy the above criteria, a foreign exchange problem might still follow, if we take into account the various time lags in the construction of projects and the commencement of production. During the construction phase, imports, and hence foreign exchange expenditure connected with the project, will initially rise at a faster rate than the savings in foreign exchange expenditure. (These issues are directly related to the problems of reserve adequacy and reserve management in the context of central planning, but are beyond the immediate scope of this study.)

Consideration of these issues leads us to a most sensitive issue—the role of foreign aid during the transition period. The only way to bring some clarity to the discussion of this question is if we bear certain important considerations clearly in mind. First, it can rightly be argued that, *other things being equal,* an augmentation of domestic resources by foreign resource inflows is in theory one way of speeding up the domestic rate of growth and the transformation process. However, the truth is that in practice other things are never equal. Indeed, *we have pointedly argued* that in the present situation of these economies, foreign capital inflows have served to reduce the rate of domestic accumulation, to extend the role of foreign ownership, foreign techniques, and foreign decision-making in the national economy, and in many other ways to perpetuate underdevelopment. In the context of the transition, the question therefore arises *whether socialist aid irrespective of the intentions of the donors and the recipients* can avoid the manifestation of other malformations.

The second point is that, in practice, foreign aid in most underdeveloped economies *already plays a crucial role* in the growth process. Even in a "transitional" state such as Tanzania, foreign aid—most of it from China—has accounted for over 50 percent of the government's development expenditure over recent years. Thus we find that the prevailing levels of actual dependence on foreign aid are already very high.

Third, our own strategy of transformation stresses domestic resources being brought into use to satisfy domestic needs. The main propulsive elements of expansion are clearly to be focused on the internal system, and foreign aid cannot be as important as the domestic surplus in making resources available. Where foreign aid and foreign exchange become *particularly* crucial is in *the knowledge of techniques and processes that are initially required* and are not available at home. Selective importation of these, and local adaptation to resources and needs (as the examples of China and Japan show) may be the only practical basis for initiating the early phases of indigenous technological development.

Fourth, the question of foreign aid always has to be evaluated in terms of the domestic alternatives. Foreign aid, if it induces a dynamic process of dependency and *extensive reliance on foreign technology of whatever sort, is clearly unacceptable to our strategy.* As we have argued, the technologies of all the present-day industrial economies have grown and logically responded to their own resources and to their own domestic needs. For any country to be extensively reliant on such a technology, even that of other socialist countries, would clearly represent a failure to develop an indigenous technology as the organic link between domestic resources and domestic needs. Thus the main cornerstone of our strategy would be removed.

To the extent, therefore, that foreign aid is required, the preferences clearly ought to be for knowledge of the processes and techniques initially required to produce the basic materials and the basic goods of the society. But such processes, techniques, and plants are to be relied upon only as *initial* ways of starting production. The subsequent dynamic developments must follow from the creative movement from simple selection to adaptation to local requirements, and thence to innovation. This can only occur in the context of an explicit strategy which focuses on local resources for local use in serving local needs.

Whatever final political choice is made concerning foreign aid from the socialist bloc, it should be borne in mind that in general a dependence on the socialist bloc will be directly influenced by the size of the gap between required and domestically available technology and the initial inelasticity of output on the basis of domestic resource use, of the transforming sectors. For such assistance to be of maximum benefit, therefore, it is important that *the activities to which it is directed do not require as a long-term and permanent feature foreign exchange outflows to maintain the transformation process.* In our strategy these are minimized insofar as practicable because the major investment criterion is intensity in the use of domestic resources. The obverse of this criterion is the minimization of the foreign exchange content of domestic expenditure. As a rider, we can add that significance of the foreign exchange constraint will be reduced as the servicing costs of the loans are lowered—i.e., the lower the rates of interest to be charged and the longer the repayment period.

In this regard it is clear that the already industrialized socialist countries can be of great strategic importance in supporting disengagement from capitalism, economic transformation, and the sequencing of investments. However, it is important that if they are to achieve their objectives such a strategic advantage should not permit the development of dependent relationships *growing out of the sheer disparities in size, technological efficiencies, and resource availabilities.* These can only be avoided if the planning frame is as outlined above. It is only in this situation that foreign assistance does not promote dependence, but contributes strategic additions to local resources in order to promote transformation.

In conclusion we make two observations. First, the problems raised here help to highlight the profound interdependence of trade, foreign exchange management, and technological know-how. The trade structure, with all its distortions, is but a manifestation of the wider and more basic deformed structure of the economy. Despite this, the existing trade structure continues to play a crucial role in the early phases of transformation, which indicates that the planning of external economic relationships is one of the most fundamental and immediate tasks to be tackled. The impact of this of course varies with the de facto technological gap and the prevailing domestic inelasticity of output in the transforming sectors. Among the existing small underdeveloped economies, this variation appears to be not insignificant.

Second, with regard to the sequencing of investments, it

should be mentioned again—largely to reassure the "practical men of affairs"—that while our discussion has taken place on a theoretical level, we are not suggesting an outright abandonment of the techniques of project selection as a decision aid. The techniques of project selection have their obvious, if limited, uses. Projects have to satisfy efficiency criteria. They have to be weighted for their foreign exchange, employment, and income effects, etc. Given the pattern of demand and the range of materials which have to be produced, the search is clearly for priorities within this particular vector of possibilities. But such priorities cannot be established independent of the final uses to which the base materials are to be put. The result is that the regulation and control of demand becomes integrated into the whole question of project choice. An *independent weight* must be given to the economic configuration which is being established. In this sense, project analysis is objective—not because it is neutral, as the neoclassicists argue, but because it conforms to the objective of economic transformation. The choice of project is *teleologically* linked to the economic structure which it is intended to establish.

Notes

1. See A. Hirschman, *The Strategy of Economic Development*, and P. N. Rasmussen, *Studies in Inter-Sectoral Relations.*
2. For some of the main literature see F. A. Von Hayek, ed., *Collectivist Economic Planning;* O. Lange and F. Taylor, *On the Economic Theory of Socialism;* M. Dobb, *Welfare Economics and the Economics of Socialism,* chapter 9.
3. See L. V. Kantorovich, *The Best Use of Economic Resources,* and V. U. Novozhilov, *Problems of Measuring Outlays and Results Under Optimal Planning.*
4. Kantorovich, ibid., p. 122.

5. Data cited in J. Wilczynski, *The Economics of Socialism*, p. 41.
6. There is of course some interaction between eventual uses and the method of calculation.
7. I. Little and J. Mirrlees, *Manual of Industrial Project Analysis.*
8. E. Preobrazhensky, *The New Economics*, p. 297.

8

Converging Needs with Demand: The Second "Iron Law" of Transformation

So far in our discussion of economic strategy, we have established the need for certain lines of action to ensure the progressive convergence of the pattern and structure of domestic demand, domestic production, indigenous technology, and domestic resource use. Since the circular relation of production-consumption-production holds in every economic system, it remains for us to conclude our discussion of economic strategy by examining some of the major issues involved in seeking a progressive convergence of the demand structure of the community to its needs.

Needs and Demand

Insofar as in economies based on specialization—and more so in fully developed capitalist market economies—consumer demand largely expresses the actual purchasing power in the possession of individuals, it is obvious that where there are such distortions of the economic system as highly skewed income distributions, private ownership of the means of production (together with the usual inheritance laws which perpetuate this), private appropriation of the social product, etc., demand in this sense will not always adequately express the needs of the people in that society. Indeed, in the rich industrialized capitalist economies, despite the high levels of private product per capita, one glaring manifestation of this is often found in the so-called paradox of "private affluence and public squalor."

In this connection, experience seems to have shown that as further and further increases in the absolute levels of per capita income take place in the industrialized capitalist countries, and as the spread of material output widens to encompass more and more of their population, it is likely that the contemporaneously determined subsistence requirements available to the population at large will tend to rise. The result is that, despite marked sectors of deprivation (e.g., black minorities in the United States), people become, by and large, free from crude physical deficiencies of protein, health care, clothing, shelter, and recreation. In poor economies, rising per capita product has not significantly reduced the immiseration of the vast bulk of the population. While it is true that pockets of high-level consumption exist, and that almost all of the cities in these desperately poor countries are characterized by islands of incomparable affluence and ostentation, nevertheless the societies are marked by the acute divergence between the basic needs of the population at large and consumption expenditure. This divergence not only reflects the inequities of income distribution, as would be expected, but also the low levels of absolute income per capita, thereby signifying the considerable underdevelopment of these countries' productive forces.

These juxtaposed social realities have been accompanied by tendencies toward the progressive homogenization of consumption patterns within the industrial economies. In the last few decades these tendencies have been stimulated by extensive spending by firms in the capitalist center on advertising and promotion around the world. Inevitably, the well-to-do of the underdeveloped economies have been drawn into this web of increasing socialization of consumption patterns, and have in turn transmitted these influences to the local population through their own life-styles—a development further aided by the flood of "similar" local advertisements and promotional techniques. As the multinational firms have expanded their operations locally, they have tended to establish a "local sales program," little more than a slight adaptation to the local scene, using black and brown faces instead of white in the same advertisements.

We have so far devoted relatively little attention to the problems involved in attempting to interpret the community's needs. Yet this is obviously of fundamental importance for the efficient and equitable planning of the demand structure. The reason for this omission is quite obvious: the concrete historical situation confronting each state and its planning machinery demands the creation of unique mechanisms for determining this. There can be no dogmatic solution to such a problem, since it is largely in the manner and form of its consumption that a society expresses its values, beliefs, prejudices, and fears. Therefore, given the considerable interaction of noneconomic factors in determining consumption, this inevitably has to become the area of analysis and strategy least susceptible to purely theoretical analysis or to specific suggestions.

Given the requirements for a specific social interpretation of needs, it follows that the mechanisms for interpreting a community's needs can and will involve varied degrees of democratic participation in their application. But between the two extremes of infallible bureaucratic fiat and the cajoling, manipulation, and consequent exploitation of weaknesses which characterize capitalist methods of advertising, methods must be found to satisfy the requirements of both planning and individual taste. Our own preferences are for the maximum public participation and democracy in framing the society's consumption patterns. This can be achieved outside of the *laissez-faire* approach to the market as an allocative device, but success with alternative methods, which follow upon the relegation of the market to a subsidiary role, depends not only on quick decisions to abolish the obvious inequities of the market, but also on the strength and ability of the political process to involve people in the forms of distribution which replace market dominance.

Despite the obvious limitations on any prescriptions which can be made outside of a specific historical and cultural situation, it is still possible to generalize from historical experiences about some of the broader priorities that are likely to emerge, and we shall attempt a few such generalizations later.

Toward Public Consumption

In our strategy, planning of consumption requires simultaneous operations on at least three different levels. First, basic materials have to be planned in relation to the basic goods required, as we have already indicated. The main planning decisions involved here are what basic materials are to be used in relation to the basic goods required, conditioned by the extent and nature of resource availability and by the cultural preferences of the community. Thus the same basic good—e.g., housing—can be made with wood or cement, aluminum or steel, clay or glass. To be efficient, planning choices have to reflect both domestic resource availability and the cultural traditions of the community in the construction and design of the places people live.

We have also touched upon the second necessary level of planning of consumption. This relates to the determination of the size of the consumption fund in relation to production and accumulation. Such a decision requires efficient planning choices about: (1) the overall savings ratio, (2) the size of the wages fund, (3) the planning of price levels to ensure that the total value of goods and services is equal to the purchasing power of the consumers, and (4) the establishment of regulatory procedures which ensure that balance in individual markets is preserved. The normal practice would be for this to be achieved through price variations and manipulation of turnover taxes imposed between production and retail prices. Such regulatory provisions require a considerable independence of retail price formation and producer prices. This separation of the two areas of economic activity is the only way the country can avoid the transmission of the powerful influences of the retail market onto the investment program.

The third level at which the planning of consumption has to take place is in the determination of the *desired composition* of final consumption goods and services. It is frequently not fully realized to what extent planning at this level is related *to the manner in which consumption goods are made available.* We have previously indicated that, given the basic scarcities which will most definitely continue during the transition period, some form of market for retail goods and services will also have to exist. In practice, if and when this does occur it will further become necessary for the bulk of the community's income to be distributed individually—i.e., in the form of money wage payments. Once the economic system is thus organized, *individual incomes and individual choices will be in a position to exercise quite considerable influence on the manner of distribution of final goods and services.*

Under these sorts of economic arrangements, many of the characteristics of distribution in the pre-transition period will be carried over. Furthermore, it is exceedingly likely—as indeed experiences in Eastern Europe have so far demonstrated—that such a system of individual wage payments, combined with the exercise of private influence on the composition of consumption goods, can only be sustained by the extensive use of material incentives. These incentives are usually directed at improving the quality of individual effort, which, under these arrangements, is held to be the main basis for improving labor productivity. The result is that *need,* which is basic to the socialist ideal as a distributive principle, becomes relegated to the background.

These developments are not surprising, resulting as they do from certain logical and social imperatives. Thus, if society finds it necessary to operate a system of material incentives as the principal means of improving labor effort and efficiency, then for the monetary rewards offered by the various enterprises and approved by the state to be attractive, they will have to be matched by the availability of consumption goods and the smooth operation of the principle of allowing extensive consumption to take place, as a matter of private choice. Similarly, if we reason from the other end, when private choices determine the composition of consumption, and where these choices are exercised through the market, then *incentives of a material kind are necessary if the consumer is to be able to improve his own level of material welfare in that society.*

Now, it is very important for us to be realistic in considering this very basic and fundamental contradiction of societies in transition. Decentralization, direct democracy in consumption, maintaining the level of accumulation necessary to effect a transformation of the economic structure, added to a situation where consumption goods are scarce, will always require some form of market and money wage system through which the distribution of final products will take place. *It is impossible to conceive of a workable alternative which will attain all these objectives simultaneously in the context of scarcity.* The existence of a retail market and a labor market are the only ways in which supply-demand balances of this sort can be maintained. It is true that the existence of a population which is highly motivated politically would reduce the importance of these considerations, but the question still remains as to how direction is to be given to implement the consensus arrived at, even by the most highly aware population. The correct answer to these problems cannot be allowed to be an emotional objection to the market and material incentives, etc. Rather, it is necessary to devise ways of planning which will enable a society *to minimize the impact of the market, private incomes, and private choices on the manner and form of distribution of final products.*

Certain elements of the planning process tend in this direction. First, in the context of comprehensive planning, decisions about the overall savings/consumption ratio of a society are usually made at the highest and most general social and political levels. As a consequence, the direct influences of the market in determining these macroquantities are usually minimal. Second, the same can be said about the determination of the size of the wage fund and hence the total output of consumption goods. The experience in socialist countries has been for these sorts of decisions to be the result of a complicated and drawn-out process of social and political interaction. Third, the absence of private property and the removal of private sources of substantial unearned incomes (which follow on the socialization of the major means of production) eliminate the most important bases of income differential, as experiences in capitalist countries show.

In addition, these basic policy decisions are not only usually made outside the frame of reference of the market and therefore generally in response to social and political objectives, but they are also combined with progressive policies aimed at narrowing the spread of earned incomes. Thus, while it is true that incentive payments, etc., tend to lead to disparities in income levels because of the operation of the labor market, there is in these societies a consciousness of the need to undertake deliberate policies to prevent significant disparities: in the Soviet Union, for instance, official policy has strongly supported deliberate efforts to narrow the range of wage differentials.

The general effect of policies of this sort is to set in train powerful social tendencies toward the minimization of the area of effective influence of the market. In addition, there is one further policy measure of immense strategic importance which can be applied: *the progressive generalization of the principle of collective or social consumption*, by which we mean the provision of more and more goods and services to satisfy the community's needs, in such a manner as to make the price of commodities and hence the level of individual consumption unrelated to the cost of goods and services.

In neoclassical welfare theory, consumer satisfaction is maximized when the marginal rate of substitution in the consumption of commodities by the consumer is equal to the price ratios of the commodities. Until the consumer reaches this position, his or her satisfaction can be increased through rearrangement of consumption patterns, and this constitutes the rational basis for giving the consumer *free choice*. It is only through such *free choice* that the maximization of consumer welfare will be assured. If the maximization of individual welfare coincides with the maximization of social welfare in the community (because there is no divergence between private and social marginal rates of substitution and private and social costs), the community has achieved its optimal consumption pattern. The case for *free choice* as a condition of maximizing welfare has received considerable support in the literature. As Dobb has pointed out:

> We have seen in our discussion of *optimum* conditions that there is a *prima facie* case on welfare grounds, first for allowing consumers to spend their incomes freely and without restriction, because in this way individual variations in tastes and in wants will obtain the fullest satisfaction, given the pattern of supply and of prices confronting them . . . [This proposition] is fairly obvious, and is indeed sufficiently noncontroversial to need no further elaboration.[1]

If we accept the above position, the case for providing goods at relative prices which *do not* reflect the relative costs of production has to be justified by its proponents. There are, however, a number of recognized exceptions to this rule. Two of the most important are situations where, as a result of ignorance or irrationality, undesirable commodities are consumed; and situations where consumption has external effects. The most obvious example of the former is drugs, but clearly the same can be said for most of the purchases in capitalist societies that take place as a result of highly manipulative and pressurized sales techniques. The necessity of having legal "safeguards" in the form of hire-purchase and credit-sales legislation in these countries is ample testimony to the gullibility of consumers in these situations. The second type of exception applies to situations where the consumption of goods can have strong negative or positive consequences for the community as a whole—beyond the effects on the individual consumer. Thus we have cases where consumption of some goods leads to negative consequences—such as congestion and pollution—which affect the rest of the community in an undesirable way, or to positive consequences—such as health control and education—where the effects on the rest of the community can be beneficial. These exceptions, however, do not deny the *prima facie* superiority of this consumption welfare test. Thus Dobb argues:

> The conclusion is evident that there will be a considerable number of cases where, for good reason, public policy would hold it desirable to *refrain* from bringing relative prices into strict alignment with relative costs . . . Perhaps one should hasten to repeat, in order to obviate misunderstanding, that to say this is *not* to contend that such a rule (about equating consumers' price-ratios and cost-ratios) should be lightly jettisoned or disregarded. To suggest that consumers' sovereignty should be a limited one and subject to restriction is not necessarily to call for its dethronement. In many cases, indeed, one might well ask who if not the consumer himself is capable of judging best what contributes to his own welfare? We have seen that there are numerous cases where such a presumption is justified: where there is good reason for supposing that his individual verdict is not to be trusted, either because he lacks sufficient information, or because there are effects of his own consumption on others of which he takes no account (or insufficient account). There seems to be no reasonable ground for treating individual desires as an ultimate beyond which there can be no appeal, or consumers' sovereignty as possessing some kind of value *per se*, (i.e., apart from its own estimated consequences for general welfare). To do so would clearly be arbitrary and untenable. *But what does seem to be reasonable ground for asserting is that the individual's estimate of his own needs can be taken as presumptive evidence, and as sufficient evidence in the absence of sufficient reasons to the contrary.*[2]

One category of goods which has extended the range of the above exceptions considerably is the category of so-called public goods. A public good is one whose production costs are decreasing rapidly, so that increased use of the good will entail zero or insignificant cost increases. Examples include communications, parks, meteorological services, etc. Here, because of the decreasing cost function, ordinary market rules cannot be applied in a way consistent with social efficiency, and the problem of the public good becomes one of "where to draw the line." Under capitalism, it is the line between the state sector and private interests profiting from the private provision of the commodity, while under socialism it is the line between collective and private consumption.

These arguments were formulated by Dickinson in the context of socialism to establish three major categories of goods and services which are amenable to collective consumption.[3] These are: (1) commodities which serve social purposes and are generally collectively consumed (e.g., police, electricity, roads, etc.); (2) "satisfactions less definite in character than goods and services, which cannot be divided or graduated among individuals"[4] (e.g., public health, police, etc.); and (3) a miscellaneous category of goods which, despite their amenability to private appropriation, may nevertheless be provided collectively. The key economic characteristic of all these goods is that at high income levels the price and income elasticities are zero or very low, clearly allowing for the avoidance of "wasteful" consumption.

Our approach to collective consumption is very different from the above. In the first place, in underdeveloped economies the number of important items falling under the definition of "exceptions" can be considerable. The external effects of industrialization or rural water supply, for example, are significant, and these alone can command the bulk of the society's investment funds! Second, the goods with zero or low price and income elasticities in the developed economies are not the same as those in the underdeveloped economies because of the obvious differences in the levels of income in the two. Thus, housing, furniture, and basic foods all have very high income and price elasticities in the underdeveloped economies, whereas in the developed countries the secular decline in these elasticities is quite noticeable.

The third and most important point is that the rationale for our approach is much more basic and comprehensive. It is essentially designed to create situations conducive to an extension of the scope of cooperative living, working, and consuming, in order to reduce the sheer mercenariness which threatens to accompany the acquisition of material goods in any society. For our own part, therefore, a deliberate policy aimed at the progressive expansion of the range of socially and collectively consumed commodities is required to reduce the distributive role of the market, minimize the real impact of income and wage differentials, narrow the scope and influence of money wage payments in the determination of consumption, and allow for the introduction of rational, collective values in the composition of consumption, and ultimately production as well. In this way we can define the long-term dynamic aim as the reduction of the role of surplus accumulation as the supreme object of the economic process. A *necessary* condition for this is an increase in material output to such a level of abundance that the problems of basic scarcity recede rapidly. But, at this stage, *sufficient* conditions necessitate that the social forces capable of initiating the transition to *need* as the basic distributive principle already exist. The likelihood of this increases as these developments are seen as, and are therefore planned to be, extensions of the values of the society.

Thus our approach to collective consumption is essentially a dynamic one which recognizes that consumption responds to, and helps to shape, the values of a society. However, if these values are to develop continuously, intergenerational welfare linkages will have to be made. The principle of progressive social and collective consumption explicitly seeks to do this. The starting point is to see the purpose of the transition period as linked with the development of a society where *need* becomes the basic distributive principle, and *production for use, not profit* the object of all economic activity.

Basic Needs and Transformation

One of the major purposes of economic development under socialism is the collective improvement of the material welfare of the broad mass of the people. Generalizing from human experience, it appears as if the level of material welfare hinges largely on the output and consumption of certain tangible and intangible products. The intangibles are mainly education, recreation, and travel, together with the usual array of medical, cultural, and social services. The tangibles are largely adequate housing, food, clothing, a proper living environment, and the service of such important consumer durables as transportation, electronic entertainment equipment, and durable household goods (furniture, washing machines, refrigerators, etc.).

Obvious as these broad priorities in consumption would seem to those who have known nothing but poverty, it is unfortunate that there is much implicit romanticization of poverty in the economic literature. Things that economists find indispensable in their own households automatically become luxuries for the nation at large. A moral verity has come to be imputed to deprivation! These commodities are only luxuries at that point in time when production is geared to the select consumption of these products. To see the situation otherwise is to impose a static conception on the process of transformation and to deny the capacity of the economy to achieve a broad-based increase in the level of material output.

It would be unfair, and indeed a crude caricature of the argument as presented here, to suggest that we are recommending the abandonment of, let us say, a steel mill for a motor-car assembly plant. On the contrary, it is simply intended as a reminder that the material advantage of such basic material production as a steel mill lies in its intended use for building houses, cars, washing machines, schools, hospitals, etc. There is in each decision to produce a basic material the implicit necessity to plan the use of the basic goods that will ultimately be consumed. On this basis, the items listed above constitute an important range of priorities. This is so because they are either immanent to man's physical and psychological requirements (e.g., health, recreation), or because the experience of those who are materially better off is already generally known and is expressed in the aspirations of those who are not. While it is undoubtedly true that a socialist society ought to struggle against the undesirable aspects of the global homogenization of consumption along the lines of capitalist affluence, the chances of real success in this are not very good for any single small society that has been, as a result of the colonial process, open and dependent. We might wish that the lead in the development of consumption patterns, as indeed in production, had not been taken by the capitalist countries, but to waste time regretting this would be wishful ahistoricism.

We have already indicated that the specific composition of consumption goods cannot be determined a priori. Nevertheless, there are several important dimensions to the priorities which should be highlighted. First, most of the goods we have listed are ideal from every standpoint as items of collective consumption. Social services, education, public transport, housing and household effects—all of these can be planned so that they are made available as collective goods, so that the role of need as the fundamental distributive principle is strengthened.

Second, production aimed at the satisfaction of these needs constitutes an important additional element in the investment program. The major investment requirements are in the *field of construction* (houses, buildings, etc.) and since industrialization, rural reorganization, population shifts, and so on will all occur at an increased rate, an additional focus is on *urban/rural development and design.* The great significance of these areas of economic activity is that evidence from other countries suggests that their rates of expansion do not depend very heavily on absolute income levels, but rather on the *rate* at which industrial activity expands and household incomes grow. As a result, a broad-based stimulation of construction activity can be achieved at low levels of per capita income.

The construction industry is also one of the most flexible of the major industries in its input mix. Its natural resource content is flexible (wood, clay, cement, glass, aluminum, plastic, steel, etc.) and therefore amenable to planning to conform to the natural resource endowments. And its combination ratios of fixed equipment and labor are flexible, again allowing for adaptation to emerging scarcities. Finally, its scale of operations is flexible (large, medium, small), without significant changes in the economies yielded, allowing for considerable locational adaptation. In view of these advantages, it is possible to plan this sector in order to be: (1) labor intensive; (2) natural resource intensive; (3) conducive to high rates of growth based on high rates of industrial development; and (4) adapted to a scale of operations suited to its particular location.

This particular part of the investment program can therefore be planned so that it will have the largest impact on the initial labor surplus situation and at the same time contribute substantially to the reduction of urban/rural differentiation. In addition, in terms of sheer ability to be organized as an activity of mass involvement, self-help, and community endeavor, there is nothing superior to basic construction activity. It is for this reason that it has been widely used in those socialist countries (e.g., China and Cuba) where political motivation and involvement are high. It should be noted that we are not being so naive as to suggest that such a pattern of activity involving self-help and community programs only brings benefits and is costless, in the neoclassical sense that given massive unemployment the marginal social cost of labor is zero. On the contrary, from a social standpoint, and in the context of comprehensive planning, there is always a cost that arises from any attempt to bring human and other resources to bear on the provision of the community's needs, and it is the social evaluation of those needs that determines the true benefits of such activities.

One further observation is worth making here. Given the basic and fundamental needs for houses and household effects, social services, and transportation, the progressive provision of these items in a planned economy forms an important compensation to households when the pressures to raise the levels of social surplus are great. Indeed, it constitutes highly appreciated evidence of real improvement, because of its obvious and direct impact on the standard of living. Moreover, if communal self-help activity turns out to be a key element in the organization and development of this sector, it also fosters great pride and sense of achievement within communities.

The strategic advantages of the construction industry, which derive from its capacity to absorb labor on a large scale, are also to be found in such services as transportation and recreation. Internal travel satisfies the needs of the domestic population, while travel by visitors from abroad in the act of satisfying their needs brings in an important resource, foreign exchange. Unfortunately, the expression of the need for travel, recreation, and vacation has been confined to the global movements of the relatively rich and well-to-do. In the typical underdeveloped economy, tourism is often seen as *the* fastest growing economic activity, and while this is often true, equally often this growth is measured by the increase in numbers of visitors and the economic impact therefore multiplied out of all proportion. The following factors must also be taken into account: (1) that these visitors often arrive on foreign carriers; (2) that the arrival of these carriers requires heavy overhead expenditures in airports, harbors, and other communication facilities, in game parks, etc.; (3) that the visitors' expenditure in the domestic market has a high import-leakage (which is to be expected, given the structure of these economies as we have examined them); (4) that there is extensive foreign ownership and control of the major hotel and recreational facilities; and (5) that racism, self-abnegation, and servility accompany tourism in poor countries. Given all these, it is difficult to see either the economic justification for this policy, or its merits from a social standpoint, despite the obvious enrichment of a few.

In the context of these historical developments, the struggle against tourism is therefore usually one aspect of the wider struggle against economic and cultural imperialism and dependency.[5] This is unfortunate, since the rapid worldwide growth of tourism, travel, and recreation suggests that it is an important element in a fuller and more relaxed life. If it were possible for transportation charges to be low, accommodation simple, flexible, and cheap, and the attraction oriented toward physical relaxation and an enjoyment of the people and their culture, travel could constitute an important source of foreign exchange earnings—not only from the rich capitalist countries, but from other friendly and neighboring states, as well as from the socialist countries, where this practice has not greatly grown. It is unfortunate that, given the capitalistic anarchy under which these industries have so far developed, they have come to symbolize the worst abuses of dependency and virtually to negate strategies of disengagement. Yet it remains true that, with careful planning, travel and recreation could be an important source of acquiring what is a crucial bottleneck resource during the transformation process—foreign exchange. It is a pity that it is the spectacle of a "Hilton" that prevails.

It can be seen from this brief review of the sort of broad consumption priorities we feel are likely to emerge as an expression of the needs of the community that their impact on the investment program will be considerable. But all these activities rest on a base of material production—on the basic materials sector and on other elements of the capital goods sector. They therefore represent the inextricable interrelationships of consumption and production. It is because of this that the progressive spread of the principle of collectivity in consumption, particularly in these priority areas, will serve to reinforce the importance of the social needs of the community as a major impetus to organizing the use and development of its productive forces.

Choice and the Variety of Needs

We shall conclude this chapter with a brief discussion of some of the problems of choice and variety of needs as they relate to consumer welfare issues. In the neoclassical literature it is widely assumed that consumers exercise sovereignty over the economic process. If this is so, then not only will their exercise of "free choice" in the matter of consumption lead to maximum individual welfare, but this choice is necessary if the society is to move toward its optimum conditions of resource use. Free and competitive markets leading to Pareto-type rational allocation of resources presuppose the free and rational exercise of individual choice. Given this argument, it follows logically that a restriction of choice, other things being equal, is in effect a reduction in the economic welfare of the community below Pareto top-level maxima. Now, in the face of this, it would be as well to admit that, for small economies, a strategy such as we have outlined implies strong limits on the "variability" of choice of product during the transition period. The problem we face is therefore how this should be interpreted.

One way of beginning is for us to recognize at the outset that—whatever the theoretical merits of the case for private adjustments of marginal rates of substitution of consumption to price ratios in the market, as the condition of maximizing satisfaction—in practice such consumer sovereignty as this implies is little more than a myth in capitalist countries. Given the widespread existence of monopolistic elements in these economies and the vast inequalities in income and wealth which prevail, it is impossible for the consumer to dominate the economic process. In addition, there are also all the techniques of advertising and selling through the mass media, which have developed comparatively recently but which have nevertheless succeeded in establishing a mode of operation in which manipulation of the consumers' preferences is the rule rather than the exception.

The point about all the factors that impinge on the consumers' sovereignty is that they are inherent to the economic order from which they emanate, and there is therefore no real possibility of consumer sovereignty being established in these circumstances. Freedom of choice is much more apparent than real, for the real extent of freedom to choose ultimately depends upon the nature of the existing social order. This point has been argued effectively by Baran:

> Just as it makes no sense to deplore war casualties without attacking their cause, war, so it is meaningless to sound the alarm about advertising and all that accompanies it without clearly identifying the *locus* from which the pestilence emanates: the monopolistic and oligopolistic corporation and the non-price-competitive business practices which constitute an integral component of its *modus operandi* . . . the issue is rather *the kind of social and economic order* that does the molding.[6]

The second point to bear in mind is that, in the context of our transformation strategy, the apparent restrictions of choice for some are designed to facilitate the *planned* expansion of choice for others. In particular, "free choice" is a purely theoretical notion for those who have been historically marginalized by the process of underdevelopment, and who, therefore, lack the *sine qua non* for exercising choice—the purchasing power to acquire the commodities and services they need. Thus, for example, if standardization of products proves necessary in order to achieve efficient output runs, it should be realized that simply by making production of transformative materials possible, this policy will bring products which hitherto could not be "afforded" within the reach of many. The implications are far reaching, since here the question of choice is linked with the attained levels of income and its distribution, as well as with the productive base from which these incomes derive.

In neoclassical theory, such a deliberate narrowing of the range of choice represents losses in economic welfare and is therefore condemned. But if, as in our case, the narrowing of choice is accompanied not only by an increase in output, but also by a narrowing of divergences in the structure of domestic output, domestic demand, and the needs of the broad mass of the population, surely welfare, in any meaningful sense, must be enhanced.

The third and final problem, one which will always confront efforts at planning the convergence of needs and consumption, is determining how variable in fact a person's needs are. On the one hand, there is the widespread view that needs grow unendingly and are infinite in their variability. If this were so, then the policies we suggest, aimed as they are at the progressive extension of public consumption, would be faced by a similar progression in the variation of the population's needs. The result would be that society would always be confronted with the fact that it could only collectively consume a certain range of goods and the policy would always have a limited applicability. On the other hand, there is the view that the historically revealed variety of needs is not as great as is generally assumed. Thus Mandel, drawing on the work of Mumford, has argued as follows:

> Let us take first the question of the alleged variety of needs. Any moderately serious study of anthropology and history will show, on the contrary, how remarkably stable they are: food, clothing, shelter (and in certain climatic conditions, warmth), protection against wild animals and the inclemency of the seasons, the desire to decorate, the desire to exercise the body's muscles, the satisfaction of sexual needs, the maintenance of the species—there are half a dozen basic needs which do not seem to have changed since the beginnings of *homo sapiens*, and which still account for the bulk of consumer expenditure. To these we may add needs for hygiene and health care . . . and needs to enrich one's leisure . . . and we have almost exhausted the list of consumer expenses even in the richest countries of the world, on the basis of a small number of basic needs.[7]

While the evidence still remains somewhat inconclusive, we are inclined to the latter view as being a more accurate interpretation of man's development. We believe that the progressive spread of collective consumption will not be permanently eluded by the growth of an infinite variety of newer needs. In any event, it would seem to us that, given the low level of incomes which prevails in underdeveloped economies, there is a wide range of products which the population at large does not consume in appropriate amounts. These are commodities such as housing, public health, recreation, nutrition, and education, which would, under any criteria, be amenable to collective consumption. Thus the prospect exists of establishing in the early stages of transformation a predominant tendency toward the principle of collectivity in the consumption of commodities.

Collective consumption, because it eliminates the operation of the market, does not mean consumption by administrative fiat. On the contrary, the capacity of collective consumption to raise the levels of welfare in the community depends on the extent to which democracy can prevail in framing decisions about consumption. Surprisingly, as Robinson has pointed out, many of the techniques of the capitalist countries can be used to improve our understanding of consumers' needs. Her suggestion serves to re-emphasize Baran's argument quoted above, that it is the manner in which these techniques are used—the social order from which they emanate—rather than the techniques per se that determine their character. Thus it is easy to agree with Robinson that:

> The true moral to be drawn from capitalist experience is that production will never be responsive to consumer needs as long as the initiative lies with the producer. Even within capitalism, consumers are beginning to organize to defend themselves. In a planned economy the best hope seems to be to develop a class of functionaries, playing the role of wholesale dealers, whose career and self-respect depend upon satisfying the consumer. They could keep in touch with demand through the shops; market research, which in the capitalist world is directed to finding out how to bamboozle the housewife, could be directed to discovering what she really needs . . . No one who has lived in the capitalist world is deceived by the pretence that the market system ensures consumer sovereignty. It is up to the socialist countries to find some way of giving it reality.[8]

As this chapter makes clear, it would be incorrect to attempt to specify the detailed composition of consumption from general principles because the determination of the precise details in each society is largely an empirical matter. All that we have attempted is to indicate the importance of the principle of collectivity in consumption and the transformative significance of some of the broader priorities of consumption that are likely to emerge. We are thus concerned with the principles which should guide the convergence of needs and demand; and, above all, we believe that the correct determination of these principles is crucial to the development of socialist relations in production. Need as a distributive ideal, and production for "use not profit" as a productive ideal, both depend upon the dominance of social needs over all material and economic processes. Nevertheless, while these are the ideals, the small underdeveloped economy during the transition period is likely to be characterized by the persistence of dependency and by norms of distribution rooted in underdevelopment. The only way to contain these is through the early implementation of our suggestions. As experience in the industrialized socialist economies shows, if not dealt with from the outset, the contradiction between a socialist mode of production and pre-socialist forms of distribution will become acute. This will always happen if, in the building of a socialist society, we do not take care to stress the vital importance of the intergenerational growth and development of social forms.

Notes

1. M. Dobb, *Welfare Economics and the Economics of Socialism*, p. 208 (emphasis in original).
2. Ibid., pp. 220-21 (our emphasis).
3. H. D. Dickinson, *Economics of Socialism*. For a discussion of his contribution see Dobb, ibid., pp. 223-26.
4. Ibid., p. 53.
5. There is virtually an unlimited list of such abuses: in Africa there is the promotion of the continent as a "wild-life" paradise, with little or no projection of the peoples and their culture, aspirations, etc.; in many metropolitan capitals, marketing strategy requires that representatives of the underdeveloped countries be white, so as to act as an inducement to visitors; the existence of luxury beach hotels (even in "socialist" Tanzania), and the juxtaposition of these facilities with poor villages in such a way that even the electricity and pure water

supplies brought to these "remote" spots by-pass villages less than a couple of hundred yards away; the importation, under "special" exemptions where import regulations exist, of special foods for the tourist—"Miami steak" flown into Jamaica; and so on.

6. P. Baran, *The Political Economy of Growth*, pp. xiv and xvi (our emphasis).
7. E. Mandel, *Marxist Economic Theory*, p. 660. This conclusion is based in part on L. Mumford's work, *Technics and Civilisation.*
8. J. Robinson, "Consumer Sovereignty in a Planned Economy."

Part 3

Relations of Production and Forces of Production

9

Problems of Political and Social Interaction

In this chapter we propose to develop further our consideration of two major social issues, both of which have run throughout our earlier analyses. The first of these relates to the advocacy of economic integration as a strategy for overcoming the constraints of smallness; the second concerns the nature of the contradictions likely to emerge during the transition period.

Integration, Size, and Dependence[1]

The rise of self-determination and the movement toward national independence have brought into sharp relief the importance of national size as the context in which national relations of production evolve. Of course, when we study the history of nation states, it can readily be seen that national size, even in such elemental terms as geographical area, has not been constant. For much of the history of nation states, conquest has played a crucial role in the observed enlargements and contractions in size. At present, in light of the existing nature of the global and national conflicts generated by the struggles between the possessors and the dispossessed, national conquest as a general means of territorial expansion can be ruled out for the smaller nation states among the underdeveloped countries, which are our major concern. International integration, political and economic, has become the principal form of struggle for the enlargement of nations.

It is evident that insofar as the size of national markets, the level of national skills, and the availability of other national resources do constitute important constraints on the capacity for national development, political struggle, aimed at political and economic union over a wider geographical area, has considerable potential importance in overcoming these constraints. In this section we shall argue that political and economic union—as they have tended to evolve in practice and as they will continue to evolve—will not make a significant contribution to easing any of the major constraints of size. Moreover, when evaluating the possible contributions of political and economic union to increasing the effective size of nations, it seems to us that the real issue is whether existing states are more likely to be able to forge meaningful integration arrangements among themselves, as opposed to the prospect that historical circumstances may require these states to go it alone in their attempts at socialist transformation. It seems to us far more likely that many of the small underdeveloped areas will have to advance toward socialism in relative isolation from their neighbors, rather than in the context of a broad sweep of nations simultaneously moving in that direction. Of course, as the numbers of these states increase, and as socialism advances on a broad front, the scope for the effective integration of neighboring states will be greatly enhanced. In a sense, therefore, the narrowing of present options is a transitional phenomenon of the world order.

Judging from the sheer number of recent integration arrangements among the underdeveloped economies, there would seem to exist a considerable drive toward the merging of nation states. Several complex forces appear to lie behind this movement, but at the base of each is the deep sense of sharing, the common historical experience, felt by wide sections of the population of the underdeveloped countries. Unfortunately, this historical experience has, more often than not, been founded and molded on colonial domination of national life. In many instances it has also been reinforced by ethnic, religious, and other cultural affinities. Thus the Pan-African movement, or the idea of Arab unity, are deeply rooted in these affinities, and are struggles to overcome and contain the divisive tendencies of colonialism and imperialism.

Given the way social classes are formed in underdeveloped and dependent situations, the sense of oneness and unity that exists in the population at large has inevitably become an object of manipulation by the ruling classes of these countries. Forever preaching unity, these social classes are nevertheless *objectively* the main supports of the processes of fragmentation and disintegration of these societies. How could it be otherwise? The dominant social classes have historically developed and derived their ultimate support in the context of their relationship to imperialism. Their major contributions, therefore, are in the direction of a perpetuation of dependency relations. As such, they cannot in any *objective* sense be seen as the instruments of the international political and economic integration of these societies; indeed, a movement in this direction must have as a basis the downfall of all such classes.

The principal form the manipulation of the broad-based support for unity has taken is the practice of sponsoring government strategies seeking cooperation in order to enlarge national markets. Such enlargement, it is argued, is the necessary precondition for, if not the main instrument of, economic development, because foreign and indigenous capital will not be attracted to the transformative industries as long as the national markets of the individual nations are too small to make it worthwhile and profitable. Economic integration, if not political integration, should therefore be pursued with the objective of enlarging the national market available to capitalists through unification of hitherto discrete national markets. Economic integration replaces national import substitution with protection and import substitution at the regional level; it neither requires nor presupposes attempts at regionally coordinated action to alter the relations of production generated by underdevelopment. In effect, it is more of the same. An early statement by Prebisch succinctly rationalizes the economic basis of this approach:

> The stage of easy substitution is past. It was relatively simple to substitute domestic production for imports of individual items of current consumption and of some durable consumer and capital goods, and there is little margin left for substitution in this field in most of Latin America. We are now moving into the stage of import substitution in respect of intermediate or durable consumer or capital goods, which, besides being difficult to manufacture, require markets much larger than those of the individual Latin American nations.[2]

One of the factors that has strengthened support for policies of economic integration is the widely reported and assumed "success" of the European Economic Community. Governments of the underdeveloped countries frequently take it as axiomatic that if national markets are unified, success, although not necessarily on the scale of the European Economic Community, will naturally follow. No cognizance is taken of the enormous differences between the social systems and circumstances involved in the European integration movement and their own. In Europe, a wider market can improve the rate of growth of output and productivity because the relations of production which *already exist* derive much of their incentive to produce and innovate from the operation of the sort of market mechanisms that already prevail. Presented as the "forces of competition," wider markets in fact allow for the opposite of competition: they are the prelude to further cartelization and concentration of monopoly capital. Accordingly, unification of national markets strengthens the already existing driving forces of capitalism. In the underdeveloped economies similar circumstances simply do not exist.

These developments in favor of integration have their theoretical rationale in the neoclassical economic theories of customs unions, and in Western political theories of neofunctionalism. These theories assert that the degree and nature of economic integration can be measured by the extent to which markets are unified, and that there is a supranationalization of legislative and administrative functions of the integrating units. Thus, we find that customs union theory ranks the association of countries from simple free trade areas to economic union, and the factors which differentiate each stage are the rules and regulations which permit a unified market. A free trade area is simply the freeing of regional trade barriers without a common external tariff; and a common market is a customs union plus a common market for the "factors of production"; and so on. These hierarchical rankings either "create" or "divert" trade. The former is good for the nation, the union, and the world, while the latter is bad. Trade creation occurs when, as a result of competition among the different national producers in the region, there is a shift from a relatively higher-cost to a lower-cost source of supply. Trade is diverted when, as a result of the formation of a union, a higher-cost source of supply is able to capture the regional market. This occurs when, with the aid of the protected regional market, one or more national producers within the region can replace extraregional suppliers.

These concepts are associated with Viner.[3] As close study shows, they focus exclusively on competition and supply shifts among *existing* producers. Even in the context of static neoclassical trade theory, it can be seen that they ignore "demand" effects, or that they assume that commodities continue to be consumed in the same proportions after the formation of the customs union as before.[4] As a consequence, there have been subsequent attempts to incorporate demand into the analysis by allowing for shifts in consumption, following on the obvious changes in selling price which occur if output shifts from one source of supply to another and if the level of tariff protection varies. But this has not altered the static and partial characteristics of the analysis, as it only allows for the analysis and development of customs union theory to take place in terms of intercountry and intercommodity substitutions. Both of these, of course, are discussed only in terms of simple demand and supply analysis—

even the so-called dynamic effects which neoclassical theory usually encompasses in their concessions to a growing economy (e.g., balance of payments effect, terms of trade effects, etc.) have not been systematically integrated into the analysis.

We can see from this highly condensed exposition that the theoretical bases of customs union theory have nothing whatsoever to do with the social and political context of underdevelopment. Yet it has been precisely such crude rationalizations of existing theory that have formed the "scientific" basis for evaluating the prospects of integration in the underdeveloped economies! This has led to certain ridiculous situations. Thus, if economic and political integration are measured by the extent to which the "rules of exchange" and the "rules of supranationalization of legislation" allow for a common market and common executive and legislative action, then arrangements such as the British Empire—with its more-or-less free movement of capital and labor, its consistent tariff regulations, commercial law, and "unitary" government—should be considered as having been a highly integrated area. Not even neoclassical economists would accept this, despite its logic in terms of their analysis. It is thus evident that this problem cannot be resolved until it is realized that *economic and political integration cannot be analyzed abstractly outside of the context and goals of the integration movement itself.* In other words, the theory of integration "must be an integral element of a theory of economic and social transformation and not simply an adjunct of the microeconomics of static location theory."[5]

In summary, in the social context of underdevelopment, current movements toward political and economic integration do not, and indeed cannot, represent attempts at meaningful integration. The analysis involved carries with it the explicit assumption that the methods and instruments of integration have no social validity apart from the goals and objects of the integration process. *It follows, therefore, that unless the goals of economic and political integration encompass the coming together of national states with the objective of changing the relations of production and developing the level of productive forces, then any method or instrument of integration in use will only contribute to the perpetuation and possible deepening of the underdevelopment process.*

This basic point may be brought out by a brief examination of some of the more general consequences of the present integration movements around the world. As we have pointed out, the dominant focus of the worldwide movement toward integration has been the liberalization of trade (i.e., the formation of customs unions and free trade areas) as the basis for widening national markets and thereby extending the permissive area of "free" exchange of goods. Judging by developments so far, there seems to be an assumption that the larger market will, of and by itself, offer the necessary incentives to the formation of an indigenous capitalist class and/or the attraction of foreign capital on a large enough scale. These will then be the sources of the needed large-scale investments in the transformative industries. But it is already evident that the process has not occurred in this way. The widening of the markets has not been large enough or secure enough to attract foreign capital in these newer directions. Instead, what has happened is that the existing multinational firms, which already dominate the incipient manufacturing activities of these countries, have begun to rationalize their plant facilities in the region, trying to avoid some of the worst excesses of duplication while seeking to maintain and even expand their share of the export market, disguised in the usual form of assembling knocked-down imports. In addition, they have sought to secure their investments by seeking to minimize nationalist reaction in any given state, using the fairly obvious tactic of playing off one national petty bourgeoisie against another.

That the main beneficiaries so far have been the multinational firms is not by any means an unexpected occurrence. One of the principal characteristics of the Third World countries is the minimal extent to which they trade with each other, integrated as they are into the production and consumption needs of the metropolitan countries. A program to unify the national markets is faced with the stark reality that the countries produce very little that can be sold to each other. The only significant exceptions to this rule are the output of the newer multinational firms catering to high-income consumers, and the output of mass consumption foods. The former accounts for the gains which have gone to the multinational fabricating industries, but the latter is faced with the fact that existing integration arrangements do not usually fully include agricultural commodities. Where agricultural protocols exist in the various treaties, they are frequently confined to a recognition and restatement of previous exchanges between food deficit and food surplus areas in a given region. Thus the exchange of rice, fats, and oils (which existed before the integration arrangements), and the sale of seasonal surpluses in the Caribbean, presently form part of that region's agricultural protocol attached to the Free Trade Area Treaty.[6] In other cases, historical exchanges of food have followed the search for high prices, even when the exporting territory has been deficient in its own food supplies; and, as in the case in East Africa, the *prohibition* of unauthorized movements of livestock and cattle constitutes an important form of regional collaboration.

In organizational terms, the main momentum behind these arrangements lies in the bureaucracies which have been created to service them, the multinational firms which benefit from them, and allied pressure groups of private interests, such as the various local Chambers of Commerce and Manufacturers Associations. The result has been that all too frequently, despite the existence of the latent and widespread sense of unity we referred to, these agreements remain extremely shaky and fragile. Thus the Central American Common Market was supposed to have been working extremely well because of the strength of the regional bureaucrats, the famous *tecnicos.* It was claimed that they were succeeding quietly and stealthily in bringing the territories together with a minimum of fuss and political intervention. As if to prove that nothing serious can be achieved by stealth, this agreement—long the darling of the integrationists, and frequently boasted about in the Western literature as the most successful regional agreement in the underdeveloped world—fell apart in July 1969 after a football game and the ensuing war between Honduras and El Salvador.[7]

Other highly touted arrangements have also proven to be very fragile. Thus Arab "unity" has come and gone with tragic frequency. States are combined, separated, and recombined in the same routine fashion as the announcements which greet them. That these dramatic swings in national policy have little or no major internal consequences is testament to the absurdity of the entire process. Some unions are often politely forgotten (e.g., Ghana-Mali-Guinea) while others, despite long colonial experience in coordinated administrative and political action, can be rendered impotent by a single coup, as in the East African Community.

In many of these unions, because the emphasis has been on freeing trade, some of the universal characteristics of trade tend to replicate themselves within the regions. Thus the countries which were initially favored by the multinational firms have been able to reap most of the benefits of expanded intraregional commerce. In the absence of coordinated national planning and production strategies by the various national governments, the benefits from union, to the extent that they do come about, are confined to the expanded exchanges of assembled manufactures. The unequal bilateral and intraregional balances of trade which unfailingly emerge, lead to strong disagreements over the sharing of the "gains." Instead of seeing that most of these gains are being absorbed by the multinational firms, the governments frequently quarrel among themselves over the sharing of the remainder. The few cases where these integration agreements include clauses pertaining to the joint establishment of new industries, thereby indicating a concern with joint planning and new investments, instead of with trade liberalization, have usually become bogged down in disputes over sharing the benefits of the industries and over their location. Thus the famous Kampala Agreement of the East African Community, which was to have heralded new and very significant departures in economic integration arrangements among underdeveloped countries, has never been put into effect.[8]

The combined consequence of all these developments has been that old rivalries, nurtured in the colonial era of "divide and rule," have compounded each other and multiplied beyond proportion the problems of cooperation among nation states. Given political structures which do not allow the people to participate in their own national governments, let alone in the various new integration institutions and structures, the regional bureaucracies soon become the main foci of "integration" activity. Lacking a political base among the people, these bureaucracies come to see their role as the simple accumulation of "functions" that give the appearance of unity. Thus numerous regional associations begin to proliferate in a way which testifies to the emphasis on symbols rather than substantive unity. As a result, we have regional associations of nurses and doctors rather than comprehensive regional efforts and programs to battle disease and sickness, or we have an emphasis on highly publicized regional activities such as motor car rallies!

In the process of socialist transformation, integration can only play a meaningful role if it is based on simultaneous changes in the relations of production and the development of productive forces over contiguous areas. The prospect of this occurring seems very unlikely. Thus the case remains strongly in favor of a strategy designed to maximize reliance on national resources and national political capacities. Present integration arrangements cannot, by the very nature of the social processes at work, be considered a real alternative to the socialist transformation of production relations, in each country, as the necessary condition for developing the level of productive forces and transforming the structure of production. This does not, of course, lead to the conclusion that the state in transition should not rely on trade and cooperation agreements with other Third World states. Indeed, the opposite is true: agreements and cooperation should be pursued in such a way as to fit them into planning and transformation requirements so that trade can play an important role in the strategy of turning international relations away from capitalism. But the warning of present dangers should be ever clear. As Rodney has observed in his study of Africa, these dangers have been historically conditioned:

> From the fifteenth century onward, pseudo-integration appeared in the form of the interlocking of African economies over long distances from the coast, so as to allow the passage of human captives and ivory from a given point inland to a given port on the Atlantic or Indian Ocean. For example, captives were moved from Congo through what is now Zambia and Malawi to Mozambique, where Portuguese, Arab or French buyers took them over. That was not genuine integration of the economies of the African territories concerned. Such trade merely represented the extent of foreign penetration, thereby stifling local trades.[9]

It is clear that a preoccupation with the "formal legal structures and procedures" of the various integration efforts in the underdeveloped world would be mistaken, in terms of trying to evaluate their possible impact on the size of nations and hence their capacity to transform themselves through the growth and development of an indigenous capitalism with the aid of the state. Meaningful integration is not possible under present circumstances, not because cooperation among underdeveloped countries is undesirable, but because of the *objective* position of the dominant classes who presently make such decisions and initiate the lines of cooperation. Their position is in fundamental contradiction with the requirements of the transformation of the existing relations of production. Until this contradiction is resolved, productive forces cannot be fully developed to the point of alleviating want, hunger, and disease. Given the historical relations of these classes to imperialism, all they can achieve is the reinforcement of the dependency links between the industrial metropoles and the various national economies. In this sense, as Rodney has observed, "such trade merely [represents] the extent of foreign penetration."

Contradictions and the Mode of Production

In the course of presenting our economic strategy we have referred to at least three sets of major contradictions which are certain to be of crucial importance in determining social relations during the transition period. These are: (1) the contradiction posed by increasing rural differentiation, (2) the contradiction which centers on the simultaneous operation of a comprehensive planning system and markets in certain important areas of economic activity and which extends into the conflict between the mode of production and the mode of distribution; and (3) the urban/rural contradiction. Drawing on the experiences of other socialist countries during the transition period, it seems to us that from the onset of attempts to restructure the social relations which govern production, the utmost importance has to be attached to the nature of the "choices" made in the way in which these contradictions are to be resolved. Yet these experiences have also shown that the sheer power of specific historical experience to narrow the freedom of such "choices" should not be underestimated. Even in revolutionary situations, it seems that men cannot act very far outside of their own historical traditions. Because of this, we feel that there are strong grounds for believing that a consciousness and analytical awareness of the issues presented here are the most important means of guaranteeing that the right choice will be made and that the society will proceed to struggle against the systematic reproduction of social inequities and social injustices during the transition period. Accordingly, in this section we shall concentrate on expanding some of our earlier comments on these contradictions, while at the same time referring to others.

Given the historical unevenness of social development, it is no surprise to find that the nature of the contradictions represented by *class differentiation in the rural areas* varies significantly from country to country. In some of the African rural areas, where there have been strong traditions of communalism and where only comparatively recently have subsistence economies been drawn into the orbit of the cash-crop export economy, although rural differentiation clearly exists, its significance differs substantially from that of other areas, particularly some of the latifundia areas of Latin America and Asia. But, whatever the precise degree of the existing levels of rural differentiation, the dynamics of rural change in the underdeveloped economies are such that the forces of increasing rural differentiation cannot for long remain incipient. Consequently, the urgency of these problems remains acute.

There have been two recent sets of public policies in many of the Third World countries which underline the pervasive threat of rapidly growing rural differentiation. The first has been presented under the guise of "progressive" farmer policies, and the second has been in the form of "cooperative" agriculture. The idea behind the "progressive" farmer approach is to identify what are termed dynamic entrepreneurial elements in the rural economy and to concentrate state support on them in the hope that their eventual success will have far-reaching "demonstration effects" throughout the rural economy. This approach has usually been the prelude to the growth of state-supported capitalist farming. Not infrequently, therefore, we find that the "progressive" farmers are closely identified as supporters of the ruling party and, judging from revelations following changes in government, have often been close relatives of public servants and government ministers. These "progressive" farmers frequently begin to move out of traditional agriculture and into supplying certain types of high-protein foods (chickens, etc.) for the urban elite. The entrenchment of these capitalist elements in the rural areas, supported by public funds and facilities, has often been accompanied by the dispossession of the small peasant holders and by rampant land speculation leading to high prices and rents. As the experience of the Soviet Union indicates, these "kulaks" come to play a decisive role in the process of transition.

Now it is clear that while during the transition period the state will have to fight against all forms of capitalist farming relations and their accompanying abuses, to be successful such a struggle has to be pursued with the support of the broad mass of the peasantry. As we saw in Chapter 5, this approach has long been the mainstay of socialist thought, if not practice. Ruthless and undemocratic approaches to the solution of this problem are bound to be counterproductive: the history of Eastern Europe is replete with experiences which show that such approaches can only result in extensive sabotage of the transition efforts. Farmers have been known in these circumstances to withhold food, to destroy agricultural machinery, and to sabotage essential food supplies to the towns wherever they can. In this confrontation, even though the socialist state might succeed in overcoming the intransigence of the peasantry, socialism itself will nevertheless be very much the loser. Thus the rural transformation of the relations of production is likely to be slow and painstaking, *constituting what might very well be considered the most important test of the mobilizational capacity of the worker/peasant alliance.*

The second set of policies—the support of certain forms of "cooperative" farming—usually involves very little real cooperation. The usual practice is for the cooperatives to be confined at most to marketing and credit organizations. There is rarely any real cooperation in production, ownership of rural resources, and innovation in farming techniques. Because of their basically nonsocialist character, positions of authority within these cooperatives, and even the access of particular cooperatives to credit, etc., often become objects of political patronage. Further, what is particularly significant during the transition period is the dominance of what has been termed *outside leadership* in running and organizing these cooperatives. The whole system of selection and guidance, the organization of extension services to farmers by the state, and the methods of extending services and rural communication, reduce these cooperatives to mere appendages of the state. Instead of more cooperation at the grassroots level, this *outside leadership* serves to undermine the basis of true democracy and to strengthen the dependent characteristics of the society, because *outside leadership* supports a situation where order and direction are seen to be the product of outside forces, beyond the compass of the people themselves. This has profound consequences on attitudes toward authority and change, which may seriously endanger attempts to democratize the production system.

The problems we are faced with in dealing with the theoretical problems of class contradictions in the rural economies of the small underdeveloped economies include not only the wide variations which exist among these societies in their types of rural organization, but also the wide variation of rural types which can exist in any one economy. This coexistence of various social formations (e.g., model cooperatives, peasant small farms, middle peasants, landless laborers, settlement schemes, plantations, large estates, and government farms) means that a diversity of solutions will have to be found, even though the basic principle remains that all solutions must be consistent with our stress on democracy and participation, and with the form and content of output. As Mandel has correctly pointed out in his discussion of agriculture and distribution during the transition period:

> A single solution valid for all these diverse situations cannot be found. But the two principles from which any solution ultimately has to start are these: no socialization (whether *de facto* or *de jure*) of enterprises is justifiable unless the technical conditions make possible a higher output this way than private enterprise can get; and no socialization is justifiable unless the small proprietors (small producers) agree to it, either from conviction or from material interests, or (what is, of course, the ideal situation) from both motives at once.[10]

Instead of merely saying "higher output" as Mandel does, we would stress *higher output of the new form and content of production* advocated in this study. As we have shown, in the context of underdevelopment and the struggle to transform society, the quantum and composition of output are indivisible entities.

In the socialist literature, *the contradictions of plan and market, production and distribution*, play a central role in the theoretical discussion of the transition period. This is particularly noteworthy in the Sweezy/Bettelheim exchanges and in Mandel's discussion of the transition period. Let us quote Mandel once again: "The contradiction between the noncapitalist mode of production and the bourgeois norms of distribution is the *fundamental contradiction* of every society transitional between capitalism and socialism."[11] While not attaching the same fundamental importance to this contradiction as Mandel does, its importance in theoretical discussion can nevertheless be seen from Sweezy's comments:

> The very term "market-socialism" is self-contradictory, the market being the central institution of capitalist society and socialism being a society which substitutes conscious control for blind automatism. But this does not mean that the term is inappropriate: the phenomenon which it designates is also self-contradictory. And it is precisely this inner contradiction which impels the market socialist societies toward capitalism.[12]

In rebuttal Bettelheim observes:

> The "plan/market" contradiction is not—cannot be—a fundamental contradiction: it designates neither a class contradiction (a political contradiction) nor an economic contradiction (a contradiction between social relations in effect on the economic level), but certain variable consequences of these contradictions and the "places" where these consequences manifest themselves. To be more precise, I would say that the "plan/market" contradiction indicates, in a metaphorical way, a contradiction between two "areas of representations," two "stages."[13]

We do not propose to take up the discussion of this particular theoretical issue, since it involves a conceptualization of matters which are of lesser importance to us. Basically, the importance attached to these issues stems from a preoccupation with socialism in Europe, and, given the social formations of the dependent, underdeveloped, neocolonial economies, it should be no surprise to find that the transition stage there gives rise to different sorts of fundamental contradictions. Yet it remains true that, whereas this might not be *the* fundamental contradiction as Mandel argues, it is nevertheless a very important one in all transitional states. It is, therefore, fitting to recall here some of the features of the strategy we outlined which are intended to provide mechanisms to solve the contradictions between plan and market, production and distribution.

In particular, we have emphasized the importance of immediate moves toward having the principles of social and collective consumption govern consumption. The progressive spread of collective and social consumption of goods will lead to the progressive reduction of the role of money wages in determining the use of the community's resources and the distribution of the output of consumption goods. It will also help to marginalize the overall impact of the market on economic activity. Second, we have stressed the need, at every stage, to actively support the development of democracy and popular participation in the management of production and distribution as part of the wider effort to democratize social relations within the society. This means that the process of revolutionizing the political and social order is a continuous one, involving the constant struggle at all levels of social existence against dependency relationships, authoritarian attitudes, and over-bureaucratization. We have made this point while stressing the *totality* which has historically governed the operations of social institutions in most of these countries. Now, we are not by any means underestimating the difficulties of achieving this, both in terms of internal and external considerations. In particular, we are not trying to understate the mortal hostility of the capitalist camp toward all efforts to radically transform the relations of production. The examples of Cuba, Vietnam, and North Korea are too vivid to let us think otherwise. Nevertheless, we do believe that given the complexity and comprehensiveness of the history of dependency, neocolonialism, and underdevelopment, their successful eradication cannot be achieved by lesser efforts than those we have espoused.

To these two major principles which should guide strategies to cope with the contradictions of production/distribution and of plan/market, we would like to add the importance of developing *democracy and participation at work.* This contributes toward the reduction of the contradiction between socialized production relations and material incentives to produce. Material incentives work against efforts to expand the public consumption of goods, since for material incentives to mean anything, they have to be accompanied by support of individual choices to govern consumption. In this way, therefore, they strengthen the role of the market in the transition period and further remove us from being able to establish *need* as the basic distributive principle. This is true because material incentives pander to the commercialization and mercenariness of social intercourse, negating most of the ethical and moral principles of socialism, and fostering the alienation of the worker from his work and life situation.

The third contradiction, *the urban/rural contradiction*, is a rapidly developing one which is already immanent to the present anarchic pattern of growth in most underdeveloped economies. The historical tendencies of concentration of activities in the cities, and the immiseration of the rural areas, have led to a phenomenal growth of urbanization and a regional pattern of activities which reflects the power and interests of international capitalism. With the economy functioning to ensure that local production is geared to servicing and satisfying metropolitan needs, the spatial differentiation of these activities must inevitably be a response to these influences. The conflicts between agriculture and industry, urban and rural economy, are deeply intertwined with these basic social forces. It is only through our strategy, which requires a reordering of these priorities, that we can generate the necessary preconditions for a rational and equitable approach to the solution of the problem of urban/rural differentiation. That is why our basic strategy is not predicated on making any such explicit distinctions and then developing policies to contain them. We have taken the more positive approach of planning the dynamic convergence of domestic needs and domestic production. Any trivial sectorization of the economy into agriculture and industry thus becomes progressively artificial.

The strategy we have outlined has been premised on the progressive spread of industrial techniques to all areas of economic activity. It is important to note that, so far, history has shown that all instances of national industrialization have been initiated and directed from "above" and have been accompanied by significant urban growth. It is indeed difficult to imagine the absence of a considerable amount of direction from "above" in the initiation of a strategy as comprehensive as the one we have outlined. With this in mind, it is clear that the urban/rural contradiction presented here is fundamentally inseparable from the other two contradictions mentioned above. Initiation and direction of industrialization from "above" raise the prospect of bureaucratization and threaten to further entrench authoritarian traditions bred under colonialism. Struggle for democracy at all levels is the only effective safeguard against these tendencies. Thus, an approach to the solution of this contradiction has to be based on as much local democracy and decentralization as possible. Often, however, this policy might in practice conflict with others, as in those states with strong tribal, ethnic, or other forms of local and regional differentiation, where there would be great need to opt for the promotion of a strong state, via centralization, in order to combat these centrifugal tendencies. Once again, it is worth noting the power of specific historical conjunctures, and therefore the utter impossibility of specifying a priori rules to govern every situation.

The problem of the urban-rural contradiction becomes particularly acute when two other factors are taken into account. First, a socialist government of the people, in the typical underdeveloped economy, must at this stage be based on a strong alliance between the peasantry and the workers. While numerically the peasantry is often in the majority, because of its "transitional" characteristics as a social stratum—i.e., progressively being forced off the land under capitalism to become landless laborers and eventually the urban proletariat—much of the ideological leadership and stability may have to come from the numerically weaker working class. At the same time, since these economies are predominantly agricultural, most of the surplus generated for material development will be drawn from the rural economy. These tendencies affect the productive base of the alliance itself. Socialist experience in Europe is again useful, particularly as this indicates that this particular conflict has occupied a central position during the transition period. Generally, the policies pursued in socialist Europe have tended to discriminate against the peasants in their own stated interest of overall national development. But the consequences of this have been considerable and today are reflected in the lagging of output and comparative inefficiencies in the rural areas. In turn, these have created pressures on the availability of foreign exchange. Even China, which has attempted to deal with this problem differently by placing much greater emphasis in the early stages of development on the urban/rural balance and on decentralization, has not been able to develop without the pressing constraint of a deficit in food supplies and the consequent need to rely on food imports from the capitalist countries.

Again, we argue that the solution to these contradictions relies heavily on the correct choices being made from the very outset when power has been seized. Experience has shown all too clearly that wrong decisions can be rapidly compounding in their ill effects as history proceeds.

In every society there are two overriding antagonistic contradictions. The first is the contradiction between the level of development of the productive forces and the nature of the social relations which govern production. The second is between the productive and material base of the society and the "superstructure" of its organization (political, economic, and social), and the social, cultural, and psychological attitudes these generate. This is why we have argued that underdevelopment can only be *objectively* explained in terms of the present conjuncture of social relations and the development of productive forces on a world scale, and it is why we have also stressed the need to proceed on the basis of the *co-terminous development of productive forces and changes in the relations of production in the development of social-*

ism. This approach has been a revolt against the widespread tendency to romanticize poverty and idealize the virtues of rural life in the Third World countries. This tendency is all the more regrettable since it is clearly the lack of conformity in the development of productive forces and relations of production which is at the base of the drive toward social revolution in the underdeveloped economies. History has demonstrated that existing social relations cannot develop and control the technico-material basis of the society so as to bring an end to poverty. Indeed, much of our discussion in Part 1 sought to highlight this basic lack of conformity. But, as Marx has pointed out:

> At a certain stage of their development the material productive forces of society come in conflict with the existing relations of production, or—what is but a legal expression for the same thing—with the property relations within which they have been at work hitherto. From forms of development of the productive forces these relations turn into their fetters. Then begins an epoch of social revolution.[14]

Given the way social forces have operated in the underdeveloped countries, it seems that two fundamental contradictions of the transition period should remain after the relations of production have been brought into conformity with the requirements of raising the level of productive forces. *The first is the contradiction between social and state ownership of the means of production, and the second is the contradiction between the juridical form of ownership of the means of production and the structure and content of production.* There is a shortsighted tendency everywhere to equate state ownership with socialization, and it is nowhere more noticeable than in the underdeveloped countries; it derives in large measure from the basic weaknesses of their economic structures. With the local means of production firmly under foreign ownership, the anti-imperialist struggle against this domination is not clearly seen as only a stage in the development of socialism at home. Frequently, this gives rise to a tendency to equate the extent of socialization with the extent of state domination of the "commanding heights" of the economy.

While we have indicated the prevalence of this confusion, it should not be taken to imply an underrating on our part of the importance of state control (i.e., national control) over the existing structure of production. It is highlighted here in order to focus attention on the nature of the state and the ruling classes who are in command.

This confusion between social ownership and state ownership is similar to the confusion among those who concentrate on the legal and juridical control of the productive base of the social system, for ostensibly socialist purposes, while ignoring the crucially important considerations of the structure and composition of output. This latter, and prevalent, view contains the disguised assumption that progress cannot be made in diversifying the structure of production of these economies because they are too small and their resources too limited. Its roots are firmly entrenched in the dependency characteristics of the society, and in the way social attitudes and the whole superstructure of dependency operate. It is a contradiction derived from the neocolonial mode of production.

Because of the pressures of rapid change and adjustment during the transition period, it is likely that many of these contradictions, where they do exist, will be "resolved" by a movement to highly centralized planning. Such a "resolution" is merely the suppression of these contradictions. What is also particularly dangerous from our point of view is that experience has shown that centralized planning, in the early stages, seems to yield highly significant results in the technico-economic development of the society. One factor which definitely favors this is that in the early stages of transformation the economic system is not sufficiently complex to allow for much uncertainty in priorities and lines of action. "Information" is readily obtainable, in the sense that an easy command can be established over the flow of information to the center. While this creates certain types of difficulties—as, for example, in the Soviet Union, where experience indicates that the information suppliers, because they are also implementors of plan directives, tend to protect their areas of action and achievement by hiding reserves, understating their spare capacity, raising the input/output ratios, etc.—in general, in the early stages these difficulties are overshadowed by the dramatic increases in material output.

However, as the economic system becomes more complex, the difficulties posed by trying to "contain" these contradictions in this manner multiply because after the period of extensive growth and major structural change is over, the material problems of the economy emerge in the form of maintaining efficiency via marginal adjustments in the economic processes. As these contradictions multiply, different solutions have to be sought, and presently, in the socialist countries, the solutions are being sought in the form of decentralization. *But, as we have argued, a tendency toward decentralization, which is but the by-product of the growth of wage differentials, material incentives, and the spread of individual appropriation of the product, is no real solution, since it is not consistent with the ethical and moral precepts of socialism.* Such an approach fails to promote worker control over the objects of production and the work situation. As we have also pointed out, such failure is deeply rooted and lies in large measure in the wrong "choices" having been made at the onset of the struggle to transform these societies; while the wrongness of these "choices" is itself explained by the historical forces operating at the particular time.

Thus, if we are to achieve a consistency between the mode of production and the mode of life in the transition period, careful attention has to be paid to devising strategies to deal with the problems as we have posed them here. It is in this fundamental sense that our strategy is rooted in the explicit requirement of a co-terminous development of the forces of production and the relations of production. For us, these forces and relations of production extend into the way of life of the entire community and are the only bases for bringing security from deprivation, developing a creative relationship of the people to their environment, eliminating dependency characteristics in social relations between the people, and bringing an end to all forms of alienation within the society.

Notes

1. For a fuller discussion by the author of some of these issues see H. Brewster and C. Y. Thomas, "Aspects of the Theory of Economic Integration"; "Cuestiones Téoricas Planteadas por la Integración Economica Regional"; and *Integration and Ideology.*
2. R. Prebisch , *Towards a Dynamic Development Policy for Latin America*, p. 66.
3. See J. Viner, *The Customs Union Issue.* For a short survey of the literature see R. G. Lipsey, "The Theory of Customs Union: A General Survey."
4. See R. G. Lipsey, ibid.; J. E. Meade, *The Theory of Customs Union;* and F. Gehrels, "Customs Union from a Single Country Viewpoint."
5. Brewster and Thomas, "Aspects of the Theory of Economic Integration," p. 113.
6. See the Caribbean Free Trade Area Treaty, CARIFTA Secretariat, Georgetown, Guyana; and *CARIFTA and the New Caribbean*, also prepared by the Secretariat in Guyana.
7. For details see M. S. Wionczek, "The Rise and Decline of Latin American Economic Integration." An idea of the sort of sentiment which the Central American Common Market has generated can be seen from the following: "Even though practical results are as yet modest, there have been several efforts to secure economic union among developing countries—notably the Latin American Common Market, East African Common Market, West African Customs Union, Central African Customs and Economic Union, and the West Indies Federation. Of these, the Central American Common Market has been the most successful integration effort." (G. M. Meier, *Leading Issues in Economic Development*, p. 569.)
8. For general details on the institutional and legal bases of the East African Community, see I. D. diDelupis, *The East African Community and Common Market*, and the Kampala Agreement (Tanzania Information Service, Dar es Salaam, 1964).
9. W. Rodney, *How Europe Underdeveloped Africa*, p. 122.
10. E. Mandel, *Marxist Economic Theory*, p. 647.
11. Ibid., p. 572 (our emphasis).
12. P. Sweezy and C. Bettelheim, *The Transition to Socialism*, p. 5.
13. Ibid., pp. 35-36.
14. K. Marx and F. Engels, *Selected Works*, vol. 1, p. 363.

10

The Economics of the Transition Period

In this final chapter, we shall not attempt to summarize what has been said—some readers may indeed feel that we have already summarized issues requiring tomes of their own. Instead, we shall make a few brief and very general observations about the main areas of our endeavor.

First, we would like to make a few observations about the general field of inquiry we have attempted to explore. We attempted to establish in the beginning the extent to which socialist economic theory has neglected theoretical issues raised by the requirements of an economic strategy for the transition period. In indicating the historical and social factors which account for this neglect, we did not intend to overlook the fundamental contributions made by the empirical and theoretical studies carried out in the various socialist states since 1917. We have been more concerned with the specific failure to develop any sort of theoretical apparatus to cope with the problems of transition in the small underdeveloped economies during the neocolonial phase.

We have focused on the small underdeveloped economies because they represent the vast majority of states in the present world order and because the establishment of capitalist relations of production does not seem capable of providing a framework for the development of their productive forces—although we would accept the possibility that in theory capitalism can succeed in the isolated cases of the large economies, such as Mexico, Brazil, India, in developing indigenous productive forces to the point where widespread poverty will be ruled out. In particular, this development may occur through the initiation of relatively advanced forms of industrialization. Such a position does not, of course, indicate a preference on our part for capitalism, but merely acknowledges that the historical evidence is not sufficiently conclusive at this stage for us to rule out absolutely and unequivocally the possibility of other "capitalist successes," such as Japan. Other people have shared this uncertainty. Thus Sutcliffe observes: "It has become (perhaps too hastily) almost an axiom of recent socialist writing on Third World development that further independent capitalist industrialization is not possible."[1]

The main reason for our not precluding such development is that in the large underdeveloped economy which is generating an increasingly large demand for capital goods, market incentives may be sufficient to stimulate the necessary investments to create an adequate range of Department I branches of production. If such development occurs, we see it as taking place with the active support of the state machinery. That is why we have indicated that in the neocolonial situation the state is not merely the *object* of class conquest, but is also the *instrument* of class creation. It is because technico-material conditions favor the development of the productive forces that state capitalist relations may generate a sort of development, without a revolution in social relations of production, which will take the society beyond capitalism. In the small underdeveloped economy, however, the social cost to the population at large of undertaking a transformation along these lines (particularly where the benefits are to be appropriated by a capitalist class) is prohibitive.

This brings us to our second observation. Our explicit recognition of size as the background against which social relations of production and productive forces are organized is consistent with both socialist thought and historical experience, because social relations have historically been organized within the context of nation states, while national independence and self-determination have been tremendously progressive historical forces in our time. With the break-up of the colonial empires, the size of the new states inevitably constituted an important element in their social development. We have stressed the social determination of size, and we have strongly repudiated the view that size can be interpreted as an expression of the force of nature: one only has to observe the impact of war and conquest on the size of nations to see how little this is so.

Despite these historical developments and an existing world order in which small underdeveloped economies predominate, we have abundantly documented the extent to which both socialist and neoclassical economists are negative about the possibilities of transforming the material base of production of the small underdeveloped economies. But if under both neocolonialism and socialism the technico-material bases of the society are considered to be too limited to "afford" transformation, then the situation which confronts us is the one in which these countries are either condemned forever to remain neocolonial appendages or, at best, can only be transformed as a by-product of socialist transformation of the large states in the present world order.

We can only accept this view for those situations where the transformation and development of the productive forces are being attempted by way of state-aided development of an indigenous capitalist class. Such a class will not have the political and social capacity to mobilize and organize the productive forces of the community in a way capable of eliminating poverty. Indeed, we argued at some length in Chapter 3 that even the so-called high-growth states of this sort have not generated a truly transformative capacity, despite their "export successes," and their rapidly rising per capita incomes. In contrast, however, we believe that transformation becomes possible in the context of a strongly entrenched worker/peasant alliance seeking to establish a socialist society—despite the widely held (and quoted) views that even then they cannot have a modern and highly differentiated economic structure. That is why we have addressed our attention to these countries.

One basic question we have tried to deal with is how, given that underdevelopment can only be *objectively* explained in terms of the existing conjuncture of social relations of production and the level of development of productive forces, the dependent characteristics of the economic structure of the small economy fundamentally manifest themselves. Our answer is that these characteristics are to be found in the workings of an economic system which divorces domestic production from domestic resource use, and domestic demand from domestic needs. As far as we are concerned, therefore, these economies are distinguished by the fact that they do not have the necessary, let alone the sufficient, conditions for the development of a vibrant and indigenous technology—by which we mean a creative relationship of the people to their social environment (as reflected in their needs) and their material environment (as reflected in their resources).

We have sought to extend these considerations to the view that for an economic system to exist and function as a national economic system there must first exist such basic and dynamic domestic interrelationships as domestic resources–domestic resource use and production–domestic technology–domestic demand–domestic needs. It is the absence of a dynamic convergence of these which explains underdeveloped and dependent economic structures. It is also because of this that we have found much of contemporary economic theory of little use in such fundamental areas as the determination of a rational pricing system, the operation of the law of value, the determination of basic goods, etc. When examined carefully, it is clear that all such notions implicitly assume an economic system capable of functioning with a high degree of internal autonomy.

While we have not sought to overburden this book with historical detail, it has been important that our interpretation of the impact of colonialism on indigenous productive forces and social relations be well documented. We have referred to two outstanding attempts at general historical analysis, and these in turn have drawn on scores of lesser known monographs, comments, and notes.[2] We ourselves have drawn on all of these in reaching our particular conclusions. We have often found—except possibly in the two works cited—that the authors are not fully aware of the implications of what to them is the natural order of the colonialism and imperialism they are documenting—i.e., that overseas possessions and colonies were established to service the needs of Mother Europe, and that therefore both social relations in these territories and the use of productive forces must reflect these considerations.

This matter of historical perspective is crucial to us because it above all else gives validity and power to our analysis. The power of "economic" analysis cannot rise above the validity of the historical and social reality which informs it. This is why, in criticizing existing theories of underdevelopment, we have sought to stress the extent to which their fundamental limitations lie in their ahistoricism. Although this is a rather straightforward Marxian notion, one which has been used to devastating effect in analyzing imperialist and neocolonialist social formations, it has not yet been able to transcend this focus and construct a strategy to cope with the manifestations of these particular forms of underdevelopment in the process of constructing a socialist society. And, as we pointed out, practical experience (that of Cuba, North Korea, North Vietnam, Tanzania, and Chile) has been too limited to establish clear-cut lines of practice.

Given our interpretation of the way productive forces are brought into use in the small underdeveloped economies during the present neocolonial phase, it is not difficult to see that the major requirement of an economic strategy of transformation is to plan the dynamic convergence of resource and production, demand and needs. Most of our work has centered on the elaboration of this idea. We have outlined a strategy of convergence, covering *en passant* such important issues as the nature of linkages, the role of foreign exchange and trading, pricing, the use of investment criteria, etc., in the transition period. Moreover, we have stressed again and again that convergence is not only a dynamic process, but that as such it must be put into the larger context of change and development in the society, reaching far beyond the elimination of the social formations of underdevelopment.

The economic model and strategy we have introduced can be interpreted, in some senses, as a generic variant of the "socialist" paradigm and practice of economic transformation. History has generally shown that for economies to achieve self-sustained growth in material production, they must have previously matured, in the sense of reversing the cumulative divergence of domestic production and domestic consumption. Even mature economies that trade heavily conform to this model since, for these, trade is an extension of the domestic market—there is no sharp divergence between what is produced and what is consumed. What practice has also demonstrated is that under socialism this maturity can be achieved at a much faster rate than under capitalism, and that for most peripheral economies in the capitalist system of relationships this maturity may never be achieved.

In the socialist models of economic transformation, the major focus has been on investment in heavy industry. This follows from recognition of the universal validity of the view that as economies grow, the needs of the population have to be satisfied by more and more industrial goods being supplied relative to agricultural goods, and that for both sets of goods to grow, the machines and materials used to produce the machines and materials used in the production of these goods will also have to grow. When this idea is carried over to the small underdeveloped economy, it is assumed by socialists and nonsocialists alike that these economies are too small to afford the costs of such a growth program. Much of our argument has been directed toward disproving this. The purpose of our model of industrial transformation has been twofold. First, it sought to examine the production economies of scale in order to demonstrate that an important range of heavy industry is feasible in the typical small underdeveloped economy because *the test of feasibility is whether the volume of output, where scale sensitivity is greatest, can be attained.* In both socialist and neoclassical economic theory, the focus has been on "optimum," not critical minimum, levels of output. Given the societies in which these theories have developed—where size is not a critical constraint—concern with the optimum is to be expected; but this is not, and indeed cannot, be our major concern.

The second objective of our model of industrialization has been to demonstrate the crucial importance which must be attached to the interpretation of the role of heavy industry in the underdeveloped economy. We argued that substantial transformation can be attained in the small underdeveloped economy if we narrow the heavy industry sector down to the major basic materials required as inputs into the domestic consumption of goods. This allows for the convergence of domestic resource use and domestic demand, for significant increases in the local value added in domestic production, and paves the way for the development of a vibrant indigenous technology through the localization of technology-intensive activities.

This model has been presented as constituting the most efficient sequence for transforming the material base of these societies. But while this transformation is fundamental in itself, if cultural, social, political, and psychological development is to be achieved, *it also assumes a sufficient level of prior development of these forces to make it possible to implement such a comprehensive strategy.* That is why we have had to assume the existence of a firmly entrenched worker/peasant alliance. Unfortunately, not even in Tanzania or Chile can it be honestly said that these forces have been sufficiently developed. In part, as we have suggested, this reflects the pervasiveness of capitalist influences. One of the staggering consequences of underdevelopment and dependence is the widespread lack of confidence the leadership in Third World countries has in the capacity of the people to master the environment. Despite the great contributions Third World societies have recently made to political theorizing and practice, it is not surprising that rarely has revolutionary political theory been matched by an equally radical vision of the capacity of the people to transform and master their environment. As a substitute we have had either arcadian predilections for rural life as it is—minus the kulaks—or a drive for state control of existing activities as an end in itself and as formal proof of socialization. What is also striking is that this has occurred during a period (the last fifty years) when, if anything is noticeable about human society, it must surely be the rapidity with which the material environment has been mastered and transformed where the people were *politically liberated for this task.* It is against this poverty of vision that this work has above all been directed. Political revolutions should, as a matter of course, offer the people liberation from, and mastery of, their material environment. If they cannot do this, they cannot introduce a higher mode of production. Without such a material base, increased consciousness will soon be dissipated. Revolutionary change, to be self-sustaining, must not only affect relationships between people, but also between people and their material environment. It is the achievement of both which permits the transition to a higher mode of production.

A major argument of this book is that there is no justification for the widespread belief that a social and political revolution in the small underdeveloped economies ought to be separate from economic transformation. We have sought to offer a model of economic transformation consistent with a revolutionary approach to society's transformation. *In this respect it is clear that failure to achieve economic transformation is itself proof of the failure to develop socialism.* It cannot, and should not, be excused by platitudes concerning the enduring nature of poverty, lack of skills, insufficient capital, and so on.

Ideological development and economic change in these societies have as one of their major tasks the constant struggle against the cultural and psychological dependence, derived from the incorporation into the system of Euro/American/Japanese imperialism. The pervasiveness of the view of the limited capacity of our people to master their environment is largely due to the society's internalization of Euro/American views of itself. As we have come to see ourselves only as others see us, so we have moved further from our freedom. Dependence grows, entrenches itself, and obstructs the liberating potentialities of socialism.

Our stressing the need to evaluate both the nature of the social relations which govern production and the level of development of the productive forces as expressed in the technico-organizational basis of society is a straightforward application of the Marxian idea of the mode of production. Because the mode of production expresses the ways in which the factors of production are brought together, interconnected, and combined in each particular historical epoch, the categories of productive forces and relations of production are dialectically united concepts which cannot be studied and analyzed in isolation from each other. Self-evident as this view would seem, we find that it has been dodged in analyses of the development of socialism in underdeveloped economies, mainly by focusing exclusively on the social and political relations in the society. As we have argued, this approach is an inevitable by-product of the assumption that the productive forces do not exist in sufficient magnitude and quality to facilitate drastic changes in the structure of production.

These two dimensions of the mode of production lay the basis for a transformation which affects not only social relations, the level of material development, etc., but also the very quality of human life itself. It seems to us that if there are to be changes in human nature, it is imperative to realize the comprehensive, continuous, and thoroughgoing nature of the struggle against dependency which is required. The overriding moral superiority of socialism resides in the possibility of a conscious and planned development of growing convergence between the forces of production and the relations which govern production. It is in this way that communities can rationally strive to bring about continuous improvement in the quality of life of each and all of its members.

It can be seen that such a continuous improvement in

human nature is the only way to make truly rational the idea presented here of domestic production and domestic resource use for domestic needs. Unless individuals as social beings develop to the point where they see themselves as members of a community in the pursuit of rational needs, rationality and communal objectives can never as a matter of course dominate all forms of material activity in society. Instead, we would certainly have what others fear to be an innate characteristic of men: the irrational pursuit of wealth and goods as ends in themselves. And as the economy grows we would have this blind pursuit of material objects as a substitute for the creative development of human capabilities.

We have tried to be careful in pointing out that there are certain dimensions of the transitional process that can only be correctly analyzed in a specific historical context. More generally, we share all the major assumptions stated by Sweezy in the exchanges with Bettelheim on the nature of the transition to socialism, despite their preoccupation with the already industrialized European states. These were:

> (1) There is no such thing as a general theory of the transition between social systems. This is not because relatively little attention has been paid to the subject—though this is undoubtedly true—but because each transition is a unique historical process which must be analyzed and explained as such.
>
> (2) Nevertheless, a comparative study of transition can be extremely valuable. In particular, the study of past transitions can help us to ask fruitful questions about present and possible future transitions, to recognize similarities and differences, and to appreciate the historicity and totality of the process under examination.
>
> (3) Transitions are never simple or brief processes. On the contrary, they typically occupy and even define whole historical epochs. One aspect of their complexity is what may be called multi-directionality: movement in one direction may turn back on itself and resume in a forward direction from a new basis. In some places the reversal may be prolonged or conceivably even permanent.
>
> (4) Transitions from one social order to another involve the most difficult and profound problems of historical materialism.[3]

These assumptions do not, of course, rule out the appropriate use of abstraction in order to arrive at the concrete essence of issues.

When we were considering the contradictions which are likely to emerge during the transition period, we stressed two as fundamental—that of state property versus social property and that of juridical and formal control over the means of production versus the content of such production. By doing this we were pointing out two characteristic forms of underdevelopment. One of these is that in the absence of an already established and highly developed material base, it is easy to come to see state control of existing economic activity (previously under foreign domination) as a movement in the direction of socialism. The other is that whereas in all societies the significance of an increase in output cannot be evaluated independently of the composition and distribution of that output, in the case of a society lacking the capacity to produce its own basic goods, this point holds a fortiori.

In addition, we were also highlighting the specific way in which the forms of property inherent in a particular mode of production are the bases of its social relations. Thus nationalization, which brings into existence state property while at the same time leaving the social relations of neocolonialism and its forms of appropriation and exploitation unchanged, is not a basic change in the relations which govern production. Social property requires the domination of social forms of appropriation and the exclusion of the exploitation of the labor of others. It is, in other words, the only basis for the development of equal relations of all to the means of production.

Notes

1. R. Sutcliffe, *Industry and Underdevelopment*, p. 317.
2. The two studies referred to were W. Rodney, *How Europe Underdeveloped Africa;* and A. G. Frank, *Capitalism and Underdevelopment in Latin America.*
3. See P. M. Sweezy and C. Bettelheim, *On the Transition to Socialism*, pp. 107-8.

Bibliography

Abbott, J. "The Efficient Use of World Protein Supplies." *Monthly Bulletin of Agricultural Economics and Statistics,* vol. 21 (June 1972).

Arrighi, G. "International Corporations, Labor Aristocracies, and Economic Development in Tropical Africa." In R. I. Rhodes, ed., *Imperialism and Underdevelopment.* New York: Monthly Review Press, 1970.

Arrow, K. J., et al. "Capital-Labor Substitution and Economic Efficiency." *Review of Economics* (August 1961).

Bagchi, A. G. "The Choice of Optimum Technique." *Economic Journal* (September 1962).

Bain, J. S. *Barriers to New Competition: Their Character and Consequences in Manufacturing Industry.* Cambridge, Mass., Harvard University Press, 1956.

Balassa, B. "Tariff Protection in Industrial Countries: An Evaluation." *Journal of Political Economy* (December 1965).

Baldwin, R. E. "Secular Movements in the Terms of Trade." *American Economic Review, Papers and Proceedings* (May 1955).

Baran, P. A. *The Political Economy of Growth.* New York: Monthly Review Press, 1957.

Baranson, J. "Automotive Industries in Developing Countries." IBRD, Staff Occasional Paper Number 8 (1967).

——. "Integrated Automobiles for Latin America." *Finance and Development* (December 1968).

Beckford, G. *Persistent Poverty: Underdevelopment in the Plantation Regions of the World.* New York: Oxford University Press, 1971.

Bernardo, R. M., ed. *The Theory of Moral Incentives in Cuba.* Birmingham: The University of Alabama Press, 1971.

Best, L. "Size and Survival." In N. Girvan and O. Jefferson, eds., *Readings in the Political Economy of the Caribbean.* Jamaica: New World Group, 1971.

Bhagwati, J. "A Sceptical Note on the Adverse Secular Trend in the Terms of Trade of the Underdeveloped Countries." *Pakistan Economic Journal* (December 1960).

Boeke, J. H. *Economics and Economic Policy for Dual Societies.* New York, 1953.

Bognár, J. *Economic Policy and Planning in Developing Countries.* Hungary: Akadémiai Kiadó, 1968.

Boorstein, E. *The Economic Transformation of Cuba.* New York: Monthly Review Press, 1968.

Brewster, H. R. and Thomas, C. Y. "Aspects of the Theory of Economic Integration." *Journal of Common Market Studies* (December 1969).

——. "Cuestiones Teóricas Planteadas por la Integración Económica Regional." *Demografía y Economía*, vol. II, no. 3 (1968).

——. *The Dynamics of West Indian Economic Integration.* Institute of Social and Economic Research, University of the West Indies, Jamaica (1967).

——. *Integration and Ideology: Towards an Integrated Theory of International Integration.* Mimeo, 1972.

Bruton, H. J. "The Import Substituting Strategy of Economic Development: A Survey of Findings." *Pakistan Development Review* (1970).

Chenery, H. "Patterns of Industrial Growth." *American Economic Review* (September 1960).

Chenery, H. and Taylor, L. "Development Patterns Among Countries and Over Time." *Review of Economics and Statistics* (November 1962).

Chenery, H. and Watanabe, T. "International Comparisons of the Structure of Production." *Econometrica* (October 1968).

Chang, Chu-Yuan. "Growth and Structural Change in the Chinese Machine-Building Industry, 1952-66." *China Quarterly*, no. 41 (January-March 1970).

Cliffe, L. and Saul, J., eds. *Socialism in Tanzania.* Nairobi: East Africa Publishing House, 1972.

Corden, W. M. "The Structure of a Tariff System and the Effective Rate of Protection." *Journal of Political Economy* (June 1966).

Dhar, P. N. and Lydall, H. *The Role of Small Enterprise in Indian Economic Development.* New York: Asia Publishing House, 1961.
De Jong, H. W. "The Significance of Dumping in International Trade." *Journal of World Trade Law,* vol. 2, no. 2 (March/April 1968).
Dekker, G. "Climate and Water Resources." In G. Wolstenholme and M. O'Connor, eds., *Man and Africa.* London: Churchill, 1965.
Demas, W. *The Economics of Development in Small Countries (With Special Reference to the Caribbean).* Montreal: McGill University Press, 1965.
Di Delupis, I. D. *The East African Community and Common Market.* London: Longman, 1970.
Diáz-Alejandro, C. F. Book Reviews. *Journal of Economic Literature,* vol. XI (March 1973).
——. "On the Import Intensity of Import Substitution." *Kyklos* (1965).
Dickinson, H. D. *Economics of Socialism.* Select Bibliographical Reprint Series. Oxford: Kelley, 1939.
Dobb, M. *Papers on Capitalism, Development and Planning.* London: Routledge and Kegan Paul, 1967.
——. *Soviet Economic Development Since 1917.* London: Routledge and K. Paul, 1966.
——. *Welfare Economics and the Economics of Socialism.* Cambridge: Cambridge University Press, 1969.
Emmanuel, A. *Unequal Exchange: A Study of the Imperialism of Trade.* New York: Monthly Review Press, 1972.
Flanders, J. M. "Agriculture Versus Industry in Development Policy." *Journal of Development Studies* (April 1969).
Frank, A. G. *Capitalism and Underdevelopment in Latin America.* New York: Monthly Review Press, 1967.
Gallo, E. and Katz, J. M. "The Industrialization of Argentina." In C. Veliz, ed., *Latin America and the Caribbean: A Handbook.* New York: Praeger, 1968.
Gehrels, F. "Customs Union from a Single Country Viewpoint." *Review of Economic Studies* (1956-57).
Girvan, N. *Foreign Capital and Economic Underdevelopment in Jamaica.* Jamaica: Institute of Social and Economic Research, 1971.
Gourou, P. *The Tropical World: Its Social and Economic Conditions and Its Future Status.* London: Longmans, 1961.
Hagen, E. *The Theory of Social Change: How Economic Growth Begins.* Homewood, Ill.: Dorsey Press, 1962.

Harbison, F. and Myers, C. A. *Education, Manpower and Economic Growth.* New York: McGraw Hill, 1964.

Hayter, T. *Aid as Imperialism.* London: Penguin Books, 1971.

Helleiner, H. "Socialism and Economic Development in Tanzania." *Journal of Development Studies* (January 1972).

Hirschman, A. O. "The Political Economy of Import Substituting Industrialization in Latin America." *Quarterly Journal of Economics* (February 1968)

——. *The Strategy of Economic Development.* New Haven: Yale University Press, 1958.

Hobsbawm, E. J. *Industry and Empire: An Economic History of Britain Since 1750.* London: Weidenfeld and Nicolson, 1968.

Hoffman, W. *The Growth of Industrial Economies.* Manchester: Manchester University Press, 1958.

Huberman, L. and Sweezy, P. *Socialism in Cuba.* New York: Monthly Review Press, 1969.

Islam, N. "Comparative Costs, Factor Proportions and Industrial Efficiency in Pakistan." *Pakistan Development Review* (Summer 1967).

Jalée, P. *The Pillage of the Third World.* New York: Monthly Review Press, 1968.

——. *Third World in World Economy.* New York: Monthly Review Press, 1969.

Jewkes, J. "Are Economies of Scale Unlimited?" In E. A. G. Robinson, ed., *Economic Consequences of the Size of Nations.* New York: St. Martin, 1963.

Kantorovich, L. V. *The Best Use of Economic Resources.* Cambridge, Mass.: Harvard University Press, 1965.

Karol, K. S. *Guerrillas in Power.* London: Jonathan Cape, 1971.

Kindleberger, C. P. *The Terms of Trade: A European Case Study.* (New York, 1956).

Kuznets, S. *Modern Economic Growth: Rate, Structure and Spread.* New Haven: Yale University Press, 1966.

Lange, O. and Taylor, F. *On the Economic Theory of Socialism.* Minneapolis: University of Minnesota Press, 1938.

Lee, D. H. K. *Climate and Economic Development in the Tropics.* New York: Harper, 1957.

Leff, N. H. *The Brazilian Capital Goods Industry, 1929-64.* Cambridge, Mass.: Harvard University Press, 1968.

Leff, N. H. and Netto, A. D. "Import Substitution, Foreign Investment and International Disequilibrium in Brazil." *Journal of Development Studies* (April 1966).

Lenin, V. I. "On Cooperation." In *Alliance of the Working Class and the Peasantry.* Moscow: Progress Publishers, 1955.

——. *Selected Works.* Moscow: Progress Publishers, 1970.

Levitt, K. "Canada, The World's Richest Underdeveloped Country." *New World Quarterly*, vol. 4, no. 2 (1968).

——. *Silent Surrender.* Canada: Liveright, 1970.

Lewis, W. A. *Aspects of Tropical Trade, 1883-1965.* Stockholm: Almquist and Wicksell, 1969.

——. *The Theory of Economic Growth.* London: Allen and Unwin, 1955.

Li, Cho-Min. "China's Industrial Development, 1958-63." In R. MacFarquar, ed., *China Under Mao: Politics Takes Command.* Cambridge, Mass.: M.I.T. Press, 1966.

Lipsey, R. G. "The Theory of Customs Unions: A General Survey." *Economic Journal* (September 1960).

Little, I. and Mirrlees, J. *Manual of Industrial Project Analysis*, vol. 2. Paris: OECDI, 1969.

Livingstone, I. "Industry Versus Agriculture in Economic Development." *Journal of Modern African Studies* (September 1968).

Lloyd, P. J. *International Trade Problems of Small Nations.* Durham, N.C.: Duke University Press, 1968.

Macario, S. "Protectionism and Industrialization in Latin America." *Economic Bulletin for Latin America* (March 1964).

Magdoff, H. *The Age of Imperialism.* New York: Monthly Review Press, 1969.

Mandel, E. *Marxist Economic Theory.* New York: Monthly Review Press, 1968.

Marx, K. and Engels, F. *Selected Works.* Moscow: Foreign Languages Publishing House, 1958.

McClelland, D. *The Achieving Society.* Princeton, N.J.: Van Nostrand, 1962.

McIntyre, A. "Some Issues in Trade Policy in the West Indies." In N. Girvan and O. Jefferson, eds., *Readings in the Political Economy of the Caribbean.* Jamaica: New World Group, 1971.

Meade, J. E. *The Theory of Customs Unions.* Amsterdam: North-Holland Publishing Company, 1956.

Meier, G. M. *International Economics of Development.* New York: Harper and Row, 1968.

——. *Leading Issues in Economic Development.* New York: Oxford University Press, 1970.

Mesa-Lago, C., ed. *Revolutionary Change in Cuba.* Pittsburgh: University of Pittsburgh Press, 1971.

Mishan, E. J. "A Survey of Welfare Economics, 1939-59." *Economic Journal* (1960).

Montias, J. M. *Economic Development in Communist Rumania.* Cambridge, Mass.: M.I.T. Press, 1967.

Mumford, L. *Technics and Civilisation.* London: Routledge, 1934.

Myrdal, G. *Economic Theory and Underdeveloped Regions.* 1957. Reprint; London: G. Duckworth, 1964.

Nkrumah, K. *Neo-Colonialism, The Last Stage of Imperialism.* New York: International Publishers, 1965.

Nove, A. *An Economic History of the U.S.S.R.* London: Allen Lane, 1969.

Novozhilov, V. V. *Problems of Measuring Outlays and Results Under Optimal Planning.* New York: IASP, 1969.

Nurske, R. *Problems of Capital Formation in Underdeveloped Countries.* New York: Oxford University Press, 1953.

Pratten, C. F. "Economies of Scale for Machine Tool Production." *Journal of Industrial Economics* (April 1971).

Prebisch, R. *Toward a Dynamic Development Policy for Latin America.* New York: United Nations, 1964.

Preobrazhensky, E. *The New Economics.* New York: Oxford University Press, 1965.

Rasmussen, P. N. *Studies in Inter-Sectoral Relations.* Amsterdam: North-Holland Publishing Company, 1956.

Raj, K. "Role of the Machine Tools Sector in Economic Growth." In C. H. Feinstein, ed., *Socialism, Capitalism and Economic Growth.* Cambridge: Cambridge University Press, 1967.

Reno, P. "Aluminum Profits and Caribbean People." In R. I. Rhodes, ed., *Imperialism and Underdevelopment.* New York, 1970.

Ritter, A. R. M. "Growth Strategy and Economic Performance in Revolutionary Cuba: Past, Present and Prospective." *Social and Economic Studies,* vol. 21, no. 3 (September 1972).

Robinson, J. "Consumer's Sovereignty in a Planned Economy." In A. Nove and D. Nuti, eds., *Socialist Economics.* Harmondsworth: Penguin, 1972.

Rodney, W. *How Europe Underdeveloped Africa.* Dar es Salaam and London: Tanzania Publishing House and Bogle L'Ouverture Publications, 1972.

Rosenberg, N. "Technological Change in the Machine Tool Industry, 1840-1910." *Journal of Economic History* (December 1963).

Rweyemamu, J. "International Trade and Developing Countries." *Uchumi*, vol. 1, no. 1.

——. *Underdevelopment and Industrialisation in Tanzania.* New York: Oxford University Press (forthcoming).

Seers, D. "The Role of Industry in Development: Some Fallacies." *Journal of Modern African Studies* (December 1963).

——. "The Stages of Growth of a Primary Producer in the Middle of the Twentieth Century." In R. I. Rhodes, ed., *Imperialism and Underdevelopment: A Reader.* New York: Monthly Review Press, 1970.

Sheahan, J. "Import Substitution and Economic Policy: A Second Review." *Research Memorandum* (Center for Development Studies, Williams College, Williamstown, Mass.), no. 50 (August 1972).

Shivji, I. "The Silent Class Struggle." In *Proceedings of the Sixth East African Social Sciences Conference.* Tanzania: University of Dar es Salaam, 1970.

Silverman, Bertram, ed. *Man and Socialism in Cuba: The Great Debate.* New York: Atheneum, 1971.

Simantov, A. "Economic Problems Affecting Agriculture in Europe and Policies Called For." *Kyklos*, vol. XIX (1966), Fasc. 2.

Spulber, N. *Soviet Strategy for Economic Growth.* Indiana: Indiana University Press, 1964.

Sraffa, P. *Production of Commodities by Means of Commodities.* Cambridge: Cambridge University Press, 1960.

Staley, E. and Morse, R. *Modern Small Industries for Developing Countries.* New York: McGraw Hill, 1965.

Strassman, W. P. *Technological Change and Economic Development.* Ithaca: Cornell University Press, 1968.

Sutcliffe, R. B. *Industry and Underdevelopment.* London: Addison-Wesley, 1971.

Szentes, T. *The Political Economy of Underdevelopment.* Budapest: Akadémiai Kiadó, 1972.

——. "Status Quo and Socialism: Comments on Shivji's Paper (The Silent Class Struggle)." *Sixth East African Social Sciences Conferences.* Dar es Salaam, Tanzania, 1970.

Tanzanian Economic Society, Uchumi. *Towards Socialist Planning.* Dar es Salaam: Tanzania Publishing House, 1972.

Thomas, C. Y. "Meaningful Participation: The Fraud of It." In D. Lowenthal and L. Comitas, eds., *The Aftermath of Sovereignty.* New York: Doubleday, 1973.

Travis, W. P. *The Theory of Trade and Protection.* Cambridge, Mass.: Harvard University Press, 1964.

Tshume, A. Article in *The African Communist*, no. 51 (1972).
United Nations. *Patterns of Industrial Growth, 1938-58.* New York, 1960.
———. *Pulp and Paper Prospects in Africa and the Near East.* New York, 1966.
———. *Pulp and Paper Prospects in Asia and the Far East.* New York, 1962.
———. *Pulp and Paper Prospects in Latin America.* New York, 1955.
———. *A Study of the Iron and Steel Industry in Latin America.* New York, 1954.
Vaitsos, C. V. "Transfer of Resources and Preservation of Monopoly Rents." Paper presented to Dubrovik Conference of the Harvard Advisory Service (April 1970).
———. "Bargaining and Distribution of Returns in the Purchase of Technology by Developing Countries." *Institute of Development Studies Bulletin*, vol. 3, no. 1 (October 1970).
Viner, J. *The Customs Union Issue.* New York: Carnegie Endowment, 1953.
Von Freyholdt, M. *The Workers and the Nizers.* Tanzania: University of Dar es Salaam, Department of Sociology, 1972.
Von Hayek, F. A., ed. *Collectivist Economic Planning.* London: G. Routledge and Sons Ltd., 1935.
Wells, J. *The Construction Industry in East Africa.* Tanzania: University of Dar es Salaam, Economic Research Bureau Paper: May 1972.
Wheelwright, E. L. and McFarlane, B. *The Chinese Road to Socialism.* New York: Monthly Review Press, 1969.
Wienhold, H. *On Socialist Transformation of Agriculture.* Seminar Paper, University of Dar es Salaam, 1972. Mimeo.
Wilczynski, J. *The Economics of Socialism.* 2nd ed. London: George Allen and Unwin, 1972.
Williams, E. *Capitalism and Slavery.* London: Andre Deutsch, 1964.
Wionczek, M. S. "The Rise and Decline of Latin American Economic Integration." *Journal of Common Market Studies*, vol. IX, no. 1 (September 1970).
Yaffey, M. J. *Balance of Payments Problems.* Tanzania: Economic Research Bureau, 1970.
Yudelman, M. "Agricultural Development in Tanzania." In *Seminar on Foreign Aid and Rural Development in Tanzania.* Government of Tanzania, 1970.
Zalla, T. *Dairy Development in Tanzania.* Tanzania: Economic Research Bureau, University of Dar es Salaam, 1972.

Zarembka, P. "Manufacturing and Agricultural Production Functions and International Trade: United States and Northern Europe." *Journal of Farm Economics*, vol. 48.

Index